M000318048

T H E
INTEGRAL
INTAKE

THE
INTEGRAL
INTAKE

A Guide to Comprehensive Idiographic Assessment in Integral Psychotherapy

ANDRE MARQUIS

Routledge
Taylor & Francis Group
New York   London

Disclaimer: All clients' identifying information has been altered in order to protect their identities. Thus, please note that any resemblance between the examples in the text and any real persons, living or dead, is purely coincidental.

Routledge
Taylor & Francis Group
270 Madison Avenue
New York, NY 10016

Routledge
Taylor & Francis Group
2 Park Square
Milton Park, Abingdon
Oxon OX14 4RN

© 2008 by Taylor & Francis Group, LLC
Routledge is an imprint of Taylor & Francis Group, an Informa business

Printed in the United States of America on acid-free paper
10 9 8 7 6 5 4 3 2 1

International Standard Book Number-13: 978-0-415-95766-3 (Softcover)

Except as permitted under U.S. Copyright Law, no part of this book may be reprinted, reproduced, transmitted, or utilized in any form by any electronic, mechanical, or other means, now known or hereafter invented, including photocopying, microfilming, and recording, or in any information storage or retrieval system, without written permission from the publishers.

Trademark Notice: Product or corporate names may be trademarks or registered trademarks, and are used only for identification and explanation without intent to infringe.

Library of Congress Cataloging-in-Publication Data

Marquis, Andre, Ph. D.
    The integral intake : a guide to comprehensive idiographic assessment in integral psychotherapy / Andre Marquis.
        p. ; cm.
    Includes bibliographical references and index.
    ISBN 978-0-415-95766-3 (softcover : alk. paper)
    1. Transpersonal psychotherapy. 2. Transpersonal psychology. 3. Consciousness. I. Title.
    [DNLM: 1. Psychotherapy--methods. 2. Consciousness. 3. Professional-Patient Relations. WM 420 M357i 2007]

    RC489.T75M37 2007
    616.89'14--dc22   2007025227

Visit the Taylor & Francis Web site at
http://www.taylorandfrancis.com

and the Routledge Web site at
http://www.routledge.com

Michael J. Mahoney, Ph.D.

1946–2006

I lovingly dedicate this book to Michael Mahoney,
the most inspiring teacher, the wisest mentor,
and the dearest friend I ever could have hoped for.
I have never felt more understood by anyone else.
I miss you and will continue remembering
all that we shared, from passionate inquiry, new ideas,
and our experiences in meditation and relationships
to food, wine, and nature walks—but most of all, our
interbeing. Your living was a loving, shining work
of heart. Thank you, thank you, thank you.

- **Andre**

Contents

Foreword by Elliott Ingersoll   ix

Preface   xiii

Acknowledgments   xvii

1   Some General Assessment Foundations   1

2   Integral Theory: The Metatheory Behind the Integral Intake   23

3   Quadratic Assessment   45

4   The Spectrum of Development, Pathology, and Treatment   61

5   Development Lines and the Integral Psychograph   103
    With E. Scott Warren

6   States of Consciousness, Personality Types, and the Self   131

7   Putting It All Together: Interpreting Clients' Responses and Treatment Planning (Case Examples)   169

8   Research: Past and Future Developments   239

9   Conclusion   259

Appendix: The Integral Intake   263

References   277

Index   287

About the Author   293

CD Contents   295

Foreword

More and more these days I wander around with the sense that counseling and psychotherapy, as we have known them, are dead. Like the madman in Nietzsche's parable about God being dead, I find that sharing this idea brings odd looks, laughs, and occasionally derision. Andre Marquis is one of the few friends and colleagues with whom I can share such thoughts—he understands the difference between what is theoretically interesting and what is of clinical utility. He understands the difference between a partial truth and a vision for the field. More important, he understands the difference between a vision of symptom remediation and a vision for healing the soul. Even the most positivistic among us can no longer afford the luxury of living and working by partial truths if we aim to facilitate real healing from psychological suffering. As our species faces unprecedented challenges, the mind is put under unprecedented pressure that cannot be accounted for in any one approach to treating psychological symptoms. Mental health professionals are overly specialized, and such specialization, while offering useful distinctions about the psychological trees, lacks a vision of the forest of the psyche. In this current volume Dr. Marquis offers us a way out that is practical, radical, and necessary.

Our traditional approaches to counseling and psychotherapy are dead (or at least dying) because they are based on static assumptions about what it means to be human reflected in carefully preserved, but partial, psychological maps. While these partial maps are reified in training programs and elite institutes, they are largely ignored in the therapeutic marketplace, which is driven by economic agendas that are not even mentioned in graduate training. Analytic, behavioral, humanistic, transpersonal, and integrative revolutions have come and gone, leaving barely a ripple on the ocean of mainstream therapy. Our largely unread professional journals increasingly try to wring quantitative sense out of partial views of counseling and psychotherapy, but here again the partial nature of the endeavors is never brought together in a way that is meaningful for the clinician.

The current fragmentation in our ideas about psychological wellness and healing is also reflected in the disciplines supposedly devoted to the mind. As the historian of psychology Daniel Robinson (1995) stated, "In its current form, psychology is so various, so partitioned into separate provinces, that the nonspecialist might pardonably conclude that there is no unified subject at all" (pp. 3-4). This fragmentation is due in part to the assumptions that separate the clinicians from the researchers, those who fancy themselves scientists from those who fancy themselves healers. So we continue with the proliferation of theories that reflect only a small fraction of the human experience, and then almost apologetically try to pull them all together with "integrative" or "transtheoretical" systems that have all the grace of dragging a bag of watermelons up a mountain. Of course, the tendency to ignore the fact that we cocreate reality through overly concrete interpretations of our maps is characteristic of humanity. Jung (1960) noted that "everyone makes for himself his own segment of world and constructs his own private system, often with airtight compartments, so that after a time it seems to him that he has grasped the meaning and structure of the whole. But the finite will never be able to grasp the infinite" (p. 139). Even those of us in the mental health fields get excited by a promising study, and before the next issue of the journal is printed there are seminars, devotees, popular workshops, and the industry of criticism. As Jane Loevinger (1987) reflected, "Once any view becomes widely accepted, many people have a stake in contradicting it, one way or another, and others are deeply invested in defending it" (p. 130). So here we are, defending different maps, often mistaking them for the actual territory of the human psyche, then battling to the death (or until retirement) for our perspective.

Andre Marquis has modeled a better way in this volume. It is a truly integral book that has taken a bold map of the human experience and carefully crafted it into a workable set of instructions that guide the therapeutic process from start to finish. While recognizing that the finite cannot grasp the infinite, Dr. Marquis has skillfully interpreted

Ken Wilber's "theory of everything" into an elegant intake process. He has offered an approach that invites everyone to the table—those who reify a particular theory in practice, those who want to integrate theories for practice, and those who believe we can do better.

The Integral Intake: A Guide to Comprehensive Idiographic Assessment in Integral Psychotherapy begins at the beginning, offering a map that serves as an efficient way to assess clients while providing a framework that guides treatment negotiations, the therapist's conception of the ways a client may express growth as well as symptoms, and even ways to seek out thorough supervision. The material is nicely balanced between theoretical underpinnings, practical application, and case studies that help the reader pull both together and then move on to actual work with the intake instrument.

While the integral map unpacked in this volume is perhaps the most ambitious map of human growth and development that we have, Dr. Marquis describes the theory and its application in elegant and practical terms that should appeal to novice and veteran clinicians alike. I believe this book will also appeal to those researchers among us who try to keep up to date with clinical approaches. Both researchers and practitioners are considered in this volume. Dr. Marquis has not only proposed a map but also researched the terrain and provided his intellectual genealogy for the reader. In addition, he has conducted research on the instrument that is the foundation of this book—the Integral Intake form. Unlike proponents of many of the passing psychological fads feigning scientific rigor, Dr. Marquis has completed research on his intake and continues to investigate its effectiveness in clinical settings.

We are at a time in the evolution of counseling and psychotherapy where we must integrate and synthesize the wisdom of our heritage, jettison unnecessary baggage, and move forward in a synergistic manner with tools for clinical work that embrace the whole client. Such tools will certainly require more of the clinician using them. The clinicians willing to work on the cutting edge of healing will find The Integral Intake a valuable tool to start with—perhaps a tool to start a real revolution that directly enhances the level of care our clients receive and breathes new life into our work as we see our clients with fresh eyes and hearts.

Elliott Ingersoll, Ph.D., PCC

References

Jung, C. G. (1960). The structure of the psyche. In R. F. C. Hull (Trans.), *Collected works: Vol. 8. The structure and dynamics of the psyche.* Princeton, NJ: Bollingen.

Loevinger, J. (1987). *Paradigms of personality.* New York: Freeman.

Robinson, D. N. (1995). *An intellectual history of psychology* (3rd ed.). Madison: University of Wisconsin Press.

Preface

In 1984, Ken Wilber published two groundbreaking articles that introduced the most comprehensive model of psychological developmental to date. Even more significant, he suggested that each developmental stage is associated with specific psychological or psychospiritual pathologies and that each of those pathologies is optimally treated with different therapeutic treatment modalities (1984a, 1984b). Over the past 20 years, Wilber has continued his philosophical, psychological, and spiritual theorizing, and his 20-plus books are now published in more than 30 languages, making him the most translated American academic author and arguably the most systematically comprehensive contemporary philosophical thinker (Visser, 2003; Schwartz, 1995). Unfortunately, much of the psychotherapeutic community remains unaware of this powerfully integrative system, integral theory (Wilber 1999d, 2000b), which is not only theoretically elegant but also clinically elucidating and pragmatically helpful.

The Integral Intake is a psychotherapeutic intake assessment based upon Wilber's "all quadrants, all levels" (AQAL) model. This book will provide the reader with an exposition of integral theory and the AQAL model as well as an explanation of how to use the Integral Intake. My primary goal in creating the Integral Intake was to help clinicians more comprehensively assess their clients so that the therapy they plan and enact is enhanced. My primary goal in writing this book is to provide clinicians with a complex yet parsimonious conceptual system—integral theory—with which to organize a tremendous breadth and depth of information about a client into a meaningful and practical case formulation. As such, I tried to strike a balance between conceptual clarity and practical utility in order to help both therapists in training and more experienced therapists obtain and organize clinically relevant information so that richer understandings of clients and their problems inform the planning of optimally therapeutic courses of treatment.

The Integral Intake can be used in any health-related profession, from counseling, psychotherapy, and social work to psychiatry and nursing, and in almost any setting, from community health clinics and hospitals to schools and private practices. Given that members of different professions usually conceptualize with different theoretical constructs (biomedical disease in contrast to an unhealthy social system, an issue of moral disengagement, or a lack of satisfying relationships) or focus predominantly on only a few of the many clinically relevant factors involved in people's pathologies and/or suffering, a comprehensive, integrative system such as integral theory not only improves the effectiveness of each practitioner but also facilitates interdisciplinary communication and therefore greater potentials for multidisciplinary resources and treatment.

The Integral Intake is an idiographic, biographical, multidimensional assessment instrument, the meaning of which will be described in Chapter 1, along with other general assessment issues. From the perspective of integral theory (which is introduced in Chapter 2 and more fully explicated in Chapters 3 through 6), comprehensive and holistic conceptualization of clients seeking counseling and psychotherapy requires understanding four distinct *quadrants* (perspectives) of each client: the client's internal experience, the client's externally observable behavior, the client's culture, and the client's social system; quadratic assessment is the focus of Chapter 3. Also essential to integral assessment are developmental issues, including *levels* (stages) and *lines* (aspects of people that develop, such as cognition, needs, identity, morality, etc.), *states* of consciousness, and personality *types*, all of which will be explicated in Chapters 4 through 6 and illustrated in Chapter 7 with two extensive case studies.

Merely obtaining the maximum amount of information from clients is not all that therapeutic assessment and intake interviews entail. The five components of integral theory previously mentioned (quadrants, levels, lines, states, and types) provide the primary orienting framework with which integral therapists organize a conceptualization of clients that is even more comprehensive than biopsychosocial formulations (Short, 2005; Ingersoll, 2002; Engel, 1977; Campbell & Rohrbaugh, 2006). Integral theory synergistically integrates the best of both conventional, time-honored psychotherapeutic knowledge and practice with that of more cutting-edge, provocative issues, such as suprapersonal states of consciousness and post-postformal stages of development.

Another critical component of therapists' initial contact with, and assessment of, clients involves establishing a therapeutic alliance; this issue is addressed in several places throughout this book. Likewise, practical examples are infused in each chapter—from different ways of using the Integral Intake (paper-and-pencil format versus a guide to a semistructured or structured interview) to treatment planning, *DSM* diagnoses, and the integral psychograph—to illustrate the connections between integral theory and integral practice. Chapter 8 discusses research that has been performed on the Integral Intake and other idiographic assessment instruments as well as plans for further research on, and refinements of, the Integral Intake. Chapter 9 briefly concludes the book.

Several different versions of the Integral Intake are included as PDF files on the companion CD at the end of this book; those versions include Spanish and French translations for those health care providers who work with people who are more fluent in those languages than in English. Also included is a psychiatric version of the Integral Intake, modified by David Leavitt, M.D., which entails a more comprehensive medical evaluation and psychiatric review of symptoms that more quickly points toward a *DSM-IV-TR* diagnosis, for those clinicians who are so inclined. In order to accommodate the additional psychiatric queries without creating an Integral Intake that is overwhelmingly long, Dr. Leavitt deleted some of the queries on the standard Integral Intake that he deemed less critical for those clients who are more severely impaired. Another form on the CD that accompanies this book is a letter to new clients that explains the rationale behind their completing the Integral Intake. Whether you use the form exactly as it is on the CD or use it as a guide to creating a similar letter that more readily fits your style of assessing clients, the letter is also included for your use. I encourage you to use the Integral Intake—in whatever version is most suitable to your needs—and welcome any feedback you would like to provide, as I intend to continue revising it based upon not only further controlled research but also clinicians' experiences of using it.

The primary beneficial features of the Integral Intake are its overall helpfulness, comprehensiveness, and efficiency (gathering pertinent information in a reasonable amount of time). More specifically, it assesses clients' culture and diversity issues, clients' spirituality, clients' environments, and what is most meaningful to clients far more comprehensively than any other assessment instrument (Marquis, 2002, Marquis, Holden & Hupfeld, in press). Most mental health professionals agree that these previously neglected areas of assessment are, in fact, critical to fully understanding clients and thus creating optimal treatment plans.

Integral theory and the AQAL model have been informing the work of psychotherapists for more than two decades now. Integral counseling and psychotherapy have been the focus of an entire issue of the peer-reviewed journal *Counseling and Values* (2007), numerous peer-reviewed articles, and numerous professional conference presentations; Ken Wilber was invited to present at the 2005 Evolution of Psychotherapy conference (but could not attend due to health reasons); weeklong seminars on Integral Psychotherapy at the Integral Institute have drawn large audiences of psychologists, psychiatrists, counselors, social workers, and nurses from all over the world; and work is under way on the *Handbook of Integral Psychotherapy* (Marquis & Ingersoll, in progress). Nonetheless, integral assessment and therapy will continue to develop. Thus, I welcome feedback on the Integral Intake so that future revisions will even better help us to help those we serve. I hope you find this book and the Integral Intake intellectually stimulating and practically helpful.

Andre Marquis

Acknowledgments

Integral theory is, among many other things, a theory of development. I would like to here express my gratitude for three passions of mine—people, music, and nature—that have been influential in my own development.

As someone working to develop an integrative approach to counseling and psychotherapy, I am of course indebted to those whose work I integrate. Among those inspiring authors are Michael Mahoney, Robert Kegan, Diana Fosha, Paul Wachtel, Robert Stolorow, Irvin Yalom, Rollo May, Erich Fromm, Adi Da, and Brother David Steindl-Rast, as well as James, Freud, and Piaget. No other writer, however, has influenced my intellectual work more than Ken Wilber, without whom I would not have initiated this book. Although I am not certain that all of what follows would meet with his complete approval, I do know that most of it would not have come to fruition without his unique work. My appreciation extends to my psychotherapeutic colleagues at the Integral Institute: Bert Parlee, Willow Pearson, Susanne Cook-Greuter, Jeff Soulen, Tim Black, Durwin Foster, and David Zeitler. A special thank-you goes to Vipassana Esbjörn-Hargens for contributing ideas to an initial draft of the Integral Intake. Sean Esbjörn-Hargens is one of those rare beings with whom I very quickly felt like a lifelong friend. Sean's balancing of his love of nature, his emotional development, his intellectual pursuits, and his spiritual practice is inspiring to me; plus he's super fun to be with! I would not have published this book without the approval of my "soul-brother writer" and fellow integral therapy comrade, Elliott Ingersoll. Not only did Elliott provide valuable feedback on an earlier draft of this book, he is a treasured colleague, whether writing, presenting, or editing together; he's a jewel of a friend as well. As my dear friend Michael Mahoney wrote in the preface of his last book, "Deep and enduring friendships are among the most precious blessings of a human life. I have been generously blessed."

The friends I made at the University of North Texas continue to be important in my life. Jan Holden not only gave me the idea to use the Integral Intake as the focus of my dissertation and wrote the first draft of "Letter to New Clients" (included on the CD) but also allowed me to create an integral counseling specialization within my doctoral program of study. I am deeply appreciative of her generous mentorship. Kathy Oden, Paul Abney, Sarah Menninger, Zac Tureau, Rich Herrington, Leah Brew, Maggi Budd, and I were all working on our doctorates in counseling or psychology at UNT. Thank you for your friendship, your support, and all the good times we had at the cabin! Special friendships, such as the one I have with Scott Warren, are one of life's great blessings. Scott knows my good and not-so-good sides and continues to like and love me through it all. His wisdom, understanding, care, and concern have helped me through many challenging times. I shared the log cabin that was my home in north Texas with a graceful being named Lerxst, my yellow Labrador. He was not only a tangible expression of the love, beauty, and pleasure that can be experienced in life but a perfectly consistent selfobject and treasured companion. When I remember you, Lerxst, I feel happy.

I felt great sadness leaving my colleagues and friends at Northeastern State University. Kenny Paris, Alicia Casas-Celaya, Bill Schiller, Harriet Bachner, Sarah Menninger, and I shared passionate discussions and some most enjoyable parties on Alicia's deck, around Kenny's fire pit, and at my home in the Oklahoma countryside. Despite the formidable demands of an academic life, it does afford more flexibility in one's schedule than most occupations. Kenny and I took full advantage of that flexibility; whenever we could, we canoed or kayaked the Illinois River or Baron Fork Creek, enjoying the unspoiled foothills of the Ozarks, bald eagles, and a tremendous diversity of other birds and wildlife, as well as good smallmouth bass fishing.

I have landed at the University of Rochester, and I appreciate that it is providing me with not only intellectual freedom and material support but also, and even more important, colleagues with whom I truly feel I belong. Personal and professional roles meld more smoothly in the company of colleagues such as Doug Guiffrida and Karen Mackie. I was fortunate to experience the person-centered leadership of Howie

Kirschenbaum for my first year at UR; working for someone was never easier. Gerry Rubenstein warmly welcomed me and Erica into his home as if we were family. Paul Stein's knowledge of social structures is encyclopedic, his eagle eye is critical in the best sense of the word, and his compassionate commitment to a better world for all—including non-humans—is beautiful and inspiring; my thinking feels better because of the informal discussions we often share. Finally, Kathryn Douthit is a model for me regarding her seamlessly integrating her penetrating intellect and broad-ranging scholarship with her heartfelt sensitivity, dynamic spontaneity, and compassion in action. I am proud to be a part of the UR counseling faculty and grateful to share their friendship.

I want to thank my clients for their courage and dedication to grow, for demonstrating that human change processes are not abstractions, and for playing an integral role in my becoming a more helpful helper. I want to thank my students and supervisees for their trust, curiosity, willingness to tolerate confusion, and efforts to learn and develop. I truly feel privileged to be able to participate in processes of inquiry, learning, and development.

Nietzsche wrote, "Without music, life would be a mistake." I'm not sure I fully agree with the extremity of his statement, but I certainly know that music has enriched my life and transported my consciousness to realms of ecstasy that are ineffably precious. Although the music I love ranges from Stravinsky, Miles Davis, and Chick Corea to Yes, the Beatles, and John Denver, I am most passionate about the music of Bach. Bach's music brilliantly and beautifully expresses the Aristotelian notion that art imitates nature—a principle that formed the heart of Bach's concept of musical science—disclosing dimensions of body, mind, and spirit that point to the workings of nature, or perhaps, the supernatural-musical "pointing-out-instructions" if you will. I am deeply thankful for the joyful engagement and utter absorption that I am fortunate enough to experience by participating in the subtle sublimity that is Bach's music, even though my understanding and enjoyment are only partial glimpses of the goodness, truth, and beauty contained in this "music of the spheres."

What can I say about nature? I need it and am grateful that I have always been able to lose myself in it. Currently, if I am not at work or home, I am most likely on Hemlock Lake, one of the pristine Finger Lakes in central New York. Whether fishing at Finger Lake or any of the numerous streams and rivers in central New York, the peace, enjoyment, and rejuvenation that nature affords me are priceless gifts. Independently of catching anything, fishing presents me with the play of light dancing on water, the mystery of flowing waves, and the seamless changes that emerge from the rising and setting of the sun and moon.

Although I don't see them nearly as often as I would like, the distance between me and the following friends is only geographical; we are together in spirit. I met Eric Hartman when I was 16 and dating his daughter; how our friendship has continued to morph and evolve is a testimony to dynamic systems. Craig Thigpen was originally my guitar instructor; then he introduced me to Stravinsky's music, which led me through a musical revolution and a subsequent obsession—a favor I returned by rekindling his love of Bach. Leslie Grove is a dear soul, the most devoted mother I know, and an "always there" friend. She introduced me to Peter Bellonci, a "wise old man" whose daily meditation involves sculpting stone with hand tools; until I left Austin, our Friday walks around Town Lake and brunch at Magnolia Café were a precious ritual not to be missed. Chris Warren is a gentleman from an earlier age; his word, humor, and friendship are completely dependable. Living fully each day, Gaby Rösch helped teach me that a life without risks is not a life worth living.

As you would expect, my parents were significant influences on the person I am today. I thank my mother for the love and attention she consistently gave to me. She regularly and devotedly took the time to encourage my dedication to both work and what interested me the most recreationally; in the process, she instilled in me—at an early age— the value of discipline. I want to thank my father for his modeling of passionate engagement in work and recreation, for encouraging high standards, and for exposing me to the wonders of nature. As a young child fishing with a research chemist father, I also received an early education about experimental methods: vary one aspect at a time (speed of retrieval, color of lure, type of presentation, etc.) while keeping the other aspects constant (the location, depth, type of lure, etc.), record the results (we kept copious fishing logs), and observe the patterns. My dad thus provided me with my earliest scientific training. My four sisters weren't always the easiest to live with when we were children (I'm sure they'd say the same about me), but I truly enjoy their company now. Anne-Marie, a psychoanalytic psychologist, and I enjoy discussing psychotherapy. Melinda and her husband, Clint, share my passion for music and nature; if only I could keep up with them on a hike or bike ride. Natalie is a testament to personal growth and forgiveness. Julie, with whom I have the fondest memories of childhood, cares about her cats, wildlife, and their ecologies as much as anyone. I personally know of no other siblings who are closer than my brother Ro (short for Robert) and I are. Whether we're canoeing and fishing an Alaskan river, cooking together, sharing music that moves us, or a thousand miles apart, we are thankful for a very special bond that we both know will endure. Nonetheless, I wish I could spend more time with him, his wife Kristin, and their three lovely children. When I was still a child, Ro, five years my senior, suggested that I reflect upon everything I did each day—what I felt good about and what I would have liked to have done differently. He was thus the first person to encourage my being introspective.

I would also like to thank those who helped to revise and translate the Integral Intake forms: David Leavitt, M.D., psychiatrist at Boulder Community Hospital, and private practice in Integrative Psychiatry, Boulder, Colorado; Cecilia Rios Aguilar, Ph.D., assistant professor at the Center for the Study of Higher Education, University of Arizona, and Manon Hotte, M.D., director of the School of Integrative Psychotherapy in Quebec, Canada. Gaby Rösch also deserves thanks for the photo of me used on this book's back cover.

I sincerely appreciate Dana Bliss, editor at Routledge, for his interest in and encouragement of my work as well as for allowing me the freedom to write in my own style. Charlotte Roh was ever cheerful; her accommodating my wish to have a nature photo of my own on the cover means a great deal to me. You are both a pleasure to work with.

Finally, I want to express my heartfelt gratitude to my partner, Erica Crane. In addition to carefully reading each chapter and providing helpful feedback, she has been a consistent source of encouragement, balance, and love; she is also remarkably understanding and tolerant of my need to spend a great deal of time in nature, often fishing. The love and friendship we share renews my faith in the primacy of human relationships. You become more precious to me with each passing day. Together with our dog, Nelson, she has facilitated my growing in ways that I had not anticipated.

1
SOME GENERAL ASSESSMENT FOUNDATIONS

The Role of Assessment in Counseling and Psychotherapy

Most counseling theorists and practitioners agree that comprehensive assessment, in which counselors obtain as much information encompassing as many aspects of clients as is reasonable, is essential and crucial to successful counseling (Cavanagh, 1982; Eckstein, Baruth, & Mahrer, 1992; Hood & Johnson, 1991; Lazarus, 1995, 1997; Mosak, 1995; Shertzer & Linden, 1979; Wilber, 2000e). Moreover, "the ability to assess an individual is a basic skill required of all counselors regardless of the setting in which they practice" (Shertzer & Linden, 1979, p. 3). Exceptions to this perspective come from the humanists, exemplified by Carl Rogers (1957, 1961) and, late in his career, Heinz Kohut (1984), both of whom posited that regardless of what the client's problems were, the most important thing the therapist could do is communicate accurate empathy, thus rendering assessment relatively unnecessary or even a diversion from what is most beneficial to clients.

Rogers' and Kohut's perspectives on assessment, however, may be in need of revision. This can be demonstrated by considering an unfortunately not too uncommon situation: poverty-stricken, alcoholic parents whose children are growing up in an inner city and are attempting to navigate the gang scene and other forms of social oppression. Are we truly to believe that such clients need empathy more than anything else? Moreover, at times a simple change of diet, an increase in exercise, taking an antidepressant, or other biophysical—as opposed to psychological—interventions can be as effective as, or more effective than, psychotherapy (Lazarus, 1995; Leonard & Murphy, 1995; Wilber, 2000b).

Using intake assessment instruments (the term *instrument* is used synonymously with the term *inventory*) in counseling and psychotherapy is an efficient and systematic way to obtain information about clients and to subsequently tailor a counseling approach most likely to serve clients optimally (Van Audenhove & Vertommen, 2000; Beutler & Rosner, 1995; Palmer, 1997). The more information a counselor obtains, the more likely it is that the client will be deeply understood by the counselor, thus increasing the likelihood that an appropriate course of counseling will be taken, ultimately increasing the likelihood of successful outcome (Karg & Wiens, 1998).

The preceding paragraph *presumed* that some form of counseling or psychotherapy would necessarily be the most appropriate course of action for a given client. The intake assessment process not only includes elaborate, theoretically driven questions, as can be found in the Integral Intake, but also requires such fundamental questions as "Does this person need professional help?" If the answer is yes, the next question is "Is counseling or psychotherapy the most appropriate form of help for this person?" If the answer is yes again, the questions are "What theoretical approach and what specific interventions are optimal for this person with the struggles he is facing?" and "Can I competently serve this person and his needs?" Van Audenhove and Vertommen (2000) point out that the first two of these important questions are often forgotten or bypassed by many clinicians. They, and I, urge clinicians to take those questions seriously with each new potential client.

That being said, assessment also stimulates the consideration of various issues, helps elucidate the nature of the client's problem(s), may lead to alternative approaches to the problem(s), may offer potential solutions, and often allows a means to evaluate the success of counseling (Hood & Johnson, 1991; Lambert & Cattani-Thompson, 1998; Ruddell, 1997).

Without obtaining information from clients, effective counseling is impossible (Persons, 1991; Shertzer & Linden, 1979). Even existentialists (May & Yalom, 1995) and humanists who do not formally assess clients with assessment instruments are continually receiving and encoding information gleaned from their interactions with their clients. Seen in this light, how one conceptualizes this information is a function of one's guiding theory of counseling, regardless of how conscious or unconscious the counselor is of this assessment process (Fall, Holden, & Marquis, 2004; Shertzer & Linden, 1979). The question, then, is not whether or not clinicians should assess their clients, because even Rogers (1961) made assessments of his clients—along dimensions of how open to their experience they were, to what extent their ideal selves and self-concepts were congruent, and so forth: "For the person-centered therapist, the ability to conceptualize [assess] the relative degree and the specific content of one's own and one's client's relative congruence/incongruence is central to the process of counseling and psychotherapy" (cited in Fall et al., 2004, pp. 191–192). Rather, the question seems to be one of how formally, and with what degree of theoretical consistency, the practitioner approaches the process of assessment.

The issue of how formally or informally one performs initial assessments is an important one. As previously stated, all psychotherapists assess their clients in one way or another. I refer to informal assessment as the gathering of information through the process of relating to, or interviewing, the client in session, without the use of an assessment instrument or other formal structure explicitly guiding the process. Some mental health professionals opt for a more formal/structured interview in which an assessment instrument is used to guide the questions and queries the therapist asks in the interview. In contrast to informal assessment, formal assessment involves the use of assessment instruments, whether nomothetic or idiographic, that subsequently will be discussed in detail. Considering the premium assigned to brief therapy by managed care, initial assessment instruments that efficiently gather as much information as possible—ideally without requiring much time during the counseling session itself—may have considerable value for many practitioners and clients (Beutler & Rosner, 1995). According to the author of the *Handbook of Psychological Assessment*, "Managed healthcare emphasizes the cost-effectiveness of providing health services, and for interviewing, this means developing the required information in the least amount of time. This may mean *streamlining interviews by maximizing* computer-derived information or *paper-pencil forms*" (Groth-Marnat, 1999, p. 71; italics added).

Assessment as a Process

Although assessment begins with the initial contact between therapist and client, it certainly does not end there. That is to say, assessment and the entire course of therapy are inextricably and tightly linked (Persons, 1991). "Actually," writes Garfield, "assessment and treatment are intertwined and continue throughout therapy" (2003, p. 175). Moreover, in many ways, assessment *is* a form of intervention; it is the beginning of a process of evaluation of how clients feel, how they experience themselves, what they think is disturbing them, and what their strengths, resources, and best options are (Persons, 1991; Mahoney, 2003). Based upon an initial—and, one hopes, comprehensive—assessment, the therapist constructs a tentative treatment plan. As the therapy progresses, client and therapist periodically evaluate (an ongoing assessment process) how well the treatment is working and "revise the treatment plan as needed, using an empirical hypothesis-testing approach that involves a continual interplay between assessment and treatment" (Persons, 1991, p. 100).

My approach to assessment is highly resonant with Persons' (1991) "case formulation" approach in which the information gleaned from the initial assessment process is used to construct a working hypothesis regarding the nature of the potential factors, issues, and/or mechanisms underlying the client's presenting symptoms and problems. The case formulation provides the basis from which the therapist chooses the particular approach and specific interventions that the therapist deems optimal for this specific individual with these specific issues. Importantly, the case formulation is a working hypothesis that should be continually reassessed based upon information that is obtained from each subsequent session, and revised as needed.

An important caveat to the above paragraph from Van Audenhove and Vertommen's (2000) "negotiation approach" to intake and treatment choice involves the imperative need to find a match or fit between the client's perception of things and the therapist's perspective; the assessment process and construction of a treatment plan is not driven solely by the therapist. It is imperative that clinicians pay attention to how clients experience and assess themselves—what they consider their primary problems, the duration of their problems and any precipitating events, why they are seeking help at this point in time, how they classify themselves, how they relate to themselves, what they see as their strengths and weaknesses, whether they have had therapy before and what their experience of it was like, their assessments of the likelihood of changing for the better, and how they think they can best achieve their desired outcomes and goals: "the client's theory of change is often at least as important as the theory believed by the therapist" (Mahoney, 2003, p. 41; further supported by Bohart & Tallman, 1999; Hoyt, 1998). In addition, how clients interact with therapists often sheds light on their characteristic patterns of behavior, which are usually implicated in the problems for which they are seeking help (Yalom, 2002; Garfield, 2003).

To summarize, in addition to the technical knowledge and clinical expertise that counselors and psychotherapists bring to assessment, initial sessions must always:

- Include an exploration of clients' perspectives regarding both what ails them and their ideas about what might be most helpful
- Involve informing clients of your perspective on them, their problems, and the most appropriate course of treatment
- Involve a negotiation process between the perspectives of client and therapist

Although the primary goal of assessment may be to understand clients in such a way that will ultimately serve their immediate concerns and lifelong development, knowing one's self (deep self-awareness; therapist as instrument) is intimately related to deeply knowing others (Yalom, 2002; Mahoney, 2003).

Attunement

The initial contact that is established in the first session is absolutely critical to successful client outcomes. Whether described as building rapport, establishing a therapeutic relationship, creating an I-thou relationship, or forming a therapeutic "we," the early aspects of coming together are of paramount importance. As such, intake interviews (the first session) ideally constitute a form of mutual exploration of compatibility. Not only are therapists evaluating the nature of clients, their problems, and their contexts, but clients are also assessing whether or not they feel a compatibility and faith in the therapist's capacity to help them. Thus, clients should be given the opportunity to ask any questions they have—either about the process and nature of therapy in general or about how a specific therapist works (including theoretical assumptions and specific interventions used). If therapists do not feel confident that they can be of help to a given client, they should refer that client to others who are more competent with that client's problems, culture, and so forth. Moreover, if a therapist does not like a client, has difficulty relating to or empathizing with a client and his concerns, or feels negative about some dimension of the client's self-presentation, that therapist is not likely to be optimally helpful to that client. The skill of referral deserves more attention and research: not only recognizing when it is appropriate to refer a specific client, but also how to optimally communicate that decision (Wachtel, 1993; see also Mahoney, 2003, pp. 52–54).

In the first session, many therapists opt not to work from a clipboard and a standardized intake form, and many will not take notes in session (Fosha, 2000; Mahoney, 2003; Garfield, 2003). Although I inquire into and listen for any cues regarding concerns that could demand immediate attention, my overall intention for the initial session is to be as authentic and present as possible; I hope to provide clients with a (therapeutic) form of human relating that is experientially distinguishable from what they are accustomed to. Although I try to remember as many of the details of the client's presentation as I can, I am not overly concerned with tracking all of the details; clients will return repeatedly to their central concerns throughout a session or the course of therapy (Fosha, 2000; Wachtel, 1993; Mahoney, 2003).

As the first session approaches its end, I ask clients how they feel about working with me. If we have a sense of mutual optimism, I provide them with the Integral Intake and ask them to complete it before their next session (occasionally I have mailed it to clients prior to their first session if, while speaking on the phone, they express a desire to do anything they can to speed up the process and consent to answering personally sensitive questions prior to establishing a sense of trust with me). I tell clients that we will continually evaluate how our work together is progressing, and I encourage them to engage in as much self-observation and self-monitoring (of thoughts, feelings, actions, interactions, etc.) as possible.

Assessing via Paper-and-Pencil Instruments versus Clinical Interviews

It must also be remembered that "psychological assessment includes the use of clinical skills beyond the mechanical administration of tests and computation of scores ... that the measurement instrument of greatest value in the final analysis is the clinician, not the test" (Beutler & Rosner, 1995, p. 6). In fact, the assessment procedure most frequently used by clinicians is informal, not involving an instrument—the clinical interview (Beutler, 1995b). Clinical interviews can be either structured (following a predetermined format, set of questions, and order) or unstructured (depending upon the counselor's skill, competence, judgment, and creativity) (Vacc & Juhnke, 1997; Beutler, 1995b). Although practitioners more frequently use unstructured interviews, Beutler warned that the unstructured interview is "among the least reliable and potentially least valid measure used in psychological assessment" (1995b, p. 94).

Clinical interviews provide a unique condition for gathering certain types of information that would be difficult to obtain with a paper-and-pencil instrument, such as follow-up questions that search for more detailed descriptions of the client, her circumstances, and her experiences. Interviews also afford the counselor's observation of interpersonal styles and any discrepancies between verbal content and observed behavior.

With these points in mind, Beutler (1995b, p. 97) proposed what he called the "integrative, semistructured interview," which

> occupies a central role in evaluation but does not carry the burden of being the only or even the primary tool .... This conception of the interview as part of a comprehensive clinical evaluation invites the clinician to incorporate the semistructured interview into an integrative battery of assessment procedures.

In essence, such an interview is what occurs between counselor and client after the counselor has perused the client's completed biographical inventory. This would also be an appropriate way of assessing an illiterate client.

Initial research into the effectiveness of the Integral Intake also shed some unexpected light upon some of the "shadows" of assessment (Marquis, 2002). Many of the research participants—despite their enthusiasm or fondness for a given inventory—reported that they would prefer to assess their clients via dialogue or informal interview rather than with paper-and-pencil instruments. Their concerns revolved around the potential danger that clients might be "put off" by having to reveal such personal information prior to establishing a trusting and sound therapeutic alliance. I agree that this is an important and valid concern. Clinicians should use their own clinical judgment regarding which clients will appreciate filling out a paper-and-pencil inventory versus which clients would be better served by being assessed informally via dialogue; in the latter case, the therapist might use the inventory as a guide to the intake interview. Of course, the therapist can simply ask potential clients if they would rather fill out a detailed series of biographical and contextual questions or if they would prefer to have the therapist ask them similar questions in a counseling interview.

Clinical Flexibility

The issue of whether to have clients complete intake forms, and if so, when, is a complicated and critical matter. Examples abound of clients who leave waiting rooms, never to return, because they "couldn't go through" the process of writing such personal information on an impersonal form (Kottler & Brew, 2003). Thus, many clinicians opt to have their first contact with new clients focused on building a strong, therapeutic alliance. More often than not, I give clients the Integral Intake after our initial session together, for them to complete before our next session together. As you can see in the letter to new clients (included on the CD), I sometimes mail it to clients before the initial session *if* they are cognizant of what is involved and consent to that wholeheartedly (if they seem genuinely interested in diving into the process and "getting a head start").

Thus, exactly how to use the Integral Intake is up to each clinician. If you tend to have most or all of your clients complete intake forms, you can have them do that with the Integral Intake, either before or after the initial interview. Research suggests there isn't a more comprehensive, efficient, or clinically useful idiographic assessment instrument than the Integral Intake (Marquis, 2002). For those therapists who rarely or never have clients complete such forms—those clinicians whose priority is building a sound therapeutic relationship—the theoretical framework of the Integral Intake can be used either as the framework for a comprehensive semistructured clinical interview or to help remind you to eventually touch all the bases of those dynamics and factors that are relevant to each client's challenges and strengths (this may occur throughout the course of treatment; more on this in Chapters 2 through 6). Essentially, therapists have considerable freedom regarding exactly how to use the Integral Intake; they can tailor their use of it to fit their preferred style.

Nomothetic and Idiographic Assessment

When considering what type of assessment instrument to use, probably the most significant issue revolves around the choice of nomothetic versus idiographic instruments. *Nomothetic* instruments are quantitative and have been standardized and thus provide a normative frame of reference—a norm—to which the individual's scores can be compared. In contrast, *idiographic* instruments, also called "ipsative"—self-referent—instruments, have not been standardized and, therefore, use the individual as her own reference point (Beutler, 1995a). Idiographic instruments are thus more concerned with individual differences and the uniqueness of each person. As Hood and Johnson wrote, "nomothetic techniques can be more readily interpreted, but they may not be as relevant or as penetrating as idiographic methods" (1991, p. 7). Relevant to this issue, Mahoney has underscored the "certain irony in the historical fact that psychological measurements were originally developed to document individual differences, yet have come to be used in ways that diminish those differences" (2003, pp. 39–40).

The *Journal of Counseling and Development,* the flagship journal of the American Counseling Association, has for more than a decade made a deliberate and explicit move

> from a focus on test reviews to the broader concept of "assessment" . . . a general trend away from selection-oriented prediction models in which test scores were used to "predict" various attributes (achievement, career choice, etc.) to more qualitative assessment techniques designed for exploration, self-knowledge, self-assessment, and diagnosis. (Hohenshil, 1996, p. 64)

Beutler (1995a) pointed out that the preferences in human sciences for quantitative measurements and methodologies have come primarily from researchers in academia. Mahoney (1991, 2003) lamented that numbers and "quantophilia" often still bear more scientific capital and authority than idiographic, qualitative assessment. Although nomothetic measures often provide valuable means for conceptualizing clients' problems and patterns, they are far from infallible: "the limitations of numbers to capture important qualities is readily apparent when it comes to the measurement of meaning, particularly personal meaning. Quantifiable measures of persons are plentiful, but meaningful measures are elusive" (Mahoney, 2003, p. 39). Mahoney and I are not bashing numbers, mathematics, or nomothetic assessments. In any integral system, all perspectives are valued and included, yet their limitations and partiality are also recognized simultaneously. A primary limitation of nomothetic assessment is the virtual impossibility of its adequately capturing and conveying clients' personal meanings and realities in simple summary numbers and statistics.

Among the most commonly used nomothetic assessment scales in psychotherapy and psychotherapeutic research are the Beck Depression Inventory (BDI), the Minnesota Multiphasic Personality Inventory (MMPI-2), the Wechsler Adult Intelligence Scale and Wechsler Intelligence Scale for Children (WAIS-R, WISC-III), the Millon Clinical Multiaxial Inventory (MCMI), Symptom Checklist-90-Revised (SCL-90-R), and the California Psychological Inventory (CPI) (Groth-Marnat, 1999). In contrast to the "quantophilia" of many academicians are clinicians who "have become disillusioned with quantitative methods and have criticized academic psychology and measurement theorists for the failure to attend to individual idiosyncrasies" (Beutler, 1995a, p. 81). Clinicians tend to believe that idiographic assessments, such as multidimensional biographical inventories, capture more accurately the complexity of what it is to be human, attempting to attend to the whole person and her environment. Beutler also pointed out that because idiographic instruments lack quantitative demonstrations of their validity and reliability, it is important for such instruments to be theoretically grounded.

Theoretically based initial assessment instruments are few indeed. Only three have been published: the Life-Style Introductory Interview (LSII) (Eckstein et al., 1992), the Multimodal Life History Inventory (MLHI) (Lazarus, 1997), and the (constructive) Personal Experience Report (PER) (Mahoney, 2003) (the PER was not included in my dissertation research because it was published after my dissertation research was completed; Mahoney, coincidentally, was on my dissertation committee). Given the widely recognized assumption that optimal counseling is guided by theory and that assessment "is embedded within the overall context of counseling" (Ruddell, 1997), it seems surprising that a thorough search of the professional literature yielded only three theoretically based initial assessment instruments. It is an even less predictable circumstance given the following quote from Persons (1991, p. 100):

> Assessment strategies in outcome studies are descriptive and atheoretical, emphasizing diagnosis. In contrast, assessment strategies described by theories of psychotherapy are determined by the psychotherapeutic model and its constructs.... Psychological theories are not usually theories about diagnostic categories; instead they are theories about psychological phenomena and processes.

It appears that many counselors, especially those practicing in community agencies, clinics, and hospitals, use unpublished initial assessment inventories that have been designed relative both to the types of clients who most frequently seek their services and also to the types of research they are conducting. Although such approaches have utility and afford some measure of success, published theoretically grounded initial assessment instruments not only gather information efficiently and from the perspective of the counselor's guiding theory but also allow the opportunity for far greater numbers of practitioners to use them, thus affording greater possibilities for comparison and research as well as increased effectiveness. Moreover, with published assessment instruments already in existence, creating assessment instruments anew is quite like reinventing the wheel.

A final benefit of idiographic methods involves their greater economy and efficiency in gathering information about a broad range of topics by comparison with most nomothetic methods. In addition, idiographic methods allow the counselor to obtain types of information that are unobtainable with nomothetic methods. This is especially true of cultural and environmental factors, as well as qualitative, subjective information such as what is most meaningful to the client (Hood & Johnson, 1991; Mahoney, 2003).

It is important to emphasize that the Integral Intake was constructed in order to be pragmatically helpful—to increase clinical effectiveness.

It was not designed for assessment purposes in standardized research. Nonetheless, although outcome assessment is not what the Integral Intake was designed for, a study by Farnsworth, Hess, and Lambert (2001) found that client self-reports (which is the form of data obtained with the Integral Intake) are the most common source for outcome data in psychotherapy research.

Differentiating Assessment and Diagnosis

Psychodiagnosis, more commonly referred to simply as diagnosis, involves analyzing and explaining the specific problems, disorders, or pathologies from which a person suffers. A diagnosis can also include a person's strengths and other positive dimensions but more commonly focuses on a person's psychopathology, its causal origins, a treatment procedure, and a prognosis (Corey, 2001). As such, diagnosis represents a subset of the more inclusive concept of assessment: all diagnosis is assessment, but not all assessment is diagnosis (Mahoney, 2003). Others, such as Hohenshil (1996), have differentiated these terms differently; according to him, assessing involves the activity of collecting information to help one arrive at a diagnosis, which he defines as the interpretation or meaning derived from one's assessment.

It is common sense that psychotherapy should target the nature of the client's problems, struggles, and/or psychopathology (depending on how one conceives of the reasons people seek professional help—from moral frameworks of suffering, betrayals, and questions of what makes a life worth living to medical frameworks that posit biomedical causes for mental unrest) and that the treatment plan and specific interventions used should match the identified problems (Clarkin & Levy, 2004). Whereas all therapists assess their clients in some manner, therapists differ greatly in their views of diagnosis, particularly those from the diagnostic bible—the *Diagnostic and Statistical Manual of Mental Disorders* (*DSM-IV-TR*) (American Psychiatric Association, 2000). Some view *DSM* diagnoses as absolutely essential to effective therapy, whereas "others view it as unnecessary, as a detriment, or as discriminatory against ethnic minorities and women" (Corey, 2001, p. 53). At best, "the use of *DSM-IV* as a guide for psychotherapy outcome research is a mixed blessing" (Clarkin & Levy, 2004, p. 198). It is a mixed blessing because its emphasis on categorical biomedical diagnosis (Douthit & Marquis, 2006) does not attend to other crucial mediating variables such as the client's attributional style, dysfunctional attitudes, sociode-mographic characteristics, client-learned resourcefulness, positive expectation of help, and a strong commitment to treatment (summarized in Clarkin & Levy, 2004, p. 199). "I, personally," wrote Garfield, "do not attempt to make a formal psychiatric diagnosis; however, it is generally required where third-party payments are involved. Of greater concern are variables that are potentially related more closely to psychotherapy process and outcome" (2003, p. 175).

One noteworthy difference between DSM diagnoses and other forms of assessment is that the former is based upon a categorical approach in which mental disorders are classified according to types that are defined by specific criteria sets, whereas the latter may be dimensional in nature—specifying where along a continuous spectrum an individual is with regard to, for example, narcissism. As stated in the *DSM-IV-TR* (pp. xxxi–xxxii) itself:

> A categorical approach to classification works best when all members of a diagnostic class are homogenous, when there are clear boundaries between classes, and when the different classes are mutually exclusive … the limitations of the categorical classification system must be recognized.

> In DSM-IV, there is no assumption that each category of mental disorder is a completely discrete entity with absolute boundaries dividing it from other mental disorders or from no mental disorder…. It was suggested that the DSM-IV Classification be organized following a dimensional model rather than the categorical model used in the DSM-III-R. A dimensional system classifies clinical presentations based on quantification of attributes rather than the assignment to categories and works best in describing phenomena that are distributed continuously and that do not have clear boundaries.

Clearly, the benefits of conceptualizing clients' developmental and presenting issues along dimensional spectra—in contrast to assigning them to an either-or category—provides many clinical benefits. This will be further addressed in Chapters 4, 5, and 7.

Of course, some clients desire a diagnosis, for several different reasons. First, clients often use their diagnoses as explanations for their ways of being. Second, when a mental health professional provides a diagnosis, clients tend to perceive that the professional has confidently and accurately identified the problem, which is often the first step in successful treatment. In contrast, most psychotherapeutic treatment approaches, even the majority of those on the list of "empirically supported treatments," tend to be highly experimental and nonspecific. In other words, those approaches that are deemed effective tend to be effective with individuals diagnosed with a wide range of problems/mental disorders (Marquis & Douthit, 2006; Westen, Novotny, & Thompson-Brenner, 2004; Westen & Morrison, 2001). Thus:

> Diagnoses appear to be serving functions other than specifying the best form of treatment. My concern is that, through the proliferation and continuing entrenchment of a pathology-centered diagnostic system, our personal and collective tendencies toward categories are being exploited in ways that do not optimally serve our clients or our professional focus. (Mahoney, 2003, p. 41)

Biographical Inventories

Biographical inventories, also called personal data records, personal history questionnaires, biographical data inventories, and personal/biographical data banks, are self-report questionnaires developed as alternatives to in-person interviews. Two advantages of such inventories are economy and efficiency relative to time needed to gather information because they are completed by the client outside of the session, and uniformity in format compared to unstructured interviews (Shertzer & Linden, 1979). In addition, one of the virtues characteristic of health- and wellness-oriented self-assessment is its contribution to a sense of personal responsibility (Dana & Hoffman, 1987). The responses provided by clients to such inventories provide excellent jumping-off places—leads that the counselor can further explore during subsequent sessions. Such inventories also enable practitioners to compare results among various clients, although not in terms of standard scores, as in the case of nomothetic instruments. For example, a simple frequency count of the number of hobbies written down may be significantly different between clients who are depressed and those who are not.

The value of such inventories

> depends on four factors: (1) the comprehensiveness with which the instrument asks for data regarding individual characteristics; (2) the accuracy with which the individual describes himself or herself; (3) the perspective that the instrument provides counselors, teachers, and other personnel on areas of individual characteristics and behavior that should be explored in interviews or counseling sessions; and (4) the opportunities that this technique affords individuals for obtaining an increased degree of self-understanding. (Shertzer & Linden, 1979, p. 383)

Shertzer and Linden further wrote:

> To make self-understanding and personal development a primary rather than secondary purpose of testing will require major changes in measurement instruments and technology. Such change is but in its infancy today. It is an exciting venture and represents a trend highly promising for the work of counselors. (1979, p. 538–539)

It was with that spirit in mind—to focus not merely on psychopathology, but also to emphasize the value of self-awareness and constructive developmental potentials—that I created the Integral Intake.

Multidimensional Assessment Instruments

Multidimensional assessment instruments are a type of biographical inventory that attempt to yield as much information as possible regarding the major dimensions of human experience. Although the exact content of such instruments varies as a function of the instruments' theoretical underpinnings, the goal is to obtain as comprehensive a "snapshot" as possible of the whole person and the environment in which the person resides (George, 1994). Such comprehensive approaches can also yield crucial relationships among various dimensions of the person's well-being (Marquis, 2007). Several authors have noted that assessment inventories seldom address environmental factors that might influence clients' problems and difficulties (Karg & Wiens, 1998;

Pressly & Heesacker, 2001; Shertzer & Linden, 1979). Approximately one quarter of the Integral Intake is devoted explicitly to gathering such environmental, systemic, "interobjective" information.

As previously stated, a review of the counseling and psychology literature revealed only two published, theoretically derived initial assessment instruments designed for counseling, both of which are multidimensional: the Life-Style Introductory Interview (Eckstein et al., 1992) and the Multimodal Life History Inventory (Lazarus & Lazarus, 1991).[1] It was surprising to find such a dearth of theoretically grounded initial assessment protocols, especially given that the assessment literature describes numerous structured clinical interviews (Hodges, 1993). However, as Vacc and Juhnke explained, "the structured descriptive assessment interview is not based on any particular theoretical framework" (1997, p. 471)—at least not usually. Following are brief descriptions of the LSII and the LMHI—both of which can be used as either paper-and-pencil instruments or as guides to structured clinical interviews—as well as their strengths and weaknesses.

Life-Style Introductory Interview

Central to Adlerian psychotherapy and counseling is lifestyle investigation (Eckstein et al., 1992; Mosak, 1995). Lifestyle has been conceived of as one's "personal mythology" (Mosak, 1995, p. 70): a form of personality structure consisting of the beliefs and orienting principles that people construct by four to six years of age to help them organize and understand their experience. Investigating a client's lifestyle involves exploring how the person experienced early formative influences. The focus is on one's perceptions of one's first social group, typically one's family-of-origin constellation. "Although the time reference is the past, determination of implications for the present and future is the goal of life-style assessment" (Eckstein et al., 1992, pp. 21–22).

By 1929, Adler had created lifestyle forms for young children, adolescents, and adults. He wrote that gaining information about the eighteen questions constituting the adult form would provide "extensive insight into the style of life of the individual already within about half an hour" (cited in Eckstein et al., 1992, p. 43). In 1967, Dreikurs elaborated upon those 18 questions and created a longer questionnaire, providing much of the material for the current LSII (Eckstein et al., 1992), a copyrighted instrument that may be obtained from the Kendall/Hunt Publishing Company.

The LSII begins by inquiring into the client's subjective "way of being in the world" and then has the client rate herself on the life task dimensions of work/school, friendship, love, self-esteem, and spirituality/existentialia. The majority of the inventory is devoted to exploring the atmosphere of the client's family of origin with questions such as "Who was most different from you? How? If you are an only child, in your peer group who was most different from you? How?" "Who was most like you?" and "Who took care of whom?" Next, the client is presented with 23 characteristics such as "intelligent," "conforming," and "idealistic," and the client is asked to rate which sibling is most and least characterized by each adjective. The client then describes her parents, including who was each parent's favorite child and why. The inventory ends with inquiry into the client's early recollections and any recurring dreams.

Multimodal Life History Inventory

In 1966, Arnold Lazarus wrote that

> anamnestic interviews may be considerably shortened with literate individuals by asking them to complete, at their leisure, a Life History Questionnaire... . Using the completed questionnaire as a guide, patient and therapist may quite rapidly obtain a comprehensive picture of the patient's past experiences and current status. (Cited in Lazarus & Lazarus, 1998, p. 15)

Since 1966, Lazarus' initial inventory has evolved through four versions, with each revision incorporating what was learned from field testing. The most recent version appeared in 1997 and is called the Multimodal Life History Inventory (MLHI). It is a 15-page, copyrighted inventory, and it can be obtained from Research Press.

Lazarus, like others noted before, reported that he uses the inventory as a guide in interviewing those clients who will not or cannot complete it on their own. Lazarus reportedly advises clients to complete the inventory over several days rather than trying to finish it in one sitting. After the client returns the completed inventory, the therapist should read through the completed form in her own time, noting items she wishes to pursue further in session. Clients are told they can leave blank their names or any other identifying information if that will help them complete the inventory more honestly.

Evaluation of the MLHI and LLSI

The MLHI is a rather comprehensive instrument, and Lazarus should be commended for the clarity and breadth with which he translated his theory of counseling into a means of assessment. From an integral perspective (which will be discussed in detail in Chapter 2), however, what seems to be lacking is attention to the client's physical environment, culture, spirituality, and other meaning-making dimensions. Research has also revealed that an additional weakness of the MLHI is its length, which often leads to "fatigue" and "feeling overwhelmed" in an attempt to complete it (Marquis, 2002). The question that initially guided my dissertation research was whether or not a comparable breadth of information could be gleaned more efficiently by a less lengthy instrument. The answer to that question is yes (Marquis, 2002; Marquis & Holden, in press; see Chapter 8 in the present volume). Although the LSII inquires with a bit more detail into the client's family-of-origin atmosphere, the LSII is less comprehensive than the MLHI. Moreover, like the MLHI, the LSII does not inquire into the physical aspects of the client's current environment or the client's culture. Thus, the need for a more comprehensive inventory appeared to be substantiated.

Integral Intake

From an integral perspective, (comprehensive assessment) involves at least two aspects, (developmental) and (quadratic.) Developmental issues of clients are extremely relevant to clinicians' choice of treatment modalities. However, after more than a year of inquiry, research, and much consultation with developmental researchers such as Don Beck, Susanne Cook-Greuter, and Jeffrey Soulen (Beck & Cowan, 2000; Cook-Greuter, 2003; Cook-Greuter & Soulen, 2007), I realized that measures of self-development—for example, the Sentence Completion Test (Hy & Loevinger, 1996) and the Subject-Object Interview (Kegan, 1982)—are extensive both in administration and scoring/interpretation, which makes them costly to clients in terms of both time and money. I thus concluded that it would defeat my goal of assessing clients efficiently (in a manner that does not overwhelm them) to formally include a comprehensive developmental dimension to the Integral Intake. Much more about assessing clients' developmental levels and lines will be discussed in Chapters 4 and 5.

Because a primary motivation in creating the Integral Intake was a balance of comprehensiveness and efficiency, I decided to emphasize the quadratic aspects of integral theory (Marquis, 2007), which is more fundamental to getting the "whole picture" of the client than formal and explicit assessment of developmental issues. Nonetheless, the Integral Intake does include a checklist of common developmental problems as well as other questions that inquire into developmental issues. Moreover, other aspects of integral counseling, such as developmental lines, states of consciousness, and personality types, are also addressed in the Integral Intake (see Chapters 4 through 7).

Diversity and Multicultural Issues

It is important to distinguish between diversity and multiculturalism. Whereas the term *diversity* involves issues of how people vary along dimensions such as ethnicity, race, gender, age, sexual orientation, religious affiliation, social class, and health status, the term *multiculturalism* demands attention to issues of power and privilege (Robinson, 1997; Cormier & Hackney, 2005). Although these terms can be defined in many ways, their meanings revolve around the notions of differential access to resources (power) and unearned advantage and thus dominance (privilege) (Cormier & Hackney, 2005).

Assessment of diverse clients—of any client from a culture other than that upon which a test has been standardized—presents numerous difficulties (Kottler & Brew, 2003; Hood & Johnson, 1991; Shertzer & Linden, 1979). Fortunately, idiographic assessments bypass most of those difficulties by focusing on the individual's uniqueness and individuality. Nonetheless, it is still imperative that the counselor proactively seek a greater understanding of diverse clients' cultural backgrounds, especially with regard to how they make meaning from their experiences. Such understanding facilitates more accurate interpretations of the meanings of the completed assessment. Thus, the client's cultural background must always be taken into account and the therapist must remain sensitive to what the client's responses mean *from the client's cultural perspective*. As will be discussed further in Chapters 2 and 3, the Integral Intake gives nearly one quarter of its attention to cultural dimensions of clients and their concerns.

If a therapist is not mindful of the client's sundry cultural contexts, the therapist may arrive at an erroneous diagnosis: "A clinician who is unfamiliar with the nuances of an individual's cultural frame of reference may incorrectly judge as psychopathology those normal variations in behavior, belief, or experience that are particular to the individual's culture" (*DSM-IV-TR*, p. xxxiv). Whether these errors involve misinterpreting specific religious beliefs or experiences as psychotic or assessing an African American, Latina, or Native American as unmotivated, inhibited, or repressed, insensitivity to clients' diversity and other ethnocentric biases profoundly interfere with our ability to optimally serve diverse clients. Bear in mind that many of these diverse clients who are seeking help feel systemically oppressed and marginalized from power differentials in society at large. At a more iatrogenic end of the assessment spectrum, therapists who are not mindful of how their position of power as a professional—especially with regard to how one acquires much sensitive information during the initial phases of therapy—can play out with those who already may feel vulnerable can reproduce in therapy the very things that are responsible for clients' seeking professional help in the first place.

The Need for Integral Assessment

Accurate assessment is critical not only in integral counseling (Marquis & Wilber, in press; Marquis, 2007; Marquis & Warren, 2004) but in all counseling, because different people—with different quadratic issues and at different stages of development—face different struggles whose resolution demands different counseling approaches and practices. The research of Van Audenhove & Vertommen (2000, p. 288; italics added) revealed that

> in most cases the psychotherapist's theoretical framework determines the specific form of intake and this in turn strongly predetermines the kind of treatment selected for a client.... There is no *metatheoretical* framework in which problems and complaints are conceptualized so that the choice of the most appropriate method for a specific client can be made.

Although the integral approach has thus far been referred to as a theory, you will discover in Chapter 2 that it is actually just the sort of metatheoretical framework that Van Audenhove & Vertommen (2000) state is needed to assess clients with the least theoretical bias possible, so that the most appropriate treatment is delivered to each client rather than providing a similar treatment to each client. As you will see, integral counselors have a metatheoretical justification for why they may practice quite cognitive-behaviorally with one client while being very psychodynamic or existential with others.

As you will see throughout this book, it is important to determine in which quadrant(s) a client's concerns predominantly originate, and what resonances may be occurring in other quadrants as a result. For example, although the significance and relevance of environmental, cultural, and spiritual issues has been acknowledged in the counseling literature, few assessments address these in a thorough manner (Karg & Wiens, 1998). Most assessments "have concentrated on the individual and the individual's specific traits, states, aptitudes, and attitudes. Little attention has been paid to the environments in which individuals function" (Hood & Johnson, 1991, p. 168). The environment (including both interobjective/systemic and intersubjective/cultural dimensions) is, of course, the bottom half of integral theory's four quadrants (see Figure 1 in Chapter 2). The Integral Intake will thus help provide an overview of not only the client but also her environment (both social/interobjective and cultural/intersubjective).

Similarly, even though 96% of the U.S. population reports believing in God or some sort of universal Spirit and 92% report being affiliated with some form of religion, most assessment instruments fail to adequately inquire into religious and spiritual dimension of clients (Marquis, 2002). Prochaska and Norcross stated that therapists are increasingly integrating religious and spiritual issues with their psychotherapeutic treatment, "but in the future religion and spirituality will be incorporated more specifically and overtly into therapy. Clinicians will include religion and spirituality as a standard dimension of clinical assessment, especially as a potential strength and social support" (2003, p. 556). As will be discussed in Chapter 8, the Integral Intake—compared to the LMHI and LSII—was evaluated as the best assessment of clients' spirituality; both rankings and ratings between the Integral Intake and LMHI and between the Integral Intake and LSII were statistically significant, $p < .001$ (Marquis, 2002; see Chapter 8).

The Integral Intake has been developed to help clinicians clarify which perspectives (quadrants) and which levels of development reflect the client's most pressing issues (Marquis, 2002). These two central aspects of integral assessment, as well as other essential dimensions of integral assessment (developmental lines, personality types, states of consciousness, and the self-system) and how to construct a treatment plan from them, will be discussed in subsequent chapters.

Conclusion

The law of the hammer states that if the only available tool is a hammer, many things will appear to need hammering. This dynamic also applies to therapists, some of whom develop proficiency in certain interventions and then use them in more situations than call for those specific interventions (Mahoney, 2003, p. 57). One of my goals was to develop a tool—the Integral Intake—that is capable of accommodating diverse clients with their sundry issues and needs, thus helping clinicians expand their theoretical and practical "toolboxes," and even assisting their choosing the optimal "tool"/treatment approach for each individual client.

Note

1. As previously mentioned, after my dissertation research was completed, which compared the clinical utility, comprehensiveness, and efficiency of the existing theoretically derived, initial assessment instruments designed for counseling, Mahoney published a book (2003) that includes an initial assessment inventory, the Personal Experience Report.

2

INTEGRAL THEORY

*The Metatheory Behind the Integral Intake**

Introduction

Integral theory is a way of knowing that helps one strive for the most comprehensive understanding of any phenomenon—in this case, assessing clients and creating treatment plans. A primary purpose of integral theory is to foster the recognition that disparate aspects of our clients and their circumstances—from biological constitution and felt sense of selfhood to cultural worldviews and social systems—are all critically influential to one's well-being or suffering, and therefore should be given attention in the assessment process be given attention in the assessment process. Applying integral theory to our practice of assessment and therapy thus guides the "real world" applications of our understandings so that we may better serve our clients and professions.

How can integral theory incorporate elements such as counseling, social work, biomedicine, psychology, and diversity studies into higher-order, unified wholes? It does this by providing a parsimonious and *tight*

---

* This chapter is an adapted reprint from Marquis' article in *Counseling and Values, 51(3)*, pp. 164–178. © 2007 The American Counseling Association. Reprinted with permission. No further reproduction is authorized without written permission from the American Counseling Association.

self-reflexive conceptual scaffold within which to order the myriad approaches to understanding and helping others, from psychoanalytic, cognitive-behavioral, existential-humanistic, and transpersonal perspectives to biomedical, sociological, philosophical, and economic ones. An integrating, unifying metaframework such as integral theory is *not* intended to minimize the significant differences we find across cultures, across systems, or between individuals from the same culture or family; this would clearly represent a disadvantage to this approach. However, in addition to acknowledging that differences are salient, vital, and add spice to life, integral theorists also search for the deep pattern similarities that pervade striking surface variations between individuals and cultures (see Wilber 1999d, 2000b). Thus, it is often said that the integral approach genuinely honors unity within diversity. The advantage of searching for unifying patterns is, in this case, to reconcile apparent contradictions between the various approaches to counseling and assessment. To do so, in my view, leads to more inclusive, holistic, and effective therapy.

Integral theory is actually a metatheoretical framework that simultaneously honors the important contributions of a broad spectrum of epistemological outlooks while also acknowledging the parochial limits and misconceptions of those perspectives. In other words, integral theory provides us with a metaperspective that allows us to situate all of the diverse knowledge approaches (from premodern to modern to postmodern) in such a way that they synergistically complement, rather than contradict, one another. What is this theoretical framework called integral theory? Simply put, it is AQAL (pronounced *ah-kwihl*).

AQAL: All Quadrants, All Levels

AQAL refers to "all quadrants, all levels," and also "all lines, all types, all states." The meaning of this will be explicated shortly. However, we begin our discussion with a description of the four quadrants.

All Quadrants: The Four Quadrants

The four quadrants are a central component of the unifying model that Wilber (2000b) developed in response to the plethora of apparently contradictory assertions by diverse disciplines and theoretical approaches. This model allows therapists to situate diverse perspectives such that they augment and complement, rather than compete with and contradict, one another. The four quadrants are formed by the intersection of

Table 2.1 The Four Quadrants in Counseling and Psychotherapy

Upper Left (UL): Interior-Individual Experience—as felt "from the inside"	Upper Right (UR): Exterior-Individual Behavior—as seen "from the outside"
• Any noteworthy patterns in the client's self-experience • Self-image, self-concept • Self-esteem, self-efficacy • Instability or stability • Joy, zest, purpose, motivation • Depression, sadness, emptiness • Anxiety, "jitters," feeling "revved up" • Political, religious, and/or spiritual beliefs and/or experiences • Consciousness as experienced as mind • The experience of, for example, depression: sadness, loss of interest in pleasurable activities, fatigue, feelings of worthlessness, difficulty concentrating, frequent thoughts of death, suicidal ideation, etc.; also how one interprets events such as the death of a loved one, divorce, profound loss, or childbirth	• Any noteworthy patterns of behavior: what specific behaviors bring the client to therapy and what specific behaviors will indicate successful outcome? • Medical disorders • Medication • Diet • Alcohol and/or drug use • Aerobic and/or strength training • Patterns of sleep and rest • Consciousness as described by neurotransmission and the functioning of brain structures • Observable changes in, for example, depression: appears tearful, no longer engages in pleasurable activities, significant weight loss or gain, psychomotor agitation or retardation, lower levels of available serotonin, social withdrawal
Lower Left (LL): Interior-Collective Culture—the group's experience "from the inside"	**Lower Right (LR): Exterior-Collective Social systems—the group's behavior "from the outside"**
• Client's experience of ethnicity • Client's experience of family dynamics • Client's meaning-making system(s) • Client's relationships with significant others, especially spouse, boss, friends, and family • The medium of the therapeutic relationship and how both the client and therapist experience their intersubjectivity • Cultural meanings assigned to, for example, depression: sick, lazy, irresponsible, heartbroken, hexed, bewitched, etc.	• Client's socioeconomic status • Condition of one's neighborhood • Environmental stressors and/or comforts; layout of household • Analyses of interpersonal dynamics, including family history • Treatment contexts (setting—inpatient/outpatient and physical nature of therapy setting; frequency and length of sessions; modality—individual/group/family therapy) • Social systems that contribute to, for example, depression: economic (poverty, drug- and gang-ridden neighborhoods); educational (poor/dangerous schools); medical (minimal access to health care—brief therapy or none at all); racism, sexism, classism, ageism, etc.

two axes: interior-exterior and individual-collective (see Table 2.1). In other words, the four quadrants are aspects of, and perspectives on, reality that yield four interrelated yet irreducible domains/perspectives. Integral theory posits that comprehensive description of any phenomenon requires that one account for these four irreducible perspectives:

- Experiential (subjective): the individual viewed from the interior
- Behavioral (objective): the individual viewed from the exterior
- Cultural (intersubjective): the collective viewed from the interior
- Social (interobjective): the collective viewed from the exterior

In a bit more detail, the four quadrants manifest as follows.

Upper Left/Experiential: Interior-Individual

This quadrant includes the subjective, phenomenal dimension of individual consciousness—any and all experiences, sensations, perceptions, feelings, and thoughts that can be phenomenologically described in "I" language. It also includes the spectrum of those impulses, occasions, and motivations of which the person is unconscious.

Upper Right/Behavioral: Exterior-Individual

This quadrant includes the relatively objective, positivistic perspective of individual structures, behaviors, events, and processes that can be scientifically described in "it" language.

Lower Left/Cultural: Interior-Collective

This quadrant includes the intersubjective dimension of the collective (Hargens, 2001). This perspective requires a sympathetic resonance common only to members of a given community—shared worldviews, customs, linguistic semantics, ethics, communal values, and other meaning-making activities that are mutually understood by members of a given culture and are subjectively described in "you/we" language. It also includes relationships with significant others, most notably one's spouse, boss(es), friends, and family.

Lower Right/Social: Exterior-Collective

This quadrant includes the interobjective perspective of systems, addressing aspects of societies such as economic structures, civic resources (education systems, employment opportunities, available transportation), governmental systems, and city planning (architectural style, spacious versus congested, available parks and other areas of natural beauty). Social phenomena are described in objective, third person, plural ("its") language. It also includes any observable interactions between the parts of a system.

For example, when seeking to understand the phenomenon of a client, each of these four perspectives yields different meanings and information necessary for a more complete understanding. This understanding, in turn, reveals that none of the four perspectives can be reduced to another perspective without violating the essential value of the former's point of view. For example, to reduce the experiences of love or anxiety (UL) to nothing but neurotransmission and brain structures (UR) is to subjugate lived experience to only what can be objectively observed and measured (privileging the brain over the mind). Likewise, to ignore recent breakthroughs in neuroscience (UR) and focus solely on phenomenology (UL) or social discourses and practices (LL) would be merely the converse form of "quadrant absolutism," in which one perspective is consistently privileged over the other three.

Each quadrant provides a different, but valid, perspective for a given phenomenon. For example, therapists can use integral theory to understand presenting complaints by quadrant (Ingersoll, 2002). Referring back to Table 2.1, the felt experience of depression is inextricably constituted by UL factors including self-appraisals of worthlessness; UR factors such as sleep disturbances, EEG abnormalities, dysregulated neurotransmitter systems, and alterations of neuropeptides; LL factors, which influence both the likelihood of developing a depressive episode (a consumer culture in which energies are directed toward acquiring material goods rather than cultivating interior development) as well as how the depression is interpreted (medical disease versus inauthenticity versus hexed); and LR factors such as living in poverty and lacking appropriate mental health care. As you can see, every experience or event irreducibly has subjective, objective, intersubjective, and interobjective dimensions, and to ignore or dismiss one or more of these dimensions is to be incomplete or reductionistic. Thus, from an integral perspective, an individual's psychological development is understood as a phenomenon with at least four distinct dimensions (quadrants) that mutually constitute one another.

All Levels: The Spectrum Approach

Prior to writing his first book, Wilber (1999a) was working through a radical conceptual transformation that fundamentally involved the problem of how to reconcile some apparently diametrically opposed truth claims from geniuses as diverse as Newton/Einstein, Freud/Skinner, and the Buddha/Aquinas. Wilber was working toward his doctorate in biochemistry when he became cognizant of the different forms of "truth value" that various disciplines privilege. He realized that positivistic science is not wrong; rather, it is limited in its ability to disclose much of human experience. Most prominently, science seemed silent with regard to the meaning(s) of life. To address this issue, Wilber began an intellectual journey through the literatures of science (from physics and chemistry to psychology and sociology), philosophy (Eastern and Western, premodern, modern, and postmodern), and religion (Eastern and Western, belief-based and contemplative). He quickly found himself immersed in multiple truth claims, methodologies, and practices, each apparently contradictory, from figures as diverse as Plato, the Buddha, Descartes, and Freud. "I felt they were all saying something true," wrote Wilber, "but that none of them had it entirely figured out... . It slowly dawned on me that these people weren't all addressing the same level of consciousness" (cited in Schwartz, 1995, p. 351). Thus the question was no longer "Whose view is correct?" but "How do these differing insights fit together in such a way that they don't contradict one another?" Wilber's questioning culminated in what he called the "spectrum approach," a developmental model that, arguably, includes and honors the most comprehensive spectrum of developmental potentials, from the earliest and most basic (Mahler, Pine, & Bergman, 1975) to the most fully mature and complex (White, 1984).

In any stage theory of development, one can fall prey to an arbitrariness regarding drawing distinctions (levels or stages) in what is actually a relatively continuous process. Throughout his work, Wilber (2000b) conceptualized the basic structures of consciousness with different degrees of specificity,[1] although he usually describes them as 10 holarchical[2] spheres clustered into three broad realms: *prepersonal, personal,* and *suprapersonal.* The prepersonal realm and the personal realm are consensually corroborated by much of Western academic psychology (Freud, 1963; Kohut, 1977; Mahler et al., 1975; Piaget, 1977).

Empirical evidence for the suprapersonal realm derives mostly from the developmental taxonomies found in the contemplative traditions, both Eastern and Western (Brown, 1986; Chirban, 1986).

Wilber (1999d) used several different words to describe the basic stages of consciousness development. He uses the word *levels* to connote the qualitatively distinct nature of each stage of development, *structures* to underscore the integrated and holistic nature of each stage, and *waves* to emphasize the fluidity with which the stages flow into one another. Importantly, an individual is not *at* a particular stage or level of development. Rather, the entire spectrum of development is present, as a potential to be realized, within each individual. Moreover, these stages are viewed not as reified structures but as probability waves, suggesting not a concrete structure residing within the individual but rather that an individual's developmental level is fundamentally a function of that person's residing in a psychological space in which the probability is quite high that the specific patterns of thinking, feeling, and acting that characterize a given level of development are present and observable, whether from within or without (Marquis & Wilber, in press).

According to Wilber (2000e), in healthy development, one's sense of self or identity progresses from one stage to the next through a general process of gradually *disidentifying* with a current structure of consciousness, *identifying* with the subsequent structure, and finally *integrating* the previous structure(s) of consciousness. As such, one's sense of self frequently vacillates, sometimes reaching slightly forward, sometimes slipping slightly backward, until transformation eventually promotes a significantly new sense of self. Of course, numerous derailments can and do occur, ranging from developmental arrests/fixations to one's identifying with subsequent structures without fully integrating the previous ones (e.g., when someone identifies with rational mental processes but denies or dissociates from embodied emotional experiences).

The Prepersonal Realm

According to Wilber (2000b) children typically spend approximately their first seven years of life developing through three basic structures of development that, together, constitute the prepersonal realm.[3] The term *prepersonal* may sound derogatory to some, as it could imply that the young child is not yet a person. I certainly do not mean to belittle childhood. Rather, *prepersonal* refers to those stages of development during which a coherent, relatively stable, individuated self-sense is as yet only in the process of emerging; hence Mahler and colleagues' distinction between the psychological birth and physical birth of the human infant (Mahler et al., 1975). Psychological functioning from the prepersonal structures is primarily prerational. Newborn children enter the sensoriphysical structure in a state of psychological undifferentiation from their environment. During their first year and a half, they take their first tentative steps toward individuation by developing an identity as a physical self, separate from the environment. Then, in the phantasmic/emotional structure, toddlers develop a sense of their emotional self in which they perceive their emotions as differing from those of others and, thus, feel emotionally differentiated from others. At approximately age 3, in the representational mind structure, the child's mental self emerges: what children had known only through their senses, they are now able to represent mentally. Piaget (1977) classified this structure as preoperational, in which the capacity for symbols and language provides the child access to an entirely new world of objects and ideas in both the past and the future.

The Personal Realm

Because stages four through six involve the elaboration and stabilization of an autonomous, coherent self, they constitute the personal realm. Psychological functioning from these structures is increasingly rational. When children are approximately 7 years of age, they typically enter the rule/role mind structure, corresponding to Piaget's (1977) concrete operations. Here, the child develops the capacity to take the perspective (role) of others and thus assumes an identity as a role self, learning the rules associated with various social roles. Adolescence commences with the emergence of the formal-reflexive structure, corresponding to Piaget's formal operations. Not only is the young teenager now able to think about thinking (which allows her to introspect), but her self-structuralization is becoming increasingly reflexive, differentiated, and aware of possibilities that are not bound to appearances or conventions. All of this marks the emergence of a conscientious self—a self that is no longer content to abide by traditional roles, values, and standards without fully questioning and evaluating them for oneself. Many people live their lives centered in this stage of development (some, in fact, never fully acquire formal operational thinking). However, young adults have the potential to develop into the vision-logic structure (see the charts in Wilber 2000e, pp. 197–217). Whereas the formal-reflexive structure involves dichotomized, either/or thinking, the vision-logic structure is integral-aperspectival, allowing one to simultaneously embrace multiple, seemingly contradictory perspectives in one's attention and, through synthesis and integration, conceptualize networks of interactions among the various perspectives. At this point, cognitive development has greatly expanded, yet existential concerns often plague the individual.

The Suprapersonal Realm

Whereas the first five or six stages tend to develop without intentional effort on the part of the individual, the progressive emergence of subsequent altitudes of development tends to require increasingly purposeful contemplative (though not necessarily religious) practice.[4] Because the last four stages involve increasing disidentification from a sense of self as isolated, separate, and individual, these altitudes of development are referred to as suprapersonal—including and transcending the personal. Psychological functioning in this realm is increasingly transrational, involving immediate awareness and intuitive apprehension. I am keenly cognizant of the likelihood that the subsequent descriptions of suprapersonal altitudes may appear far-fetched, similar to New Age philosophy, and unscientific, especially to those readers who have never had an experiential taste of these domains. The skeptical or merely curious reader is urged to consult such rigorously scientific and scholarly texts as those by Austin (1998), Scotton, Chinen, and Battista (1996), Goleman (2003), and Walsh and Vaughan (1993). The importance of Wilber's (1999a, 1999b, 1999c, 1999d, 2000a, 2000b, 2000c, 2000d) contribution here cannot be overemphasized. By providing a framework that allows different data to exist in a complementary fashion, the data from millennia of spiritual communities can be incorporated to complement the data from Western psychology.

Experiences of the *para-mental* altitude of development involve the expansion of one's identity beyond what Alan Watts (1966) called the prevalent but illusory "sensation of oneself as a separate ego enclosed in a bag of skin" to include all of cosmic nature, prompting the experience of nature mysticism (p. ix). Here, one's identity unfolds as a universal self that transcends the consensual sense of space and time. This mystical sense of oneness with the gross universe is clearly distinguishable from psychotic episodes in which people lack reality testing and a clear sense of self. Rather, the universal self includes both rational and trans-rational faculties, as well as a sense of oneself as an individual organism while simultaneously expanding to embrace all natural phenomena.

Experiences of the *meta-mental* altitude of development transcend all gross referents; that is, consciousness relinquishes its exclusive anchoring to gross realms, and thus the content of these interior experiences transcends the natural universe, usually involving archetypal images, internal luminosities and sounds, and subtle currents of bliss. Here, experiences of lucid dreaming are more the rule than the exception, and one's identity often expands in a union of one's soul with deity (or other subtle archetypes); thus, one may experience deity mysticism (Wilber, 2000b).

In experiences of the *over-mental* altitude of development, one realizes the formless ground from which all phenomena—of both exterior and interior worlds—arise. These are experiences of pure consciousness, devoid of any specific content, in which bare attention itself—the root essence of mind—abides without effort, strategic manipulation, or self-consciousness. Experiencing "witness-consciousness" (Avabhasa, 1985)—a witnessing of the matrices of cosmic existence itself—one does not merely know about but also directly realizes the unmanifest source, ground, support, and cause of all of the previous levels. When such experiences are psychospiritually metabolized, one's identity abides as the unmanifest source of all arising phenomena.

By contrast, in the *super-mental* altitude of development, the "individual" transcends even the distinction between the formless ground and the phenomena that issue forth from the ground. This altitude of development is not actually a discrete altitude of development apart from any of the preceding altitudes of development but, rather, is the reality, condition, or suchness of all altitudes of development. In other words, in this ultimate unity consciousness, one realizes that Spirit and its manifestations, consciousness and its display, emptiness and form, and nirvana and samsara (the ultimate reality or truth and the conditional realm of suffering in which most people are engrossed) are all "not-two." When such experiences are metabolized, the self has retained and integrated all of its previous forms into the stable realization of its true and ever-present nature as the All.

All Lines of Development: Specific Aspects of Development

Given that integral theorists place so much emphasis on developmental issues, it seems only appropriate to ask what it is, precisely, that develops. Within the human being, different *lines* develop. That is to say, different aspects of human functioning have the potential to develop through the same basic altitudes of development of consciousness. To clarify with an example, what might it mean to say, "John's development hovers around the formal-reflexive level of development"? Part of the difficulty in addressing such a question is that different lines, or aspects, of John—such as cognitive, moral, emotional, and interpersonal—may have developed rather differentially. Thus, John's cognitive line may be extremely well developed, whereas his emotional and interpersonal lines may be significantly less developed.

Thus, adapting work from other developmental theorists, Wilber (1999d; 2000b) has described and mapped more than 20 different lines of development that each proceed sequentially, yet quasi-independently, through the 10 basic structures of consciousness. Some of these developmental lines are cognition, self-identity, object relations, morality, role taking, psychosexuality, emotion or affect, creativity, aesthetics, altruism, interpersonal, spiritual, values, needs, and worldviews. Each line manifests itself in a relatively identifiable manner at each level. However, as stated before, the lines can and often do develop at different rates. Thus, although specific developmental lines and levels unfold sequentially, *"overall development* ... is far from a sequential, ladder-like, clunk-and-grind series of steps, but rather involves a fluid flowing of many waves and streams in the great River of Life" (Wilber, 2000b, p. xvii, italics in original). Generally, Wilber (2006) notes that the cognitive line of development leads all other lines because cognition, broadly defined, determines what one can be aware of. The self line follows cognition (of the things I can be aware of, what do I identify with?). Finally, there are also self-related lines that hover around the self-sense or ego (e.g., values, morals, needs).

Although it is beyond the scope of this introductory chapter on integral theory, the reader should note that Wilber (2000b) has mapped out developmental progressions not only within the human individual but also within all four quadrants. Because holons (that which is simultaneously a whole at one level while being a part of the whole at subsequent levels) within the various quadrants are in relational exchange with each other, a detailed figure such as the one in Wilber's *Sex, Ecology, Spirituality* (2000b, p. 198) illustrates how social structures/means/ages/eras (LR) such as foraging, horticultural, agrarian, industrial, and informational correspond to cultural worldviews (LL) such as archaic, magic, mythic, rational, and centauric.

All Types: Different Ways of Being- and Acting-in-the-World

Thus far we have addressed quadrants, levels, and lines—all of which are relatively universal in nature. That is to say, regardless of one's gender or culture, every person can be viewed from the experiential, behavioral, cultural, and systemic quadrants; every person has the potential to develop through the same basic levels/structures of consciousness; and every person can be described in terms of his or her lines of development. Another important piece of the integral model is that of *types,* or personality typologies, which describe different individuals' ways of being-in-the-world. Whereas levels of development can be conceptualized vertically, typologies are horizontal dimensions.[5] In other words, a person's type—as described, for example, by the five-factor model (McCrae & Costa, 1996), the Myers-Briggs Type Indicator (MBTI) (Briggs & Myers, 1977), the Enneagram (Riso & Hudson, 1999), Adlerian personality priorities (Fall, Holden, & Marquis, 2004), or even gender—will manifest at any level of development. Whereas all individuals can develop through the same basic structures of consciousness, not all individuals will do so in the same manner, nor will all people be optimally described by the same typological system. Thus, one's familiarity with various typological systems is an important element of integral conceptualization.

The work of Gilligan (1982) illustrated some of the crucial differences between masculine and feminine types. It is not that one of these types is better or more developed than the other, but different types do develop through the life course with different emphases—in a "different voice" (p. 2), to use Gilligan's term. According to her, the masculine type tends to emphasize autonomy, rules, rights, and justice, whereas the feminine type tends to emphasize relationship, connections, responsibility, and care. Gilligan illustrated this with the story of a little girl and boy trying to negotiate what to play. The girl wants to play as if they were neighbors; the boy wants to play pirates. The little girl responds,

"Okay, you play the pirate who lives next door." Masculine and feminine types often clash while playing games. Gilligan cited an example of a neighborhood game of baseball. A boy has just been struck out and begins to cry. The other boys wait unmoved: the rule is three strikes and you're out, and a rule is a rule, period—"That's his problem if his feelings are hurt." If a girl is playing, Gilligan pointed out, she will likely urge everyone to give him another chance. The little girl is empathic and is acting in a caring manner toward the distressed boy. Because the other boys are practicing their masculine logic, grounded in justice and based upon rules and principles, they will readily allow feelings to be hurt in order to preserve the rules. Conversely, the girls, who are practicing their feminine relating, grounded in care and based upon maintaining connectedness, will often bend the rules in pursuit of protecting others' feelings (cited in Wilber, 2005a).

Thus, attending to an individual's type of personality is important because different types of people emphasize different dimensions of life. Consider how different people's journeys through the developmental labyrinth could be due to the fact that one of them is intensely feminine whereas the other is intensely masculine (gender), or one of them is highly introverted whereas the other is highly extroverted (MBTI), or one navigates life with a self-effacing style of peacemaking whereas the other tends to demonstrate a style that is primarily challenging and confrontational (Enneagram types 9 and 8, respectively).

On a less healthy note, people who meet diagnostic criteria for the *DSM-IV-TR* axis II disorders can also be conceptualized as different types. Those who meet diagnostic criteria for borderline personality disorder display a relatively consistent (even if what is consistent is their instability) way of being-in-the-world, just as those who meet diagnostic criteria for avoidant, narcissistic, or any other of the personality disorders also exhibit relatively inflexible ways of being. However, with the exception of *DSM-IV-TR* axis II disorders, it is important to remember that no type is, in general, better or worse than any other. However, different circumstances may be more easily handled or adjusted to by a certain type of person than another. Also important is an appreciation of how multidimensional our conceptualizations become when we include types. The Enneagram consists of 9 types, each of which can manifest at any of the 10 levels; 9 types times 10 levels yields a typology of 90 different personality types. And we have not yet addressed different *states* of consciousness.

All States: Different Ways of Being- and Knowing-in-the-World

Having discussed levels, or stages, of consciousness, we now need to differentiate between stages and states of consciousness. Whereas levels/stages of consciousness can also be thought of as enduring structures or traits, by which we mean relatively stable patterns of events in consciousness, *states* of consciousness are more temporary and relatively fleeting. States of consciousness fall into one of two main categories: natural and altered. The most widely recognized states of consciousness are the natural ones: waking, dreaming, and deep sleep. Any specific state can arise at any structure or stage of consciousness. For example, one can have dreams at the stage of preoperations, concrete operations, or formal operations, just as one can remain at the concrete operations stage while daily passing in and out of waking, dreaming, and deep sleep states. According to the world's wisdom traditions, these three natural states of consciousness have specific spiritual correlates. Whereas the waking state is the domain of our everyday ego, the dream state, because it is a realm created by one's psyche, provides one route to the realm of the soul (the original meaning of *psyche*). The state of deep dreamless sleep, precisely because it is a domain of pure formlessness, provides one route to the realm of causal/formless spirit. The significance of these spiritual correlates is that all individuals, regardless of their level of development, have access (even if only temporarily) to the entire spectrum of consciousness precisely because all people wake, dream, and sleep.

Altered states of consciousness, also called nonordinary states of consciousness, include experiences such as those induced by drugs or fasting, as well as those brought about by meditation or other contemplative practices. The field of psychology has paid considerable attention to peak experiences, which can occur within people regardless of their stage of development. Peak experiences are often suprapersonal experiences, in which an individual, while awake, has direct awareness of para-mental, meta-mental, over-mental, or super-mental altitudes. However, a crucial caveat to bear in mind is that although anyone at any stage of development can temporarily access suprapersonal states of consciousness, *the person will interpret those states with the developmental tools she has available.* Wilber provided excellent examples of how individuals at five different stages of development might each differentially interpret experiences of para-mental, meta-mental, over-mental, and super-mental altitudes (see Wilber, 1999c, 1999d, pp. 446–447). The important point to remember is that regardless of how profound and earth-shattering one's peak experiences appear, they are, by definition, temporary, transient, passing states: "In order for higher development to occur, those temporary states must become permanent traits" (Wilber, 1999d, p. 447). For those interested in converting temporary altered states into more permanent realizations, some form of contemplative or yogic practice apparently becomes necessary:

> Unlike natural states (which access psychic, subtle, and causal states in the natural sleep cycle, but rarely while awake or fully conscious) and unlike spontaneous peak experiences (which are fleeting), meditative states access these higher realms in a deliberate and prolonged fashion. (Wilber, 1999d, pp. 447–448)

What do altered states of consciousness have to do with counseling? First of all, it should be recognized that episodes of depression, mania, panic, delirium, and even psychoses are usually states of consciousness. Most people are not permanently depressed, manic, delirious, or psychotic, but rather pass in and out of these states. In addition, within the counseling hour, clients may be more amenable to certain interventions given their state of consciousness. If they are too "revved up," they are unlikely to be able to "sit with" what is present and deeply process what they are experiencing. Conversely, "when we exist in the ontological mode—the realm beyond everyday concerns—we are in a state of particular readiness for personal change" (Yalom, 2002, p. 127). An obvious example of the value of inducing altered states of consciousness can be seen in the work of Ericksonian hypnosis (Erickson & Rossi, 1981), eye movement desensitization reprocessing (Shapiro, 2001), or dream work (Hill, 1996). Carl Rogers was also aware of the value of the therapist's altered state of consciousness while working with clients and he wrote that "when perhaps I am in a slightly altered state of conscious-

ness in the relationship, then whatever I do seems to be full of healing"
(1986, p. 198).

The Self-System

"The *self-system* or *self-sense* (or just the *self*)," as opposed to the quadrants, levels, lines, types, or states, is "where the action is" (Wilber,
2000c, p. 548)—the dynamic *process* holding together the various
developmental lines, establishing something of a cohesive whole. The
self is the seat of a host of significant operations and capacities, such as
identification (self-identity), organization (providing a sense of cohe-
sion to one's experience), will (choosing and initiating action), defense
(the employment of defense mechanisms), metabolism (psychological
digestion of one's experiences), and navigation (one's journey through
the developmental labyrinth). Not only is it the self that balances, integrates, and navigates the sundry levels, lines, states, and so forth, it is
also the experiential center of each individual's psychological universe.
Remember, though, that the self is not reified into a "thing"—the self
is the process or activity that creates the sense of being "inside of one's
skin." I will discuss the self-system in far greater depth and detail in
Chapter 6.

Integral Methodological Pluralism

Philosophically, theories are like models or maps of territories, whereas
paradigms are more like the injunctions or practices that enact and
disclose the territories themselves. The important point is that a new
theory without new practices is nothing more than a map without a territory. The integral metaparadigm urges one not only to conceptualize
differently but to practice and/or research differently, which brings us to
integral methodological pluralism (IMP). I want to emphasize that *an
integral paradigm is a network of practices* that allows us to honor the efficacy of each epistemological approach while also recognizing that each
approach is optimal in specific situations and less so in others. All of
the available knowledge-approaches and their corresponding practices
are crucial components of an integral operating system (IOS)—an integral methodological pluralism that "touches all the bases" in an attempt
to serve the diversity of our world and its discontents. An IOS also
initiates a self-correcting, self-organizing outreach by gently remind-

ing us to conceptualize from, and work with, all four dimensions (all quadrants) of our being-in-the-world at the most appropriate developmental level of consciousness (all levels). Any genuine IOS (and there is not just one) will continually prompt us when we are not honoring an important mode of our own or others' being-in-the-world: all quadrants, all levels, all lines, all types, and all states. One of Wilber's most clinically significant theses—the notion that derailments at each stage of development result in specific pathologies and defense mechanisms, and, most important, that specific treatment modalities are optimal for developmental problems deriving from specific levels of development—will be discussed in Chapter 4.

IMP is thus a (potentially) revolutionary pluralism because it honors the validity of each discipline/counseling theory and its associated set of methodologies and techniques while simultaneously recognizing the incompleteness and blind spots of each discipline/counseling theory. IMP then takes a step beyond most multicultural, pluralistic stances by revealing precisely *how* the diversity can be unified in a more encompassing and compassionate framework (AQAL) that salvages the validity of each by relieving each of its absolutisms. When the various disciplines are genuinely integrated, we have an IMP and a correlative transformation from a partial pluralism to an integral holism.

In the introductory paragraph, I mentioned that integral theory may help therapists "better serve our clients and professions." Hopefully, the reader can see that it does this—and thus helps to heal the wounds and mend the many fractures of an increasingly fragmented world—by providing a systematic, coherent, and consistent framework that allows one to draw not only upon the entire gamut of psychotherapeutic theories and practices but also urging therapists to heal more than just psyches. I hope the reader can see that it does this by providing a systematic, coherent, and consistent framework that allows one to draw not only upon the entire gamut of psychotherapeutic theories and practices but also urges therapists to heal more than just psyches. In other words, quadratic thinking reveals the dire need to transform not just the thoughts and self-experience of individuals (UL) but also the social systems (LR) that are equally responsible for human suffering. This means that as professional helpers, we may need to begin to work toward transforming the systemic structures that promote human suffering. This call to social liberation is clearly in line with the American Counseling Association's position on advocacy, as stated in its code of ethics: "Counselors advocate to promote change at the individual, group, institutional, and societal levels that improve the quality of life for individuals and groups and remove potential barriers to the provision or access of appropriate services being offered" (2005, introduction to section C). As someone who was trained as a counselor/psychotherapist, I admit that I am not well versed in how to effect large-scale transformations in the social structures that breed poverty, classism, and racism, but I suspect that many readers will agree that truly comprehensive therapy must address all of the sources of our clients' distress and that such systemic forces generate tremendous suffering.

Conclusion

This chapter is only a brief overview of integral theory, a philosophical worldview that Walsh and Vaughan referred to as "systematic, broad-ranging, multidisciplinary, integrative, visionary yet scholarly … perhaps unparalleled" (1994, p. 18). Perhaps you feel overwhelmed; perhaps you have disagreed on some of the specific details; perhaps you are concerned that developmental models can be used to marginalize certain people (what I call developmental abuse).

If you feel overwhelmed, rest assured that this is a normal response to a first taste of integral theory. Read further in this book and consult other sources that may clarify or fill in some of the specifics that were here merely mentioned (more theoretical issues will be discussed in Chapters 3–6). Fall, Holden, and Marquis (2004) include in their book a 60-page chapter on integral counseling; in 2007 the *Journal of Counseling and Values* devoted an entire issue to integral theory in counseling; and Wilber (2000e) is an excellent introduction to integral theory applied specifically to psychology and therapy.

If you think that Wilber or I have overgeneralized, that too is possible. When a Kosmic[6] philosopher such as Wilber integrates such disparate disciplines as physics, economics, political theory, neuroscience, psychology, anthropology, and literary theory, the level of abstraction required yields orienting generalizations that may not always do justice to the detailed specifics discovered by those with more narrow research agendas. The voicing of such disconfirming details will hasten our accommodating integral theory to "fit with the facts." That is, after all, a primary manner in which knowledge develops.

Integral thinkers are not deluded to the point of thinking that we have *the* theory or *the* answers. What we do have is a conceptual map that appears to be more parsimoniously comprehensive than other theories, but it certainly is not the final word or a closed system in any way. To the contrary, integral theory, in my view, is exquisitely self-reflexive; provided that we each remain open, humble, and honest, it will continually reveal our shadows and blind spots, and it will entreat us to translate or transform the fractures within ourselves, our clients, and the world.

Regarding the potential for developmental abuse, integral theorists make a far greater number of developmental judgments than value judgments. That is to say, an individual at the vision-logic stage is not a better or more valuable person than someone at the rule/role mind stage, any more than a 20-year-old is a better person than an 8-year-old. On the other hand, all developmental theories do involve a *telos*—less of an actual endpoint than a general direction toward which growth progresses. However, the goal of integral counseling is *not* to get all clients to the highest stage possible. Rather, the prime directive of much of our work involves helping most of our clients translate as healthily as possible at the level at which we encounter them. Although I, personally, react against various forms of fundamentalism that are most common in people who have not developed beyond the rule/role mind structure (characterized by concrete operational thinking and a conventional/conformist morality), I do not think there is something wrong or inherently problematic with the rule/role mind structure. As alluded to earlier, each and every stage/structure has its own specific types of problems and pathologies.

Finally, integral therapists work with people, not stages. In fact, knowledge of the full spectrum of human development allows us to better understand, join with, and communicate with diverse people from all walks of life. Thus, understanding Wilber's spectrum model actually facilitates a more humanistic relationship with the people we counsel. Integral therapists are devoted not just to certain structures but to the health of the entire spectrum of development, which we believe is present, even if only as a latent potential, within each and every human being.

Notes

1. Wilber (2000e) defined the term "structure" as "a holistic pattern" (p. 651). As will be stressed in many places throughout this book, integral theorists conceive of structures as relatively stable, organized patterns or configurations (of mental activities, external behaviors, etc.). Wilber has described different types of structures. In contrast to transitional structures—which are replaced or negated by subsequent developmental stages (i.e., stages of moral development)—basic structures are primarily enduring structures; as such, they tend to be incorporated into subsequent developmental stages (i.e., stages of cognitive development). According to Wilber (2000b, 2000e), the basic structures of consciousness are essentially synonymous with developmental stages of consciousness. Basic structures have both deep/universal features, as well as surface/local features, an issue that I will discuss more in Chapter 4.

2. A holarchy is hierarchy composed of holons. A holon is a whole part: something that is simultaneously a whole at one level while being a part of the whole at subsequent levels. Thus, whenever one finds orders of increasing holism, one is encountering a form of holarchy: "Holarchies exist everywhere in nature: Atoms are wholes that are parts of molecules, which are wholes that are parts of cells, which are wholes that are parts of organs, and so forth" (Fall, Holden, & Marquis, 2004, p. 429). A psychological example of holarchy involves Piaget's stages of cognitive development: sensorimotor is a whole structure that becomes incorporated/operated upon by pre-operations, which is a whole structure that becomes incorporated/operated upon by concrete operations, which is a whole structure that becomes incorporated/operated upon by formal operations.

3. As with all developmental stage theories, the order of the stages is more significant than the specific ages with which various individuals realize them. Regarding cognitive development, Wilber (2000b) tended to favor Piaget. I am aware of various criticisms of Piaget's (1977) theory, from how he deemphasized the role of the social environment and children's physical activity to his underestimating children's cognitive abilities. For example, Baillargeon and De Vos (1991) found that when they altered Piaget's assessment methods, infants are capable of object permanence significantly earlier than Piaget posited. Regrettably, page constraints require my focusing more on the general arc of such developmental processes than on the myriad criticisms of stage theories in general, and more specifically the precise ages at which most children attain the various developmental capacities.

4. *Altitude* is another term that integral theorists use to describe the degree of development in a given developmental line (Wilber, personal communication, January 28, 2005). In Chapter 4, I discuss the value of the term *altitude* and describing aspects of development using the metaphor of climbing a mountain (see pages 74–75 and 90–91).

5. Although it is not completely inaccurate to conceptualize levels vertically, a better metaphor than a vertical "ladder" is that of nested concentric spheres, in which each successive level (sphere) includes, embraces, and incorporates the preceding levels (spheres) while at the same time going beyond them. Thus, the essential features of each level are honored and retained while newly emergent features unfold.

6. *Kosmic*, in contrast to *cosmic*, derives from the ancient Greek term that referred to the patterned nature of the entire universe rather than simply the physical universe or cosmos.

3

QUADRATIC ASSESSMENT

Introduction

Although developmental levels, lines, states, and types are by no means ignored, the bulk of the Integral Intake involves *quadratic assessment:* assessing the experiential, behavioral, cultural, and social/systemic dimensions of clients and their distress. Each quadratic dimension is assessed with numerous queries, including open- and closed-ended questions, Likert scale ratings, and checklists. A critical aspect of integral counseling is an accurate and comprehensive assessment of a client's quadratic profile. Therapists then use this information as a central component of the client's integral profile, which helps therapists prioritize phenomena to be addressed when initiating collaborative goal setting and treatment planning with each client.

Before inquiring into information specific to the four quadrants, the Integral Intake requests certain basic data that virtually all effective therapists inquire about in the initial session—issues such as whether or not the client has had any previous experience in psychotherapy and what her expectations and goals are for this counseling experience. Other questions that are commonly asked of clients during the initial session are "What do you hope to accomplish during your work with me?" "What brings you here?" "Why does that issue bring you here *now?*" "What dimensions of your life are going well?" and "What would you most like to change?" Questions that therapists should ask themselves during and after the initial session(s) include: "Does this person need counseling and/or psychotherapeutic services?" "Am I the best therapist for this client or should I refer him elsewhere?" "Does this client need a medical consultation?" "What type of counseling approach (e.g., CBT, psychodynamic, or person-centered) and modality (individual, family, or group) is optimal for this person?" "Is there a risk of suicide?" "How much time and how many resources does this person have and is that sufficient given my initial assessment of him, his struggles, and his life circumstances?" "What hidden agendas may this client have that I am not yet aware of?" and "How is this client's problem related to other dynamics such as his thinking and behavior patterns, biophysiology, family of origin and other cultural dynamics, and large-scale systems?"

Recall that the four quadrants represent the interior and exterior of both the individual and the collective. Although therapists do not need to understand the following technical point to assess and practice effectively, integral theorists differentiate the "view from" and the "view through." Wilber (2006) stated that all individual holons possess four perspectives through which they touch or view the world; these are the four quadrants (the "view through"). At the same time, anything—whether a sentient holon (which possesses feeling-awareness and perception) such as a horse or a nonsentient artifact (that lacks feeling-awareness and perception) such as a sofa—can be viewed from those four perspectives; technically, integral theorists term those views *quadrivia* (plural of *quadrivium*) (Wilber, 2006). Because the Integral Intake is designed for practical utility, not as a theoretical treatise, and for the sake of simplicity and clarity, I will simply refer to the four dimension-perspectives as "quadrants."

Experiential Queries: Individual-Interior

The experiential dimension involves those aspects of assessment relative to the client's phenomenological experience. It assesses each client's self-experience (including but not limited to body image, self-esteem, self-concept, self-criticism, self-hate, and capacities for self-comforting, self-compassion, and self-reflection) and the spectrum of motivations, occasions, and impulses of which the client is unaware. As such, experiential assessment includes queries such as the following:

- How would you describe your general mood/feelings?
- What emotions do you most often feel most strongly?

- Are you aware of recurring images or thoughts (either while awake or in dreams)? Yes/No If yes, please describe.
- What is your earliest memory?
- What is your happiest memory?
- What is your most painful memory?
- Where in your body do you feel stress (shoulders, back, jaw, etc.)?
- In general, how satisfied are you with your life?
  Not at all   1   2   3   4   5   6   7   Very
- In general, how do you feel about yourself (self-esteem)?
  Very bad   1   2   3   4   5   6   7   Very good
- In general, how much control do you feel you have over your life and how you feel?
  None at all   1   2   3   4   5   6   7   A lot
- Are you *presently* experiencing suicidal thoughts? Yes/No If yes, please describe.

Those examples are fairly straightforward. Some of the experiential queries that may need some clarification include the following:

- Have you *ever* attempted to seriously harm or kill yourself or anyone else? Yes/No If yes, please describe.
- Has anyone in your family ever attempted or committed suicide? Yes/No If yes, please describe.

These two queries may seem to belong in the UR and LR quadrants, respectively. After all, whether or not a client has ever attempted to kill himself or someone else is something that could be observed from the outside and agreed upon with a high degree of inter-rater reliability. Likewise, whether or not a member of the client's family has ever attempted or committed suicide is most appropriately classified as a systemic (LR) issue. The reason these two queries are placed in the UL quadrant is because of their close relevance to the fundamental issue at hand, which is whether or not the client is currently *experiencing* suicidal tendencies, which is an individual-interior (UL) matter.

- What are the ways in which you care for and comfort yourself when you feel distressed?
- How do you deal with strong emotions in yourself?

- How do you respond to stressful situations and other problems?
- Do you have ways in which you express yourself creatively and/or artistically? Yes/No If yes, please describe.
- Describe your leisure time (hobbies/enjoyment).

It could be argued that aspects of the above five queries have strong behavioral (UR) dimensions. The reader may be thinking, "Many clients comfort themselves by taking a hot bath, listening to music, or doing yoga" (which are also possible responses to the next two queries regarding strong emotions and stressful situations), all of which could be observed from the outside and thus should be behavioral (UR) queries. The reason these three queries are placed in the UL quadrant is because they are grounded, first and foremost, in the client's *experience* of distress, strong emotions, and stressful situations, and they are concerned with how the client reestablishes a felt sense (internally) of comfort, care, or whatever is experienced as healthy to the client. Finally, many of the means by which clients reestablish their sense of balance, comfort, and so on will not be amenable to direct observation from the outside: Reassuring/affirming self-talk, comforting imagery, mindful attention to strong emotions, and so on are ways of self-soothing that reveal themselves more to the client's phenomenological experience than direct behavioral observation. Regarding the last two queries above (leisure time, artistic expression), the point here is less what we can behaviorally observe (he goes fishing, she kayaks, he knits, she plays cello) than the experiential effect these activities have on the person. Moreover, beauty, art and enjoyment are in the eye of the beholder, which is to say that the meanings of these engagements do not disclose themselves to behavioral observation or objective analyses; it is largely a subjective (UL) matter.

- Have there been any serious illnesses, births, deaths, or other losses or changes in your family that have affected you? Yes/No If yes, please describe.
- Have you ever been a victim of, or witnessed, verbal, emotional, physical, and/or sexual abuse? Yes/No If yes, please describe.

Similar to the above explanation, although the two queries above could be ascertained in a relatively objective (UR) manner, therapists are usually more concerned with how clients have been affected by such illnesses, deaths, or abuse. Clients' perceptions of past traumas and losses (which are often highly subjective and idiosyncratic) are often more indicative of their current distress than the objective facts surrounding the events that could be discerned from an outside view.

Behavioral Queries: Individual-Exterior

The behavioral dimension involves those aspects of assessment involving the client's observable behavior and other relatively objective dimensions of clients that relate to their distress and potential resources for coping. Oftentimes, clients seek therapy because of specific behaviors such as substance abuse, depression-driven interpersonal withdrawal, or anxiety-fueled avoidant behaviors. Even more frequently, clients' goals and views of successful therapy often involve specific behaviors (whether a decrease in eating, smoking, drinking, or aggression or an increase in kindness, exercise, or social activity). As such, behavioral assessment includes relatively objective queries such as the following:

- Please list any medications you are presently taking (dosage/amount and what the medication is for).
- Do you have a primary care physician? Yes/No If yes, who is it?
- When was your last physical? Were there any noteworthy results (diseases, blood pressure, cholesterol, etc.)?
- Have you ever suffered a head injury or other serious injury? Yes/No If yes, please describe.
- Describe your usual eating habits (types of food and how much).
- Describe your drug and alcohol use (both past and present).
- Do you engage in some form of exercise (aerobic and/or strength building)? Yes/No If yes, please describe.

Although the relevance of the above queries is probably evident, along with why they belong in the behavioral (individual-exterior) quadrant, I will add that many clients' presenting symptoms may be due *not* to a mental illness but to a medical disorder. For example, hypothyroidism, brain tumors, and cardiac conditions can produce many of the symptoms associated with, respectively, depression, manic episodes, and panic disorders. Thus, it is imperative that biomedical conditions be screened out so that therapists and clients do not spend time with psychotherapy when what is more contributive to clients' distress is biomedical in nature. On the other hand, most therapists, and especially integral therapists, acknowledge the importance of the biopsychosocial model (Engel, 1977, 1980), which involves the notion that biological, psychological, and social dimensions all play important roles in illness and health and that each influences the others. The reader may recognize some similarities between an integrated biopsychosocial formulation (Campbell & Rohrbaugh, 2006) and a quadratic formulation. Without considering levels and lines of development, different types of people, and various states of consciousness, a quadratic formulation could be termed a biobehavioral-psychoexistential/spiritual-cultural-systemic   (UR-UL-LL-LR) formulation; it doesn't exactly roll off the tongue. Hence, I term it an "integrated quadratic formulation." Some of the behavioral queries that may need some clarification include the following:

- In general, how would you rate your physical health?
  Very unhealthy   1   2   3   4   5   6   7   Very healthy

Given that this is a client self-report, one could argue that the datum is subjective and thus "individual-interior" (UL). The reason this query is in the behavioral quadrant is that it is seeking a relatively unbiased, objective gauge of the client's physical health. Thus, if an obese client who reported hypertension, chronic pain, and frequent bouts of flu and colds circled a 4 or higher, I would follow up with something along the lines of "How do you think a medical doctor would evaluate your physical health?" which should more closely approximate an objective indicator of overall physical health.

- Describe your current sleeping patterns. (When do you sleep? How many hours per 24 hours? Do you sleep straight through or do you wake up during sleep time?)
- Do you feel rested upon waking? Yes/No

Whereas the second of the above two queries is clearly an experiential (UL) matter, it is so closely tied to the preceding query—which can be objectively evaluated in a sleep laboratory—that it is included along with that query for the sake of coherence (the intake would appear more disorganized if questions around a specific issue—in this case sleep— were not grouped together).

- Please mark any of the following behaviors or bodily feelings that are true of you:

  _____ drink too much

  _____ use illegal drugs

  _____ eat too much

  _____ eat too little

  _____ neglect friends and family

  _____ neglect self and your own needs

  _____ difficulty being kind and loving to yourself

  _____ act in ways that end up hurting yourself or others

  _____ lose your temper

  _____ seem to *not* have control over some behaviors

  _____ think about suicide

  _____ have difficulty concentrating

  _____ spend more money than you can afford to

  _____ crying

  _____ any other behaviors you would like me to know about? Yes/no If yes, what are they?

  _____ headaches

  _____ menstrual problems

  _____ dizziness

  _____ heart tremors

  _____ jitters

  _____ sexual preoccupations

  _____ tingling/numbness

  _____ excessive tiredness

  _____ hear or see things not actually there

  _____ blackouts

  _____ do you have any other bodily pains or difficulties? Yes/no If yes, what are they?

Although a few of the above behaviors (use of illegal and/or mind-altering drugs, crying) and bodily feelings (heart tremors, blackouts) could be objectively discernible from the outside (and external observation includes the use of medical instruments and other measuring devices that extend sensory observation), most of them have a significant subjective and/or interpretive component. For example, what constitutes drinking too much, eating too much, or neglecting one's self and one's own needs? Nonetheless, these checklist items are more physically related (and thus capable of relatively direct observation or measurement) than psychologically related (issues such as self-esteem, self-hate, or artistic enjoyment, which are far less amenable to direct observation or measurement).

Cultural Queries: Collective-Interior

The cultural dimension involves those aspects of assessment relative to each client's cultural experience, which includes not only ethnicity, religion/spirituality, sexuality, gender, age, and so on but also interpersonal relationships, systems of meaning-making, and all other intersubjective dimensions that are disclosed through some form of mutual understanding or sympathetic resonance that is common only to members of given cultures, communities, or groups. A unique feature of the Integral Intake is its formal assessment of each client's culture (lower left quadrant). Thus, diversity and multicultural considerations are given substantial, structured attention from the outset of integral counseling. As such, cultural assessment involves queries such as the following:

- Have you ever been a victim of any form of prejudice or discrimination (racial, gender, etc.) or felt that you were disadvantaged in terms of power and privilege in society? Yes/No If yes, please describe.
- Describe your relationships, including friends, family, and coworkers.
- In general, how satisfied are you with your friendships and other relationships?
  Not at all   1   2   3   4   5   6   7   Very
- In general, how comfortable are you in social situations?
  Not at all   1   2   3   4   5   6   7   Very
- How do you identify yourself ethnically? How important is your ethnic culture to you?
- Describe your sex life. How satisfied are you with your sex life?

- Do you have a religious/spiritual affiliation and/or practice? Yes/No Please describe.
- Describe any political or civic involvement in which you participate.
- Describe any environmental activities in which you participate (recycling, conserving, carpooling, etc.).

Those examples are fairly straightforward. Some of the cultural queries that may need some clarification include the following:

- What is important and meaningful to you (what matters the most to you)?
- In general, how satisfied are you with your religion/spirituality?
  Not at all   1   2   3   4   5   6   7   Very

Whereas most readers probably agree that meaning-making (religion and spirituality are among the primary, though far from the only, meaning-making systems) is not something disclosed to observation from the outside—and thus agree that it belongs to one of the left-hand quadrants—many of you may wonder why it wasn't placed in the upper left (individual-inside) quadrant. Although religious beliefs, worldviews, and other life philosophies reside within the minds of individuals, meaning-making activities are so inseparable from the religious/spiritual, ethnic, political, moral, and other cultural traditions in which individuals are embedded that to conceptualize an individual's meaning-making as a merely individual (as opposed to embedded in multiple cultural contexts) activity denies the vast web of intersubjective world-spaces out of which mutual understanding and even self-understanding emerge. Even though what is meaningful to me discloses itself to my experience (UL), that meaning would not—and could not—emerge and be sustained without a vast network of contextual norms and practices as well as linguistic and semantic structures that form a shared culture. Thus, if a client speaks to you in a language you don't understand, or about cultural practices with which you do not resonate, you will not understand the meanings about which the client is speaking, even though all of the words are entering your ears and brain (Wilber, 2000b).

- Which emotions were encouraged or commonly expressed in your family of origin (the family you grew up with)?

- Which emotions were discouraged or not allowed in your family of origin?
- What emotions are most comfortable for you now?

Similar to the above point regarding meaning-making, although emotions are experienced by an individual, the meanings those emotions have for that individual stem from shared intersubjective experiences, especially those that characterized early childhood experiences within one's family of origin (Fosha, 2000; Bowlby, 1988; Greenberg, 2002). For example, two people whose caregivers responded very differently to them as children when they were angry will likely have very different experiences of themselves and their anger as adults. One may feel highly empowered and righteously justified in his anger, whereas the other may feel extreme guilt and be overwhelmed by abandonment fears every time he feels even the slightest bit angry. Finally, inquiring with clients about how certain aspects of life—in this case emotions—were encouraged, discouraged, or otherwise handled in their family of origin and then inquiring as to how those same aspects play out in their current lives helps many clients have insight into and make connections between various current patterns of thinking, feeling, and behaving and their early childhood experiences. This is a large part of the rationale behind the structuring of the following four queries.

- How did your family of origin express love and care?
- How does your current family express love and care?
- How did your family of origin express disapproval?
- How does your current family express disapproval?
- Describe your romantic/love relationships, if any.
- What beliefs do you have about sex? How important to you are those beliefs?
- What are some of your most important morals? How important to you are those morals?

The above queries (love, sex, morals) are included in the cultural quadrant (collective-interior) for many of the same reasons as previously stated. Love relationships occur in the shared spaces between people; sex is something enacted with others (usually; I am recalling Woody Allen's "Don't knock masturbation; it's sex with someone I love"); and moral issues fundamentally revolve around questions of how to rightly live with and relate to others. Although aspects of love, sex, and morality may be described from an outside perspective (for example, some of today's newlyweds originally met via an Internet dating service and they have sex X many times per week), I am confident that most readers will agree that the most important aspects of love, sex, and morality—especially as pertinent to counseling and psychotherapy—will reveal themselves only to the therapist's and client's efforts of mutual understanding, rather than behavioral observation alone. Another important point is that *how* clients respond to these queries—whether on paper or via interview—is often more telling than the specific content of their reply. For example, the following exchange reveals a quadrant absolutism. See if you can tell which quadrant the client privileges:

Therapist: "What beliefs do you have about sex?"
Client: "I believe I should get it at least once every day."
Therapist: "What else is important to you about sex?"
Client: "Nothing matters more to me than getting it as often as possible."
Therapist: "What about the *being* of the person with whom you have sex or the quality of your shared experience?"
Client: "Well, I definitely care about who I have it with. I like only brunettes."

Issues of nonjudgmental acceptance aside, this client's responses reveal a behavioral (UR) absolutism—all of his replies can be described by objective observations, such as the number of times he has sex and the physical characteristics of his partners. His responses didn't allude to the qualities of the experience he prefers (UL), the internal qualities of his partners (such as being warm, caring, or their religious or political views), or their shared experience (LL). With other clients, you may encounter a neglect of other quadrants. Someone with low self-esteem and fears of abandonment may reply in tremendous detail about the behaviors of his wife (UR) and the arguments and other upsetting events that occurred between them (LL and LR) but may systematically fail to attend to his own experience (UL), which reflects a central dynamic in his style of overaccommodating to his wife because he has an insecure attachment style.

Social/Systemic Queries: Collective-Exterior

The social, also called systemic, dimension involves those aspects of assessment relative to clients' environments and systems (from familial and local to national and global) that influence the onset, course, and treatment of their problems and struggles. As stated in Chapter 2, these systems include economic, corporate, and governmental systems; civic resources (educational and employment opportunities; transportation systems); city planning (available parks and other recreational areas; aesthetics of architecture, etc.); and smaller systems, such as those characterized by family dynamics or working conditions. Thus, situations such as unemployment or unsafe living conditions (i.e., raising infants and young children in an old home with peeling lead paint) as well as any noteworthy observable interactions between parts of different social systems are addressed in integral counseling prior to or along with the upper-left-quadrant (experiential) concerns that constitute the priority, if not the sole concerns, of traditional psychotherapy. As such, social systems assessment includes queries such as the following:

- Describe your current *physical* home environment. (For example, describe the layout of your home and other general conditions, such as privacy, whether it is well lighted, whether you have A/C and heating, etc.)
- Describe your neighborhood. (Is it safe/dangerous, nice/unpleasant, quiet/loud, etc.?)
- Describe your current social home environment. (How would an outside observer describe how you get along with those who live with you?)
- Describe your work environment (include coworkers and supervisors who directly affect you).
- Do you have a romantic partner? Yes/No
- Have you been married before? Yes/No If yes, please describe.

Those examples are fairly straightforward. Some of the systemic queries that may need some clarification include the following:

- What aspects of your life are stressful to you? Please describe.

This may appear to belong to the experiential (UL) quadrant in that stress is something perceived internally by an individual. Many completed Integral Intakes have revealed that the most common response to this question involves clients' social systems. One single mother's response to the question noted that she worked 40 hours each week, was a part-time graduate student, and was raising two children and maintaining a household by herself. Her feeling tired, down, and anxious was less a matter of a mental disorder than it was of overly demanding systemic factors.

- What sort of support system do you have (friends, family, or religious community who help you in times of need)?

This query addresses a well-known fact: the course and prognosis of an individual with a mental disorder—from depression to schizophrenia—is far better for those with a sound, strong support network than for those who lack such a support system.

An Integral Taxonomy of Therapeutic Interventions

Although the primary purpose of this book is to assist therapists in assessing their clients in a comprehensive, integral manner, I want to briefly introduce a related classifying system with which to lend order and coherence to what has been a gargantuan heap of technique. An integral taxonomy of therapeutic interventions (ITTI) is an ordered system for classifying the procedural methods and practical skills used by integral therapists to facilitate their clients' healing, growth, and well-being. I chose the word *therapeutic* instead of *counseling* or *psychotherapeutic* because a client's healing and welfare often necessitate changes that are more societally systemic than the merely intra- and interpersonal changes that characterized counseling and psychotherapy for much of their early histories.

I am currently in the process of submitting a manuscript that contains an ITTI with more than 200 therapeutic interventions (Marquis, 2006). Because I want to give the reader an initial taste of the practical utility of the integral approach and because the complete ITTI contains too many interventions to fit on a single page, I am here including what I call a "mini-ITTI", Table 3.1.

I am well aware that the unifying order in this taxonomy is a function of my inclination toward integral theory. Nonetheless, I think that even those therapists who do not resonate with integral theory can still find the ITTI clinically helpful, both heuristically and by its organization of a large number of commonly used therapeutic interventions. A

Table 3.1   A Mini–Integral Taxonomy of Therapeutic Interventions

Upper Left (UL): Interior-Individual	**Upper Right (UR): Exterior-Individual**
Body	*Body*
• Gendlin's "focusing" and attunement to immediate "felt sense"	• Self-management programs; self-monitoring and recording
• Self-comforting and basic centering exercises	• Pharmacotherapy
Mind	*Mind*
• Awareness/consciousness-raising	• Cognitive restructuring[1]
• Dialogues with parts of self	• Reality therapy's WDEP system
Spirit	*Spirit*
• Meditation/contemplative prayer	• EEG biofeedback and brain/mind machines that help induce theta and delta states of consciousness
• Cultivating mindfulness, love, compassion, forgiveness, etc.	• Yoga
Lower Left (LL): Interior-Collective	**Lower Right (LR): Exterior-Collective**
Body	*Body*
• Attending to and mending ruptures in the therapeutic bond	• Basic session management skills and structure of sessions
• Finding stability in relationships	• Involving the client's social support system in at least one session
Mind	*Mind*
• Establishing the therapeutic relationship	• Social skills training
• Role playing	• Genogram analysis
Spirit	*Spirit*
• Compassionate understanding as the heart of counseling	• Serving others and engaging in social activism to promote social justice
• "Selfless service:" compassion; social interest; social liberation	• Relating responsibly to the environment

relatively quick scan through the ITTI (the complete version, not the mini-version) suggests numerous general courses of action as well as specific methods and interventions to utilize with a given client.

I do *not* mean to suggest that one needs to use most of the 200 interventions displayed in the full ITTI in order to be an effective therapist. However, if you notice that most or all of the interventions you use fall primarily within one or two quadrants, or primarily within one or two levels, you may increase your effectiveness merely by using interventions that address other dimensions—whether quadratic or developmental—of your clients. This is one of the simple meanings of an AQAL approach: touching upon all of the quadratic and developmental dimensions of our clients and ourselves (much more about the developmental aspects will be addressed in Chapters 4 and 7).

Analogous to exercising each dimension of body, mind, and spirit, paying attention to each client's "quadratic balance" is also important. For example, someone who is excessively absorbed in himself (UL) will be self-absorbed or what laypeople call narcissistic. Such an individual will often benefit by devoting time, energy, and attention to more collective endeavors, whether that is a systemic activity (LR) such as engaging in civic action and/or working to reduce environmental pollution or a cultural activity (LL) such as empathically listening to others and/or helping someone in need of assistance. Conversely, someone who is inordinately concerned about her "we," or her place within various groups/collectives (LL), is likely to be excessively conformist. This person may benefit from spending more time alone, whether in nature, meditating, exercising, or engaging in some form of art, music, reading, or any other solitary activity that provides enjoyment to the individual. Finally, excessive focus on, or preoccupation with, solely the exterior, or more objective, dimensions of life (UR and LR) can produce dissociation from oneself or from one's groups. Such a person would be served by interventions from the UL or LL quadrants: Gendlin's focusing, dialogues with parts of self or others, personal journaling, or cultivating better relationships by practicing empathy and compassion for friends, family, and others.

To summarize, as integral therapists, we scan which quadratic dimensions the client tends to ignore, avoid, or devalue, and then select specific interventions from the ignored, avoided, or devalued quadrant(s) that fit optimally for that individual's type, or way, of being-in-the-world. Elsewhere, I have argued that the "all quadrants, all levels" model of integral theory is a prime candidate for lending order to the multitude of counseling interventions and that the ITTI is one example of integral counseling's clinical utility (Marquis, 2006). Regardless of your guiding theory, the ITTI provides a fairly comprehensive classification of therapeutic treatment practices. You and your clients may be served by consulting the ITTI and considering whether or not some of the approaches from different quadrants or levels might be appropriate to each client's specific struggles (bear in mind that the mini-ITTI included here displays only about 10% of the interventions listed in the complete ITTI).

With its mission to embody a counseling approach that integrates compassionate service with the most current scientific counseling outcome and process research, integral therapy marries not only the heart and mind but also the client's experience and capacity to choose (UL), biomedical perspectives and the individual's behavior (UR), culture and meaning-making systems (LL), and the social systems in which we find ourselves (LR)— which helps therapists honor and nurture each client's body, mind, and spirit as each unfolds in self, culture, and nature.

Conclusion

This chapter has covered a sample of the material that the Integral Intake assesses. If you look at the Integral Intake itself (Appendix A) or at the examples of completed intakes in Chapter 7, you will notice far more queries than were covered in this chapter, which were merely representative of what the Integral Intake assesses. Even more important than gaining a wealth of information, the integral (AQAL) model organizes this material in a way that is coherent, understandable, and meaningful to both therapists and their clients. Another brief example of the AQAL model's capacity to organize therapeutic interventions was provided with the mini-ITTI.

Note

1. It probably seems that cognitive interventions, because they target cognitions—which occur inside an individual—would be categorized as UL interventions. Elsewhere (Marquis, 2006), I have explained why I assign cognitive interventions to the UR. In essence, cognitive approaches strive to be as objective and empirical as possible. Moreover, Beck explicitly modeled his approach after—and teaches his clients to practice on themselves—the scientific method: clients "are taught to treat their beliefs as hypotheses and to gather additional information and conduct behavioral experiments to test their accuracy" (Hollon & Beck, 2004, p. 448). All of the above characteristics signify "gaining distance from" one's thoughts—as from the outside/exterior looking in—so that one is not so involved with the matter that they cannot see their thoughts as they "really are," which is what "objectivity" is all about.

4

THE SPECTRUM OF DEVELOPMENT, PATHOLOGY, AND TREATMENT

The complexity of human change processes merits appreciation. Human development rarely follows a simple, linear path. It is more often a zigzag course, with frequent sticking points, repetitive circles, occasional regressions, and a few startling leaps and falls. The particulars may seem dizzying in their diversity, yet *there are patterns. Patterns suggest principles. Understanding the principles of human development is essential to the task of psychotherapy.*

(Mahoney, 2003, pp. 9–10, italics added)

Different theories offer varying levels of utility at different stages of client growth.

(Ivey, 1986, p. 2)

Introduction

As the first quote above suggests, issues of human development are central to counseling and psychotherapy. Moreover, human development—even though it is complex, manifests tremendously diverse particulars, and is influenced by myriad sociocultural contexts—does demonstrate patterns and principles. Those principles and patterns (structures) form the heart of developmental theories, which emerged from an attempt to better understand some basic questions regarding the nature of what it means to develop, influences on human change processes, milestones in those processes, and problems that can arise within the course of development.

Why are developmental theories—and particularly, developmental psychology—important to counseling and psychotherapy? First and foremost:

> Psychotherapy is applied developmental psychology. The therapist uses his or her knowledge of normal development to reach some conclusions about the reason for a patient's malfunctioning and how one may enter the developmental spiral either to foster or to reinstitute a more productive, or at least less destructive, developmental process ... the model of the developmental spiral provides such a framework for gauging therapeutic interventions. (Basch, 1988, p. 29)

Thus, many, if not most, of the troubles and challenges that clients present are intimately related to issues in their development.

Furthermore, meaning-making is a process that is central to human experience and successful counseling (Mahoney, 2003; Cook-Greuter & Soulen, 2007), and understanding how diverse others make meaning is greatly aided by an understanding of various developmental processes, from cognitive and moral development (Piaget, 1977; Kohlberg, 1990; Gilligan, 1982) to ego and worldview development (Loevinger, 1976; Cook-Greuter, 2003; Wilber, 2000b). Basically, not only do people vary along dimensions such as personality *types;* they also differ significantly as a function of their developmental *levels* of meaning-making (Cook-Greuter & Soulen, 2007). Whereas different types (such as the personality styles posited and assessed by the Myers-Briggs Type Indicator or the Enneagram) are emphasized as being equally valid styles, there are clear advantages, greater capacities, and more complexity associated with later stages of human development than with earlier developmental stages. To take an example, think of the activity of being a counselor. Now compare how effective two differentially developed counselors would be: one who has not developed the capacity to take the perspective of others (characteristic of Piaget's preoperational stage of development) and who has very little awareness of emotional dynamics (Goleman, 1995; Salovey & Mayer as cited in Matthews,

Zeidner, & Roberts, 2002); and another who not only can take others' perspectives and think abstractly—seeing patterns and principles that structure various clients' problems—but also has an exquisitely developed sense of intrapersonal and interpersonal dynamics that results in a highly integrated sense of emotional intelligence. Given equal training, which of the two counselors would be more effective? I think the answer is clear.

Now turn your attention to the second quote that opened this chapter; it suggests a central point of this chapter: that different therapeutic approaches are optimally suited for different individuals as a function of their developmental *center of gravity*.[1]

Rationale for the Thesis of This Chapter

A thesis of Wilber's that is central not only to this chapter but also to a significant portion of integral therapists' clinical work is that there is a spectrum of development, pathology, and treatment. Briefly stated, part of what it suggests is that "at each stage of self development, an arrest, fixation, or dissociation from that stage results in a specific pathology" (Marquis & Wilber, in press). Similar notions have been proposed by various researchers and therapists within psychoanalytic, psychodynamic, and other developmental circles (Kernberg, 1980; Kohut, 1971, 1977, 1984; Masterson, 1981; Fosha, 2000; Ivey, 1986; Mahoney, 1991). What distinguishes this part of Wilber's thesis is the more comprehensive developmental spectrum that he addresses, spanning not only the prepersonal (which the psychoanalytic tradition focused on) and personal domains (which cognitive theorists focus more on) but also the suprapersonal (which has received less serious attention in the fields of counseling and psychotherapy; a few exceptions are Jung, 1961, 1968; Assagioli, 1988; Maslow, 1971; Washburn, 1988, 1994; Grof, 1998).

Perhaps even more significantly, Wilber suggests that particular psychotherapeutic approaches are optimally suited for clients suffering from different pathologies. Ivey suggested a very similar idea, commenting that "each therapy has special strengths for coping with various aspects of client development" (1986, p. 143), but his notion is structured by Piaget's levels of cognitive development, whereas Wilber emphasizes many developmental lines. Moreover, Ivey suggested that "although all theories cover all aspects of the developmental sphere, certain theories have claimed certain portions of the sphere. That is, some therapies operate mostly at the concrete operational level, while others, such as cognitive-behavioral, appear to function at multiple levels" (Ivey, 1986, p. 170). I would strongly disagree with the first part of the previous Ivey quote. For example, the family of cognitive-behavior approaches and existential approaches does not address prepersonal dimensions of human nature, and very, very few therapeutic approaches address the trans- or suprapersonal dimensions of human nature (exceptions above notwithstanding). Ivey's basic point, with which I concur, is that it is essential for therapists to recognize and appreciate that different therapeutic approaches—like different clients—are characterized by different developmental emphases (Ivey, 1986, p. 171).

Gordon Paul posed what is now a classic question: "*What* treatment, by *whom*, is most effective for *this* individual with *that* specific problem, under *which* set of circumstances, and *how* does it come about?" (cited in Ivey, 1986, p. 140). The thesis of the spectrum of development, pathology, and treatment is a primary answer to that question. Ivey answered Paul's question with what he calls "style-shift counseling": "If your present style of counseling and therapy does not work, shift your style to meet the developmental needs of your client. Furthermore, as your client develops increased cognitive complexity, shift your style to remain with the client" (p. 140). Ivey suggests that the therapist, after assessing where a client is developmentally, "choose a counseling approach that matches the developmental level" of the client (1986, p. 140). Ivey focuses primarily on Piagetian stages of cognitive development, and his four primary styles of counseling are sensorimotor, thinking (concrete operations), feeling (formal operations), and learning level (dialectical) (p. 141). Thus, precedents for Wilber's thesis are present in the traditions of counseling and psychotherapy.

Applying a developmental perspective allows counselors to better understand and empathize with their clients. As we will see in Chapter 5, one's ego development is central to how one makes meaning, and meaning-making is crucial to the experience of well-being and the "good life." Failing to take a client's level of ego development into consideration will likely result in a counselor projecting her own manner of meaning-making upon the client, consequently failing to understand the client and his problem(s). Very often, a single developmental principle underlies a multitude of client concerns. Failing to take a developmental view renders one blind to such critical phenomena. For example, a client of mine who was a freshman college student came to counseling because she no longer felt she fit in at home or church. Not only was Jennifer experiencing more conflict at home and church, but she also had frequent arguments with her boyfriend.[2] In addition to the conflict and not feeling that she "belonged" at home, at church, or in her romantic relationship, Jennifer felt increasingly lonely and misunderstood in the same contexts that previously had so well met her needs. Some counselors might have implemented a problem-solving approach, perhaps teaching conflict resolution skills and so forth. Any number of her apparently discrete problems could have been the focus of her sessions with such a therapist. From a developmental perspective, however, I saw that Jennifer was transitioning from a previously conformist (rule/role) level of development into a more conscientious (formal reflexive) level of development. Her father was highly authoritarian and her Baptist church was likewise; her southern boyfriend upheld traditional gender roles.

It was no coincidence that she was finishing her second semester of liberal arts courses—which she reported were incredibly stimulating and were "opening up" her mind—when she began to question the rigidity and universality of the moral codes with which she had been raised. She was both encountering a diverse array of students and engaging with new ideas and worldviews, which suddenly and rather drastically altered her perception of herself and the world around her. I conceived of her fundamental "problem"—and all of its associated challenges and pain—as a developmental one and communicated the following ideas to her (not exactly as in this monologue, but the same basic ideas):

> It seems to me that in some ways you are outgrowing your family, church, and boyfriend. That doesn't mean you don't still love, need, and want them—but you are orienting or positioning yourself differently with them. Correct me if this doesn't fit, but it struck me that the very rules and structures in your family and church that once felt most comforting and inspiring are now the very things you find the most constraining and irritating. Your previously adopting the codes of various groups—such as your family and church—without evaluating those codes for yourself was developmentally appropriate. It's also developmentally appropriate that you are now concerned with thinking for yourself,

coming to your own conscientious decisions about how to lead your life, and expressing yourself even when your views differ from others'. The difficulty rests in how to do that and maintain your ties to your family, church, and boyfriend; or you may choose to find a different faith community or boyfriend.

This client felt liberated by my framing her "problem" as a normal developmental experience. As Ivey (1986, p. 2) noted, "Developmental theory has been too long separated from clinical practice." If Jennifer had seen a therapist that had construed her problems as merely relationship or family troubles and worked on communication skills, assertiveness training, or conflict resolution, a tremendous developmental opportunity would have been lost. Jennifer and I worked together for about 30 sessions, and I had the pleasure of bearing witness to her blossoming into a young woman who thought for herself, became more relativistic in her moral stances, and was excited to be alive. Her boyfriend could not tolerate her changes and they broke up. Likewise, she left her authoritarian church and began attending a Unitarian church. Though both of the losses were painful, she found enjoyment and meaning amidst her grieving. She continued to have what she characterized as "heated discussions" with her family, and she was often simultaneously distressed and excited by the dissolution of rigid rules structuring how she related to her family. When she terminated therapy, she said she felt "more alive" than she ever had before. Much of my counseling with her was simply contextualizing her experience within a developmental framework, helping her process her experience via Socratic-type dialogue, and offering feedback and empathy along the way.

Because clients' developmental levels influence how they interpret their interactions, what they construe as meaningful, what they experience as threatening, and so forth, a developmental perspective can help counselors align their ways of interacting with their clients and help them anticipate client reactions, defenses, and conflicts (Cook-Greuter & Soulen, 2007; Pearson, 2007). This is particularly pertinent given how different clients view, receive, and/or reject feedback, which is largely a matter of their ego development (see Chapter 5 for more details about this; also consult Cook-Greuter & Soulen, 2007).

According to Ivey, "providing an appropriate therapeutic environment that is matched to the current developmental level of the client may be useful in facilitating growth and change" (1986, p. 141). Thus, with Jennifer's emerging formal-reflexive capacities, much of our work was introspective and philosophical in nature. She valued that our relationship was a place where she could "sort things out for herself"—that we discussed ideas and "examined the evidence" for various viewpoints. Though she did feel more anxiety than she used to (probably because she no longer benefited from the comforts of being associated with the "one true way" to follow), she was invigorated by her new quest to develop into the person she was becoming, and she experienced her newfound freedom as intoxicating.

> Different theories of counseling and therapy may be more useful with some clients than with others; thus, the assessment of developmental status becomes an important issue. Once having determined the developmental and cognitive level of a client, it is possible to systematically plan development with and for the client. (Ivey, 1986, pp. 33–34)

Given that Jennifer was quite clearly transitioning out of a conformist/sociocentric worldview into a more conscientious/worldcentric worldview, what I offered her was very different from what I would provide a client who was highly egocentric. In the latter case, encouraging the client to take and conform to the perspective of his family and church members (provided that those perspectives were not harmful or pathological) and helping him see the downside of his acting only out of his own self-interests would constitute more of the work of therapy. For him, developing an appreciation of the value of a structure beyond himself to which he could conform would be a major transformation. By contrast, that is the very structure/level that was confining Jennifer and out of which she emerged as a more mature young woman. Thus, different interventions and approaches are needed both to support clients at their current level, helping them translate more effectively, and also to "challenge" them at their current level, thus motivating/facilitating their transforming into subsequent stages, wider worldviews, and further integration (Cook-Greuter & Soulen, 2007).

General Principles of Developmental Dynamics and Therapeutic Processes

Mahoney (1991) wrote that because life and human change processes are complex, so too must therapy be complex. Simultaneously and paradoxically, they are quite simple. After all, parents, teachers, and friends routinely facilitate others' development: "Whether we are social workers or psychologists, mental health counselors or psychiatrists, therapeutic teachers or nurses, we all work with issues of human development" (Ivey, 1988, p. xi). The first four of Ivey's core developmental constructs are:

1. Development entails a repeated pattern of separation (differentiation) and attachment (connection, identification, integration).
2. Development can potentially occur across one's entire life course.
3. Development always occurs in cultural contexts, many of which are outside of our conscious awareness.
4. "Development does not occur just at the conscious level but also at levels beyond our awareness. These levels beyond our awareness are often termed unconscious" (Ivey, 1986, p. 345).

Other developmental principles that are common to most stage theories include:

- People at a given stage rarely prefer the solutions or ways of being that characterize the previous stage(s) (Kegan, 1982, p. 56).
- Each new stage or balance brings with it the capacity to see others more fully as they are in their distinct integrity (Kegan, 1982).
- Development involves a process of an unfolding of potentials that leads to greater understanding and effectiveness, with worldviews evolving from simpler to more complex.
- Overall, human development is teleonomic, but there is also spiraling (plenty of regressions and nonlinearity; more will be said about this later in this chapter).
- Each later stage is increasingly complex, holistic, enveloping, and holarchical.
- "People's stage of development influences what they identify with, notice, or can become aware of, and therefore, what they can describe, articulate, influence, and change" (Cook-Greuter & Soulen, 2007, p. 184).

- Subsequent stages reveal an increased tolerance for ambiguity and diversity as well as increases in reflection, flexibility, and skillful interaction in the world.
- It is a never-ending process: regardless of how developed we may become, our understanding and knowledge always remain partial and incomplete.

In a nutshell, later stages of development demonstrate more behavioral flexibility, increased cognitive capacities, and a greater sensitivity to others' experiences, especially when those experiences are different from one's own. All this tends to facilitate more intimate, satisfying, and therapeutic relationships, whether professional or not (Cook-Greuter & Soulen, 2007). Although the following is a very general statement (and all generalization is, to some extent, overgeneralization), people functioning from later developmental levels can potentially understand people at earlier levels of development, whereas the reverse is not the case. In each subsequent developmental wave (*developmental wave* is synonymous with *level, stage,* or *structure;* these four terms will be clarified and differentiated in the section "A Few Distinctions," below), a person is more differentiated, more comprehensive, and more effective in resolving the dilemmas, problems, and other complexities than he was in the preceding wave (Cook-Greuter & Soulen, 2007).

Many stage theories of human development have also incorporated key Piagetian notions. For example, each stage of development includes a period of preparation, followed by a period of relatively stable achievement. According to Piaget, "development is spotty, local, and uneven. A concept may appear in one form, but take a year or more to extend itself over its possible range" (1977, p. xxv). This unevenness, or *décalage,* was thought by Piaget to be an explanatory principle for development: the more highly developed structures coexisting with the lower ones generates the conflict, disequilibrium, and dissonance that spurs further growth. The concept of "equilibration" was central to Piaget's theory. Briefly, it refers to the individual's effort to keep his or her cognitive structures in balance. States of disequilibrium are inherently dissatisfying, and the organism will do what it can to reequilibrate. Kegan refers to this concept as the "subject-object balance" (1982, p. 39).

Humans clearly have needs for connectedness, relationships, and belonging, on one hand, as well as for autonomy, individuation, and agency, on the other. Each stage of development thus constitutes something of a "balancing act," "dynamic stability," or "evolutionary truce" (Kegan, 1982, p. 44) between those mutually defining needs, with each stage representing a shift in the balance: one stage emphasizes integration/connectedness, the next emphasizes separation/individuation, and so on (Cook-Greuter & Soulen, 2007). Neither pole is better than the other. Both are needed; the tension between the two is part and parcel of evolutionary motion. In fact, according to Kegan (1982), the two greatest strivings in human experience are for (1) inclusion, connection, belonging, and communion and (2) independence, autonomy, separateness, and agency. These two yearnings appear to be in conflict, but it is actually their relation and generative tension that is most important. As said before, each stage alternately favors agency/autonomy and then communion/inclusion in its attempt to resolve the tension between them. Even if it is true that masculine types (whether male or female) tend to emphasize agency and feminine types (whether male or female) tend to emphasize communion, Wilber has stressed that "both men and women exist as agency-in-communion (as do all holons)" (2000c, p. 588).

Development and Therapy

It is widely acknowledged that even more important than assessing issues pertaining to whether or not a client and therapist can work productively together (issues of fit and goal compatibility), it is imperative that the therapist holds a developmental view that fosters an ability "to understand, respect, and work within the framework of the client's world rather than forcing the client to fit neatly into the therapist's scheme of values" (Corey, 2001, p. 24; see also Mahoney, 1991, pp. 18–19; Mahoney, 2003; Ivey, 1986). As therapists, we "must enter the world and world view of another" (Ivey, 1986, p. 133; Rogers, 1961). Because others' (perceived) worlds and worldviews are a function of their development, one can far more readily and accurately apprehend their worlds and worldviews if one understands developmental principles and how to assess their developmental altitudes: "If one is to understand others, one must understand their epistemology, or way of knowing the world.... It does little good to offer a formal operational therapy to a client who is unable to operate concretely upon the world" (Ivey, 1986, pp. 138–139). Due to the developmental essence of integral theory, an "integral constructive" approach to therapy balances the value of lessons learned from the past with the value of present action (Mahoney & Marquis, 2002; Mahoney, 2003).

In the quote at the start of this chapter, Basch referred to his model of a developmental "spiral." Interestingly, numerous developmentalists use the metaphor or model of a spiral (Kegan, 1982; Beck & Cowan, 1996; Cook-Greuter, 2003; Mahoney, 2003; Washburn, 1994; Wilber, 1999d). Even though the specific contents of Basch's developmental spiral (decision making, behaviors, self-esteem) differ from those of other developmentalists, the principles with which developmental therapists assess clients and then tailor approaches suited to where in a developmental model clients are stuck are the same: assess what normal developmental processes or tasks were not successfully accomplished/ navigated and then facilitate the client's successful amelioration of that previous deficit (whether that deficit had more to do with the person's internal world or external holding environment, culture, or social system). Furthermore, such therapists use their developmental knowledge to more fully empathize with clients' self-experience. For example, people at different developmental waves are aware of vastly different cognitive possibilities (Piaget, Wilber), value different things (Graves, spiral dynamics), and make meaning via different processes (Kegan, Cook-Greuter). Transformation for one client may involve assuming embeddedness in a relatively authoritarian structure that demands conformity and obedience (such as the army). If that client previously had been deeply egocentric, assuming an ethnocentric perspective (even if it is rigid) is a transformation indeed. However, if a client enters therapy already rather ethnocentric, what he may most need is a developmental scaffolding or pacing that fosters more autonomy and self-directedness. Thus a therapist's ability to provide different forms of environments— different "cultures of embeddedness" (Kegan, 1982, p. 118)—based upon the developmental needs of each individual is essential to effectively helping a spectrum of people. "It is the environment the therapist provides that determines the future growth and development of the client" (Ivey, 1986, p. 131).

Integral Principles of Developmental Dynamics and Therapeutic Processes

Paraphrasing Freud, yet consistent with other developmentalists such as Piaget, Kegan, and Cook-Greuter, Wilber summarized the fundamental developmental dynamic (which is also essential to therapeutic dynamics) as "where it was there shall I become " (1983, p. 67). Actually, given that Freud did not use the Latin terms *id* and *ego* but rather used the everyday German terms for "it" and "I," Wilber is closer to quoting Freud than paraphrasing his "Where id was there shall ego be." Bettelheim (1983) and Kaufmann (1992) have made similar points regarding the translation of this famous Freud quote, and Brandt wrote that "Where it was I ought to become" is a more accurate translation (cited in Loevinger, 1987, p. 41).

If you consider your "self," you will likely notice two qualitatively distinct aspects: all of the things about yourself that you are capable of observing and describing (*distal self,* experienced as "me": the objects of your awareness, such as being a husband, father, teacher, friend, six feet tall, passionate about Bach, someone who enjoys outdoor activities, etc.) and also some observing self that is aware of those descriptive components of yourself (*proximate self;* experienced as "I": the inner subject or witness of experience). Given that "I" is the subject of experience and awareness and "it" consists of all of the objects of your awareness, Freud's famous quote is essentially similar to a phrase that Wilber and Kegan both arrived at around 1980, independently of each other: "The *subject* of one stage becomes an *object* [of the subject] of the next" stage (Wilber, 2000e, p. 34). For example, sensorimotor infants identify almost exclusively with their bodies, and thus their bodies constitute who they are as subjects. As such, they are not capable of reflecting upon and observing their bodies as *aspects* of who they are; rather, they *are* body-selves. Once they develop the preoperational and concrete operational capacities of symbols and concepts, they begin to identify with mental concepts (mind becomes their subject or "I") and can now observe and reflect upon their bodies as objects of awareness. Their bodies are now object to their new subject: mind. Thus, *"the 'I' of one stage becomes a 'me'* [or 'it'] *at the next"* stage (Wilber, 2000e, p. 34, italics in original).

As was mentioned in Chapter 2, psychological development is not simply an upper-left quadrant issue; genetics, developmental histories, and the cultures and systems into which one is born may severely constrain one's choices and freedom. Nonetheless, people, like other biological systems, do self-organize themselves (Maturana & Varela, 1987; Guidano, 1987; Mahoney, 1991). As such, people can be viewed as autopoietic systems whose development throughout the life course is substantially regulated by processes of differentiation and integration through structural organizations of increasing complexity (Guidano, 1987).

> Each time the self (the proximate self) encounters a new level in the Great Nest, it first *identifies* with it and consolidates it; then disidentifies with it (*transcends* [differentiates from] it, de-embeds from it); and then includes and *integrates* it from the higher level. In other words, the self goes through a *fulcrum (or a milestone) of its own development.* (Wilber, 2000e, p. 35)

The line of the proximate self is a particularly important line for integral therapists because "proximate-self development is," in Wilber's view, "at the very heart of the evolution of consciousness. *For it is the proximate self that is the navigator through the basic waves in the Great Nest of Being*" (2000e, p. 35, italics in original). Wilber defined a "fulcrum" of development as a type of developmental milestone, and thus each new stage is a fulcrum. Analogous to the traditional definition of *fulcrum* (the point of support upon which a lever pivots), a developmental fulcrum involves the basic structures that support the generation of a new sense of self. Thus, one's fulcrum is the current probability wave around which one's functioning and way of being "teeters," sometimes reaching slightly forward, sometimes dipping slightly backward. However, *fulcrum* and the terms *level, stage, wave,* and *structure* are synonymous only with regard to the line of proximate-self development, which is most closely assessed in a formal manner with measures of ego development (more on this in Chapter 5).

Holding Environments and Cultures of Embeddedness

All development occurs within sundry social and cultural contexts (LR and LL), from caregiver-child bonds, family relations, peer groups, school, churches, and other community affiliations, all the way to national and global economic and political systems (Mahoney, 1991; Ivey 1986; Wilber, 2000b). Kegan (1982) describes in great detail the different "cultures of embeddedness"—including mothering, role recognizing, mutuality, self-authorship, intimacy—that optimally provide the qualitatively distinct "holding environments" that individuals need at each stage of development. Kegan, consistent with Wilber, emphasizes the significance of our embeddedness:

In Winnicott's view the "holding environment" is an idea intrinsic to infancy. In my view it is an idea intrinsic to *evolution*.... They are the psychosocial environments which hold us (with which we are fused) and which let us go (from which we differentiate).... There is never "just an individual"; the very word refers only to that side of the person that is individuated, the side of differentiation. There is always, as well, the side that is embedded; the *person* is more than an individual. "Individual" names a current state of evolution; "person" refers to the fundamental motion of evolution itself, and is as much about that side of the self embedded in the life-surround as that which is individuated from it. The person is an "individual" *and* an "embeddual." (Kegan, 1982, p. 116)

Many of the most fascinating aspects of development entail the occurrences and experiences between two stages of development, when people are teetering or transitioning between different ways of identifying with and understanding themselves and the world. To actually emerge into a new evolutionary balance, one must both differentiate and integrate (not just differentiate):

The tolerance won out of the differentiation from the societal is not a balanced position from which to construct the moral world (how can you be tolerant of the intolerant?) precisely because it does not represent a new evolutionary truce. It is differentiation without integration. (Kegan, 1982, p. 66)

Many developmental models refer to subsequent stages of development as "higher," a term against which many others react negatively. As I wrote in Chapter 2, such terms are developmental judgments, not judgments about the value of people themselves. Thus, a teenager is not more valuable or worthy as a person than a toddler, but most teenagers are less egocentric and more capable of resolving more complex problems than most toddlers. Relative to this notion of height or altitude, integral theorists often describe development using the metaphor of climbing a mountain. First of all, most mountains do not have only one path to their peak. Thus, different types of people, or cultures, may develop with different emphases, just as one person may prefer a steeper, shorter path or hike up a mountain, whereas another prefers the longer, more gradual path. Second, some people's goal may be not the peak but rather a beautiful meadow two thirds of the way up the mountain. Third, some paths may afford views that other paths may not, just as counseling, meditation, serving others, and conscious relationships all can foster development through very different experiences.

Despite those differences, the different paths that actually arrive at the summit must have passed through all of the same altitudes, and although the specifics (surface features) of the views from different paths may have varied, higher altitudes will disclose greater, not lesser, views. That is to say, as one's altitude increases, more of the territory below is available to one's perspective: not only the beautiful valleys and streams below, but also the darker, shadowy spots that were formerly hidden by trees and other scenery. As one nears the peak, and especially at the summit of one of the higher mountains in a mountain range, one can see beyond one's own mountain to other mountains and distant possibilities on the increasingly revealing horizon. "The more the hikers can see, the wiser, more timely, more systematic and informed their actions and decisions are likely to be. This is so because more of the relevant information, connections and dynamic relationships become visible" (Cook-Greuter & Soulen, 2007, p. 183).

However, higher altitudes are not increasingly free from problems and distress. As Piaget once said, "For every problem solved, new questions arise" (cited in Ivey, 1986, p. 161). Wilber termed this notion the "dialectic of progress," meaning that in addition to resolving old or prior problems, further development confronts one with new, potentially more horrifying ones. For example, developing into an autonomous, formal reflexive thinker may free one from falling prey to a herd mentality, but it also opens one up to existential anxieties that do not exist (at least not nearly as intensely) at conformist levels. Moreover, Mahoney emphasized that "none of us can realistically hope to arrive at a level of development that is free of problems.... Development creates new levels of difficulties, to be sure, but development also begets enlarged capacities for embracing the overall process" (2003, p. 88).

Reality therapists (Glasser, 1990) have made the analogy that if humans are front-wheel-drive automobiles, then the front wheels (which we directly influence with our steering) are our thoughts and behaviors, whereas our feelings and physiology (which are more difficult to directly influence) are the rear wheels. I would add that larger systems, from economic and political to educational and medical, are the roads and highway systems that structure where and how we drive. Of course, there always seem to be a few, rare developmental trailblazers who drive off-road. Most of us, however, are largely constrained or influenced by these larger social and cultural systems, many of which operate outside of our conscious awareness.

A Few Distinctions

A key issue is that integral theory strongly maintains that waves of development are not rigid, permanent essences or molds; rather, they are like "evolutionary grooves or habits"—relatively stable patterns of events or occasions or moments. As I wrote in Chapter 2, integral therapists view stages as probability waves, not as rigid, reified structures.

Stages, Levels, Structures, Waves

Recall from Chapter 2 that Wilber uses the term *levels* to refer to the qualitatively distinct degrees of complexity or organization that characterize the different stages of development; *structures* to emphasize the holistic, integrated nature of each stage; and *waves* to underscore the fluid confluences with which the stages meet and join with one another. Does integral theory posit basic structures? Yes. Rigid, reified structures? No.

Wilber definitely views humans as developing through stages. But what exactly is a stage model of human development? According to McCarthy, stage models specify

> an invariant sequence of discrete and increasingly complex developmental stages, whereby no stage can be passed over and each higher stage implies or presupposes the previous stages. This does not exclude regressions, overlaps, arrested developments, and the like. Stages are constructed wholes that differ qualitatively from one another; phase-specific schematic can be ordered in an invariant and hierarchically structured sequence; no later phase can be [stably] attained before earlier ones have been passed through, and elements of earlier phases are preserved, transformed, and reintegrated in the later. In short, the developmental-logical approach requires the specification of a hierarchy of structural wholes in which the later, more complex, and more encompass-

ing developmental stages presuppose and build upon the earlier. (Cited in Wilber, 2000d, p. 50)

Although Wilber agrees that each developmental line develops in an invariant sequence and that subsequent stages cannot be stably "attained before earlier ones have been passed through," people do not need to perfectly master all of the tasks associated with a stage of development in order to proceed to the next stage. As Wilber has remarked: "All you need is a passing grade [the basic, essential capacities of that stage] to get to the next stage" (cited in Schwartz, 1995, p. 359). Also, even when conceived of as integrated structures, those structures (and "structures" essentially refers to relatively stable patterns of events) are not reified. Rather, they are viewed as probability waves, full of complex dynamics such as lines, types, states, and subpersonalities. As Wilber has emphasized:

> Please remember one thing: these stages (and stage models) are just conceptual snapshots of the great and ever-flowing River of Life. There is simply nothing anywhere in the Kosmos called the [place the name of any stage of development here] (except in the conceptual space of theoreticians who believe it). This is *not* to say that stages are *mere* constructions or are socially constructed, which is the oppositely lopsided view. Stages are real in the sense that there is something actually existing that occurs in the real world and that we call development or growth. It's just that "stages" of that growth are indeed simply snapshots that we take at particular points in time and from a particular perspective (*which itself grows and develops*). (2006, pp. 68–69)

Stages of Development and States of Consciousness

People are tremendously diverse; not all differences, however, are of the same nature. For example, Todd and Babatunde may differ because they were raised in very different cultures; or they may differ because one of them is much more developed in the cognitive and moral lines and the other is more developed in the artistic and kinesthetic lines; or they may appear different at this moment because they are experiencing highly different states of consciousness (for example, one could be asleep, drunk, panicked, or having a peak experience). Ivey, like many counselors, often confuses stages, states, and lines. He mentioned that clients could move through all four stages (sensorimotor to formal operations) in a single counseling session. People do not actually develop through four (or even two) stages in a day. Rather, different lines of development may be differentially developed, so that a client may appear to exhibit very rudimentary development in one aspect (for example, morality) and advanced development in another (scientific or mathematical thinking). Similar phenomena (clients' appearing to exhibit the qualities of different stages of development) can be accounted for by distinguishing between stages and states of consciousness. For example, a client may have a developmental center of gravity that hovers around the formal-reflexive mind but experience a state of panic or intense depression during which he resorts to the type of illogical and contrary-to-evidence thinking that characterize preoperational thinking. There are a few places where Ivey seems to distinguish between stages and states, as when he is describing a concrete operational client with whom the counselor finds various deletions, distortions, overgeneralizations, and other errors of thinking or behaving that "represent preoperational *states*" (1986, p. 163, italics added). This is an important point. The basic structures are not completely stable; otherwise, they would endure even under extreme stress. Hence, developmental waves are conceived of as *relatively* stable and enduring—far more stable and enduring than states of consciousness, but also far from rigidly permanent structures.

Levels and Lines of Development

Ivey also wrote of how clients cycle through Piaget's stages of cognitive development:

> Each person who continues on to higher levels of development is also, paradoxically, forced to return to basic sensori-motor and pre-operational experience.... the skilled individual who decides to learn a foreign language ... must enter language training at the lowest level and work through sensori-motor, preoperational, and concrete experience before being able to engage in formal operations with the new language. (Ivey, 1986, p. 161)

People do not revert from the capacity for formal operational thinking to sensorimotor, except perhaps because of a brain injury or organic
disorders of the nervous system. Piaget was very emphatic that cognitive development occurs in invariant stages, meaning that everyone
progresses through the stages in the same order. At the same time, it is
true that just because an individual exhibits formal operational thinking (a stage or level of cognitive development) in chemistry and mathematics does not mean that she automatically can perform at mastery
levels in any domain, such as, in this case, a foreign language. This is
another example of the utility of Wilber's (2000e) distinguishing the
sundry lines of development that each proceed through the same basic
levels, stages, or waves of development. Ivey seems, at times, to intuit
the difference between levels and lines, such as in the following:

> All clients will be a mixture of several different developmental
> levels [different lines are differentially developed] and will most
> likely present a variety of developmental tasks that need complet-
> ing.... A client may be magical and preoperational on one level
> [in one line], concrete operational on another, formal operational
> on another, and dialectical on still another.... Due to the many
> differing developmental tasks, we are all mixtures of many, many
> developmental levels [and lines]. (Ivey, 1986, p. 162)

Nonetheless, Ivey's intuition does not seem to be consistently
expressed with the clear distinctions that characterize integral theory.
At times he distinguishes stages from states and levels from lines,
whereas at other times he fails to differentiate them, as in the case
above regarding learning a foreign language.

Still, it is true that a given client may exhibit drastically different developmental levels in different lines in a single session, as Ivey
described (1986, p. 162). Because of this, integral therapists most
frequently tailor their overall approach to a particular client to that
client's developmental center of gravity, while at times focusing attention on specific lines (as in the case of a client whose cognitive line
was extremely developed but whose emotional awareness was severely
restricted; in this case, an integral therapist might work to help him
develop his emotional awareness, even though his center of gravity was
higher than his emotional development).

"Development is the aim of counseling and psychotherapy.... Staying put, refusing or being unable to change are what development is not" (Ivey, 1986, p. 28). I agree completely, and it is also crucial to recognize that not all change is developmental or transformative. Hence Wilber's distinction between transformation and translation. Translation is *horizontal growth,* change or expansion within one's stage of development that modifies surface structures without fundamentally altering the deep structures.[3] Translation can entail learning new information, developing new skills, or transferring knowledge from one domain to another, none of which necessarily involves a fundamental shift in how a person interprets life and makes meaning (Cook-Greuter & Soulen, 2007). In contrast, transformation is *vertical development,* a transition to a new stage of development that fundamentally alters and shifts the deep structures of a person's being and functioning. Transformation involves the emergence of a new, more integrated perspective and an increase in altitude (a higher center of gravity); it is much rarer in adults than is translation because it requires a literal transformation of one's view of reality, self, and others: "In general, transformations in awareness or changes in our mental modes are more powerful than any amount of horizontal growth and learning" (Cook-Greuter & Soulen, 2007, p. 182). Ivey is also aware of this distinction and stressed it; for him, moving ahead or ascending to subsequent stages (transformation) is termed vertical development; building adequate foundations (translation and stabilization[4])—which are essential to healthy navigation of life's demands and necessary for healthy differentiation-identification-integration processes to take place—is termed "horizontal development" (Ivey, 1986, p. 8).

According to integral theory, when one actually transforms, what was formerly the subject of consciousness is now an object of consciousness. Thus, a common therapeutic intervention that integral therapists use with clients is the practice of intentionally reflecting upon their experience as objects of awareness. If you reflect upon the statement "The subject of one stage becomes an object of the subject at the next stage," perhaps you will understand how meditative and other contemplative practices can accelerate one's progression through the stages of ego development. Such theoretical notions have been corroborated by empirical research demonstrating with diverse participants—from prison inmates to college students to upper-middle-class spiritual practitioners—that practicing meditation appears to facilitate ego development (Alexander, Druker, & Langer, 1990; Walsh, 1993).

However, most clients seek translative, not transformative, change. Thus, integral counselors often work toward what Wilber (1999d) called the "prime directive": helping clients stabilize at their current level of development. That is to say, even if what a client desires most is transformation, she must first become fully grounded at her current altitude. Doing intensive transformative work when one is not fully stabilized and grounded is like building a mansion without first laying a solid foundation. An initial goal of integral counseling and psychotherapy involves assessing the client's center of gravity and helping her stabilize at that level. This involves working together with clients so that their current wave of ego development affords them legitimate meanings and allows them to function as their environment demands, from controlling impulses to relating reciprocally at home and work. Essentially, this process assists clients in being more integrated at their current stage of life. Not only does this involve helping them translate in more effective and satisfying ways, it also lays the groundwork for further development, if that is what they and the counselor mutually agree is most appropriate for them and their life circumstances. Integral counselors enjoy fostering clients' development, but our goal is not always to "get people developing." More often than not, helping them translate more effectively is what many clients define as a successful outcome.

The Spectrum of Development, Pathology, Defenses, and Treatment

Now that the groundwork has been laid, we have arrived at the heart of this chapter, which is summarized in Table 4.1 (refer to pages 29–32 in Chapter 2 for descriptions of the specific levels).

Upon reading Table 4.1, your initial reaction may be along the lines of "What I encounter as a therapist doesn't look like what that table suggests." In many regards, I agree. It would be extremely rare for a therapist to encounter clients representative of all nine levels of proximate-self development.

In fact, most forms of typical psychotherapy deal only with a few levels: mostly fulcrum-3 (which involves uncovering and integrating repressed feelings and shadow elements), fulcrum-4 (which involves belongingness needs and cognitive reprogramming of

Table 4.1 The Spectrum of Human Development, Psychogenic Pathology, Defenses, and Treatment

General Realm	Level/Fulcrum	Class of Psychogenic Pathology	Common Defenses	Optimal Treatment
Prepersonal (body)	Sensoriphysical	Psychoses	Hallucination, delusional projection, wish fulfillment	**Pharmacotherapy with psychotherapy as adjunct** (behavioral and cognitive–behavioral approaches)
	Phantasmic/emotional	Borderline and narcissistic disorders	Splitting, (projective identification), selfobject fusion	**Structure-building approaches:** object relations, self psychology (dialectical behavior therapy)
	Representational mind	Neuroses	Repression, (projection), reaction formation	**Uncovering approaches:** Psychodynamic: Jungian, ego psychology; Gestalt; focusing; (experiential/person-centered)
Personal (mind)	Rule/role mind	Script pathologies	Displacement, duplicitous transaction, covert intention, (repression)	**Script analysis** (collaborative empiricism, cognitive therapy, REBT, Adlerian, reality therapy, etc.)
	Formal-reflexive	Identity neuroses	Sublimation, anticipation, suppression	**Introspection, philosophizing, Socratic dialogue** (experiential)
	Vision-logic	Existential pathologies	Inauthenticity, deadening, aborted self-actualization, bad faith	**Existential psychotherapy** (experiential approaches)
Suprapersonal (spirit)	Para-mental	Psychic disorders	Pranic disorder, yogic illness	**Path of yogis** (sometimes temporary suspension of contemplative work)
	Meta-mental (Illumined mind)	Subtle disorders	Failed integration, archetypal fragmentation	**Intensification of contemplative practice, increased contact with spiritual teacher**
	Over-mental (Intuitive mind) Super-mental	Causal disorders	Failed differentiation, Arhat's disease	**Collaboration between student and spiritual teacher**

Adapted from *The Collected Works of Ken Wilber* by Ken Wilber © 1999, vol 4. Reprinted by arrangement with Shambhala Publications, Inc. Boston, MA, www.shambhala.com. (Note that items in parentheses were added by the present author, based upon empirical research presented in the professional literature.)

harsh scripts), and fulcrums 5 and 6 (which involve self-esteem and self-actualization). (Wilber, 1999d, pp. 17–18)

Relationship Between Levels of Development and Psychopathology

We now arrive at the issue of *how* to assess clients' levels of development and their primary psychogenic pathology—information needed in order to tailor an optimal therapeutic approach for each person.[5] Most integral therapists, and most other developmental therapists in general (Mahoney, 1991, 2003; Ivey, 1986; Guidano, 1987), assess informally rather than with paper-and-pencil tests. According to Susanne Cook-Greuter, one of the premier figures in the assessment of ego development (which is the single best standardized measure of a person's altitude or center of gravity), counselors can assess clients' developmental center of gravity and their repertoire and range of meaning-making constructs and strategies either via formal testing (such as the Washington University Sentence Completion Test, WUSCT, or the Sentence Completion Test integral, SCTi) or via "clinical acumen" (Cook-Greuter & Soulen, 2007, p. 191).

Although I will go into more detail in Chapter 5 regarding the formal assessment of clients' ego development, paying attention to the following will help you assess a client's developmental center of gravity:

- A client's use of language, which reflects thought processes. Is the client able to think abstractly? Is the client open to examining the evidence for his thoughts and opinions? Is he willing to change those thoughts and opinions and capable of doing so?
- Signs of developmental arrests or fixations, such as intense needs that appear regressive or age-inappropriate.
- The degree of differentiation and complexity in his meaning-making activities.
- How the client relates to you (e.g., reciprocally or merely as an extension of himself; countertransferential reactions you observe in yourself that you think the client is eliciting in you).
- The client's most commonly used defense mechanisms (see Table 4.1; see also Pearson, 2007).

Prepersonal Disorders

The primary criteria in assessing *psychotic* (fulcrum 1) *disorders* include disorganized thinking/speech, delusions, hallucinations, catatonic or grossly disorganized behavior, and "negative" symptoms such as avolition, alogia, or flat affect (*DSM-IV-TR*). The use of primitive defense mechanisms—such as splitting, selfobject fusion, and projective identification—and patterns of highly unstable relationships suggest *borderline and narcissistic* (fulcrum 2) *disorders*. People suffering from borderline disorders have only a remote and tenuous sense of self. More specifically, they will reveal many of the following diagnostic criteria: intense yet unstable relationships in which they oscillate between idealizing and devaluing the other; various forms of potentially self-damaging impulsivity; identity disturbances involving an unstable, incoherent sense of self; affective instability; recurrent suicidal behavior, threats, or self-mutilating; chronic feelings of emptiness; severe dissociative symptoms or stress-related, transient paranoid ideation (*DSM-IV-TR*).

Although deriving from the same fulcrum of development as borderline conditions, narcissistic clients are characterized by more of an "outline of a self" (Fall, Holden, & Marquis, 2004, p. 86), even if it is vague and often unstable. Narcissistic disorders reflect a fundamental deficit in capacities to regulate one's self-esteem. As such, the grandiose form of narcissism that is described in the *DSM-IV-TR* is only one of the two primary forms of narcissism, and probably the less common form (Kohut, 1971, 1984). Narcissistic people may be deficient in their empathic abilities, exhibit grandiosity, require excessive admiration, believe they are special and/or unique, have a sense of entitlement, be arrogant, be interpersonally exploitative, and often be envious of others (*DSM-IV-TR*). Fundamentally, they lack confidence in their ideals and ambitions and thus succumb to distractive and other addictive endeavors to alleviate feelings of emptiness, boredom, and numbness. In contrast to the grandiose form, people with fragile forms of narcissism are characterized by feelings of pervasive emptiness and boredom, in addition to deficiencies in regulating self-esteem. They often report lacking meaning, worth, humor, zest for life, and suffer broad disturbances in their systems of ideals (Kohut, 1971, p. 22). Kohut (1977) described the fragile narcissist as having developed only part of a mature self with mature selfobjects, which coexist with an archaic self and archaic selfobjects. Because they are hypervigilant about others' evaluations of them, what most would consider only the slightest judgment may be experienced by fragile narcissists as an overwhelmingly negative assault to the core of their being, resulting in either depression or disintegration anxiety (Kohut, 1984, p. 16). To ward off these negative effects, narcissists will often resort to archaic defenses—such as inappropriate withdrawal or narcissistic rage—to defend against feelings of personal annihilation.

In contrast to the previous disorders, which are often referred to as "disorders of the self" (Kohut, 1971), in the *neurotic* (fulcrum 3) *disorders*, ego functions—such as repression and a sense of self—have developed, yet the self is characterized by internal conflict. Thus, repression and projection of sexual, aggressive, and other impulses that result in symbolically disguised symptoms characterize neuroses.

Personal Disorders

Whereas neuroses are associated with defended-against conflicts, *script or role* (fulcrum 4) *disorders* primarily involve dynamics of distorted thinking, role confusion, rigid and overly harsh cognitive scripts, or "duplicitous transactions" in which covert messages and other hidden agendas are masked by different overt messages. Although script/role pathologies can be found in individuals capable of formal operational thinking, they are more reflective of concrete thinking.

Once formal reflexive qualities predominate in an individual, her self-structuralization becomes more introspective, highly differentiated, reflexive, and open to (abstract) possibilities and is no longer tied to concrete appearances (key diagnostic criteria for this level of development). However, precisely because these developmental capacities open one to new possibilities, they also present new pathologies. The *identity* (fulcrum 5) *neuroses* involve the newly budding individual who is no longer prereflexively bound to the conventions of families, friends, cultures, or nations. Erikson (1963, 1980) has probably elucidated these issues more clearly than anyone else. Here, concerns involve fears of not being strong enough to stand up for one's own principles of conscience; concerns of not being courageous enough to remain in conflict with others with whom one was once in agreement; frightened by the task of really thinking for oneself; unsure of having the endurance to continue swimming against the currents: "It can lie awake at night, riveted with worries or elated by anticipation over all the possibilities!" (Wilber, 1986, p. 116).

Wilber emphasizes that existential conflicts or perspectives occur at all levels of self-development: one can view any of the preceding stages and their pathologies as involving existential dynamics of life versus death, preservation versus negation struggles, individual responsibility versus collective "herd" mentalities, questions of meaning, and so forth. However, Wilber distinguishes existential perspectives or conflicts with the existential wave and its corresponding *existential* (fulcrum 6) *pathologies*, by which he means it is characterized by ennui and concerns regarding authenticity; self-actualization; an integration of body and mind; responsible living, choosing, willing; meaning in an apparently meaningless world; and mortality and finitude. The more common syndromes associated with existential pathologies are:

- *Existential depression:* a global, diffuse depression or "life-arrest" in the face of perceived meaninglessness
- *Inauthenticity:* defined by Heidegger (1962) as lack of profound awareness and acceptance of one's own finitude and mortality
- *Existential isolation and "uncanniness":* a strong enough self that nevertheless feels "not at home" in the familiar world
- *Existential anxiety:* the threatened death of, or loss of, one's self-reflexive modes of being-in-the-world (an anxiety that *cannot* occur prior to fulcrums 5 and 6 because the very capacity for formal-reflection does not occur until then)
- *Aborted self-actualization:* as phrased by Maslow (1971): "I warn you, if you deliberately set out to be less than you are capable of becoming, you will be deeply unhappy for the rest of your life" (cited in Wilber, 1986, p. 118)

Suprapersonal Disorders

I will not address the suprapersonal disorders because the percentage of clients who seek professional counseling or psychotherapy with these problems is quite small. In fact, research suggests that fewer than one half of one percent (.5%) of the adult population in the United States reaches the integrated stage of ego development, which itself is not suprapersonal, but more similar to Wilber's vision-logic and what Maslow described as a self-actualizing (not self-transcending) person

(Hy & Loevinger, 1996; Cook-Greuter, 2000). Readers interested in suprapersonal disorders and their treatment can consult Chapter 13 of Fall et al. (2004) and Wilber (1999d, p. 127–133, 143–149).

Relationship Between Psychopathology and Treatment

Integral therapists do posit that people at different developmental stages face different challenges, the resolution of which is optimally assisted by different therapeutic approaches, as Table 4.1 suggests. However, Wilber emphasized that

> the nine general levels of therapy that I outlined are meant to be suggestive only; they are broad guidelines as to what we can expect, based on a careful reading of the evidence compiled by numerous different schools of developmental psychology and contemplative spirituality.... There is, needless to say, a great deal of overlap between these therapies. For example, I list "script pathology" and "cognitive therapy" as being especially relevant to fulcrum-4.... Cognitive therapy has excelled in rooting out these maladaptive scripts and replacing them with more accurate, benign, and therefore healthy ideas and self-concepts. But to say cognitive therapy focuses on this wave of consciousness development is *not* to say it has no benefit at other waves, for clearly it does. The idea, rather, is that the farther away we get from this wave, the less relevant (but never completely useless) cognitive therapy becomes. Developments in fulcrums 1 and 2 are mostly preverbal and preconceptual, so conceptual reprogramming does not directly address these levels; and developments beyond fulcrum-6 are mostly transmental and transrational, so mental reprogramming, in and of itself, is limited in its effectiveness. So it is not that a given therapy applies to one narrow wave of development, but that, in focusing on one or two waves, most forms of therapy increasingly lose their effectiveness when applied to more distant realms. (Wilber, 1999d, p. 16)

I will here address this issue in a general manner. I will go into more details of how clients at different developmental altitudes benefit from different therapeutic approaches in Chapter 7.

Because psychotic, borderline, and narcissistic clients (with disorders that derive from the first two prepersonal levels of development) lack the psychological structure (i.e., ego or self) required to make their experiences cohere in a relatively stable manner—which promotes the sense of being an individuated self that is separate from yet related to others—some form of structure-building approach is most helpful to these people. Examples of structure-building approaches include those of Kernberg (1980); Kohut (1977, 1984); Masterson (1981); Linehan (1993); Stolorow, Atwood, and Orange (2002); and Stolorow, Brand-chaft, and Atwood (1987). For individuals struggling primarily with neuroses—in which disturbing symptoms arise that are symbolic of repressed, projected, or otherwise defended-against impulses—uncovering approaches are more useful. In the case of the neurotic client, he has enough psychological structure to repress, project, and so on. That is, after all, why his issues are seeking expression in symbolic symptoms such as disturbing dreams, somaticized bodily pains, phobias, and so forth. Thus, these clients do not need to build structure (as was the case with those with psychotic, borderline, and narcissistic disorders). Rather, they will benefit the most from *uncovering* what they have kept out of their awareness; hence, the general category of uncovering approaches (which spans the entire spectrum of psychoanalytic, psychodynamic, and other "depth" approaches).

The next general category of treatments involves those clients who have acquired the sense of a relatively coherent and individuated sense of self but are challenged with struggles revolving around the process of further elaborating and defining their autonomy and/or interdependence in terms of the rules and roles they abide by, and by deeper answers to questions such as "Who am I?" and "How can I live as fully and authentically as possible?" (in other words, clients with disorders that derive from personal levels of development). For clients with script pathologies and/or systematic biases in reasoning and thinking, a generally cognitive approach (such as transactional analysis, Beck's cognitive therapy, or Ellis' rational emotive behavior therapy) is most effective. For clients with identity neuroses—in which the individual struggles with establishing autonomy and self-directedness rather than merely conforming to societal, cultural, and other collective standards—an introspective, experiential, philosophical approach (i.e., Greenberg, 2002; Fosha, 2000) will likely be maximally helpful. Given that the brunt of an identity neurosis involves the epistemological and moral conclusions one arrives at through formal reflexive thinking (rather than merely swallowing conventional mandates, as is common at the preceding stages), philosophical problems are central to identity neuroses, and thus philosophical education or counseling is a legitimate and often primary component of the therapy. For clients whose primary concerns are existential in nature—such as deeply assuming responsibility for one's life, acknowledging one's mortality, isolation, freedom, and striving to live an authentic, self-actualizing life—existential-humanistic approaches (Yalom, Bugental, Perls, Rogers) are most effective.

However, if a client is dealing with transpersonal or suprapersonal issues (i.e., most conventional mental health professionals would consider her healthy, perhaps even significantly self-actualizing, but she nonetheless intuits that she could experience more joy, meaning, and interconnectedness with the Kosmos; in other words, clients with disorders that derive from suprapersonal levels of development), a Jungian approach, Assagioli's psychosynthesis, or other transpersonal approaches (e.g., Washburn, 1988, 1994; Welwood 1985, 2000) are more appropriate.

Clarifications and Cautions

The integral model is easily caricatured and distorted. Understanding developmental principles and dynamics provides powerful sources of insight into our clients and the source(s) of their suffering, not to mention the insights we gain into ourselves. However, simply reading about developmental theories will not foster improved clinical skills, and implementing the principles suggested in this chapter requires far more than merely inserting stage-relevant interventions into the therapeutic process. Integrating an intellectual understanding of developmental theories with your clinical practice will improve your effectiveness as a counselor; mere reading will not. Ideally, after a period of focused study of developmental literature (Mahoney, 1991, 2003; Kegan, 1982, 1994; Ivey, 1986; Loevinger, 1976; Cook-Greuter, 2003; Cook-Greuter & Soulen, 2007; Wilber 1999d), one must practice these principles, then reflect upon one's practical experience, continue practicing developmentally while continuing to reflect, and so on. I consider a skilled developmental clinical supervisor indispensable in this learning process, and the supervisor does not need to identify with integral theory in order to be of immense help; most psychodynamic clinicians conceptualize and practice developmentally, and individuals such as Ivey and Mahoney have strong footholds in the cognitive therapy tradition. In the same way that mental health practitioners-in-training optimally hone their clinical skills in practica and internships under skilled clinical supervisors (rather than in theoretical courses or without the benefit of seasoned supervisors), learning to practice developmentally is optimally accomplished by counseling many developmentally diverse people under the supervision of a seasoned developmental supervisor.

Many of the cautions and clarifications regarding misuses of integral counseling involve common misconceptions of stage theories in general. This section will revolve around five common critiques of—or concerns about—stage theories of development: the universality of stages; the irreversibility of stages; the idea of progression itself; linear/ladder models as stunningly oversimplifying; and the dangers of hierarchical stage theories.

Stages: Universal or Context-Bound?

Yes and Yes.   Although the idea of universal stages of development is currently about as out of vogue in academic social sciences as phrenology is in personality research, integral theory posits that the basic structures of consciousness are cross-cultural and universal, or at least quasi-universal. *The basic structures/stages/waves of consciousness represent the degree of consciousness that characterizes any given phenomenon*—in our case, people and their development. The basic structures are to consciousness what altitude is to a mountain: both are content-free, yet both also set parameters on what is possible:

> The altitude markers themselves (3000 feet, 8000 feet, etc.) are *without content*—they are "empty," just like consciousness per se—but each of the paths can be measured in terms of its altitude up the mountain. The "feet" or "altitude" means degree of development, which means degree of consciousness.... However, using "altitude" as a general marker of development allows us to refer to general similarities across the various lines, yet altitude as "meters" or "inches" or "yards" **itself has no content**; it is empty. "Inches" is a measure of wood, but nothing in itself. You do not

go around saying, "I had to stop building my house today because I ran out of inches." ...

Likewise with "consciousness" when used in this fashion. It is not a thing or a content or a phenomenon. It has no description. It is not worldviews, it is not values, it is not morals, not cognition, not value-MEMEs, mathematico-logico structures, adaptive intelligences, or multiple intelligences. In particular, consciousness is not itself a line among other lines, but the space in which lines arise. Consciousness is the emptiness, the openness, the clearing in which phenomena arise, and if those phenomena develop in stages, they constitute a developmental line (cognitive, moral, self, values, needs, memes, etc.). The more phenomena that *can* arise in consciousness, the higher the level in that line. Again, consciousness itself is not a phenomenon, but the space in which phenomena arise. (Wilber, 2006, pp. 65–68)

As such, Wilber's basic structures or waves (which are the terms listed in the "Level/Fulcrum" column of Table 4.1) are simply markers referring to some of the relatively stable patterns that developmental psychologists have observed as they assess people across their life spans. According to integral theory, the basic structures are not permanently fixed or unchanging essences, whether Platonic, Kantian, or Jungian. Rather, they are more akin to Kosmic memories or habits of evolution than pregiven molds (Wilber, 2000b).

To return to the question of the universality of the stages/structures, Wilber emphasizes that the basic structures

have deep (universal) structures and surface (local) structures (although I usually call these "deep features" and "surface features" to avoid confusion with Chomsky's formulations; also, deep and surface are a sliding scale: deep features can be those features shared by a group, a family, a tribe, a clan, a community, a nation, all humans, all species, all beings. Thus, "deep" doesn't necessarily mean "universal"; it means "shared by others," and research then determines how wide that group is—from a few people to genuine universals. The preponderance of research supports the claim that all of the basic structures, and most of the developmental lines, that I have presented in the charts [of the book *Integral Psychology*], have some universal deep features). (Wilber, 1999d, pp. 651–652)

Thus, the deep features of the basic structures represent the defining underlying organization of each level (as in the case of Piaget's sensorimotor, preoperational, concrete-operational, and formal operational stages; each of which is itself content-free) and appear to be universal; in other words, "largely invariant, cross-cultural, and 'quasi-universal'" (Wilber, 1999d, p. 50). In contrast are surface features, which are highly culturally influenced and unique to specific locales, types of people, and so forth. For example, whereas Piaget's stages of cognitive development (deep features) are universal, the surface features of the basic structures—how individuals use their cognitive development, the specific contents of their thinking, and the value assigned to different ways of thinking and knowing—will vary tremendously; they are anything but universal. Two people may share the deep feature of formal operational thinking yet express it completely differently: one does calculus, the other writes a novel—two apparently different activities, neither of which could manifest without the capacity for formal reflexivity.

Although some research has revealed cultures in which most adults do not exhibit formal-operational thinking, I am aware of no research that has found Piaget's stages to emerge in an order other than the one he proposed. Regardless of how a culture expresses symbols, concepts, and rules, symbols emerge before concepts, and concepts emerge before the rules that apply to those concepts. Likewise with moral development: conventional stages emerge after preconventional stages, and postconventional stages emerge after them, whether assessed with Kohlberg's or Gilligan's protocols. Most definitely, the details of various stage models can—and *should*—be critiqued and continually revised to accord the data. Since they are constructions, there will always be a modicum of arbitrariness regarding where the demarcations are drawn between stages. However, even if future research finds a qualitatively distinct structure of cognition between two of Piaget's stages, or that two of the stages that we previously conceived of as distinct can be understood to operate on similar principles (and thus represent only one stage of cognitive development), that would not alter Piaget's more central point that children think in symbols before they think in concepts, and that if they are now thinking conceptually, they previously thought symbolically. One of the defining criteria for asserting that a given phenomenon has, fundamentally, a universal, quasi-universal, or cross-cultural deep structure is that the specific sequence of stages emerges in a particular (invariant) order.

To summarize, the surface structures will exhibit tremendously diverse variations in the expression of a universal, cross-cultural, or quasi-universal deep structure. The basic structures are like a skeletal system, upon and around which tremendously different human bodies express themselves. According to integral theory, the emergence of the basic structures is sequential, but it is also less like a fixed mechanical process than it is like an organic, living habit.

Stages: Irreversible?

Yes and No. The directionality and irreversibility of stage emergence are central to stage theories. Referring, for example, to the transition from Kohlberg's preconventional morality to conventional morality, Kegan captures this notion: "If children develop and change their notion of what is fair, it is *always* in the direction from this instrumentality (stage 2) to interpersonal concordance (stage 3), *never the reverse*" (Kegan, 1982, p. 56, italics added). On the other hand, we would do well to remember Piaget's admonition regarding preparation and *décalage*: "Development is spotty, local, and uneven. A concept may appear in one form, but take a year or more to extend itself over its possible range" (1977, p. xxv). Because aspects of different levels of structural organization coexist, of course people's behavior and experience will not all stem from a homogeneous stage of structuralization. In fact, when developmentalists such as Kegan (1982) claim that an individual is, for example, "at stage 4" what they mean is that her center of gravity is at stage 4 and thus approximately 50% of her behaviors, thoughts, feelings, and so on reflect the characteristics of stage 4, whereas about 25% of them will reflect stage 3 and about 25% will reflect stage 5.

> To say that the self has identified with a particular wave in the Great Rainbow [rainbow emphasizes how the colors/basic structures blend into one another rather than being rigidly discrete stages] does not, however, mean that the self is rigidly stuck at

that level. On the contrary, the self can be "all over the place" on occasion. Within limits, the self can temporarily roam all over the spectrum of consciousness—it can regress, or move down the holarchy of being and knowing; it can spiral, reconsolidate, and return. Moreover, because the self at every stage of its development has fluid access to the great natural states of consciousness (psychic, subtle, causal, nondual), it can have temporary peak experiences of any or all of those transpersonal realms, thus momentarily leaping forward into greater realities. (Wilber, 1999d, p. 467)

Perhaps even more relevant to the notion of irreversibility of waves than the above points is the crucial distinction between the logic and dynamics of stage models (Habermas, cited in Visser, 2003). Whereas the *logic* of a stage model explicates a linear, sequential unfolding of stages, the *dynamics* of those same stage models explore how development actually emerges with real folks in the real world. Of course, no one actually develops as smoothly and simply as a stage model is depicted on a page; the "messiness" of human change processes (all of the various complications, regressions, fixations, and so on that arise in the course of one's life) is what the dynamic aspect of developmental theories addresses, and what any therapist or parent can attest to. Most critiques of the linear aspect of stage models are focusing exclusively on the logic of the model, as opposed to the dynamics of how that logic unfolds in a given person.

A Progression of Stages: Are Later Stages Better or More Valuable?

Yes and No. The fundamental idea in this critique is the notion that later, "higher" stages of development are uniformly more valuable or better than earlier, "lower" stages. On one hand, many of the developmental theories that are integrated into integral theory (from Piaget to Kegan to Cook-Greuter) do in fact posit that subsequent stages are not merely different from but more effective (along various dimensions) than previous stages (Cook-Greuter, 1990; Cook-Greuter & Soulen, 2007) and that those at a given stage "never" prefer solutions to problems based upon the logic of previous stages (Piaget, 1948; Kegan, 1982, p. 56). From this perspective, subsequent stages include and embrace the prior stages, yet transcend them (this is why I prefer conceiving of developmental stages not as a linear ladder but as a series of nested, concentric spheres or circles—with each larger circle including and transcending the smaller, previous ones): subsequent stages are capable of understanding the previous stages, while the reverse is not true. Thus, subsequent stages are viewed as more flexible, more complexly organized, more inclusive, more dynamic, more differentiated, more comprehensive, more capable of optimal performance in a rapidly changing and increasingly complex world, more tolerant of diversity and ambiguity, less preprogrammed and automatic, and also less defensive. For example, if a preoperational child's perception of a stable object changes because the child's perspective has changed, that child will declare that the object itself has changed. A child who has developed an understanding of how one's own perspective influences one's perception of an object will recognize that the object itself has not changed; only her perception of the object has changed, which is closer to the truth than the preoperational child's assertion. As Cook-Greuter wrote, "Higher is believed to be better because the more differentiated and the more autonomous persons become, the more they can claim that they have a [relatively] nondistorted (true) and realistic view of themselves and the world" (1990, p. 91). Nonetheless, Cook-Greuter and Soulen also acknowledge, "Yet no matter how evolved we become, our knowledge and understanding is partial and incomplete" (2007, p. 184). In Wilber's own words:

> I have rarely, if ever, used the term "progress"; I have used the terms "development" and "evolution." There is a big difference: "progress" tends to imply that development is necessarily and in all ways a positive or beneficial affair, an idea I absolutely reject. "Evolution" or "development," on the other hand, implies that, in the course of the emergence or growth of various phenomena, there is indeed a discernible differentiation and increase in certain structures and functions, but these increases *can* be used malevolently as well as benevolently.... . In short, there is a price to be paid for every increase in consciousness, and only that perspective, I believe, can place humankind's evolutionary history in the proper context. (1999d, pp. 283–284)

Thus, Wilber and other integral theorists do not deny that along with the evolution of our species came the downside of progress, including increases in the magnitude of exploitation, war, oppression, and poverty; these represent evolutionary advances (such as technological development) used for malevolent purposes. Unfortunately, humans' internal—particularly moral—development has not developed as rapidly as our external technologies have. Moreover, any developmental sequence may include "good" and "bad" aspects. For example, as one develops the capacity for formal reflexive thought, one may use one's emergent reasoning powers to deny, repress, or dissociate from one's bodily impulses and felt sensations, to which young children are usually very attuned and sensitive. In summary, an integral view of development acknowledges the dialectic of progress: at the same time that development unfolds constructive and beneficial potentials and capacities, those potentials and capacities may be utilized to achieve a host of destructive, harmful ends or purposes.

Are We as Simple as Stage Models Suggest?

One of the opening quotes of this chapter emphasizes that not only is human development exceedingly complex, more often than not it is characterized by regressions and spirals than a simple linear path. Nonetheless, there are patterns. According to Wilber (2000e), the basic waves or structures merely represent some of the more salient contours of the great River of Life, through which all human beings flow. In Wilber's words:

> Is consciousness and its development really just a stage of linear, monolithic stages, proceeding one after another, in ladder-like fashion? The answer is, not at all ... these basic waves in the Great Nest are simply the general levels through which numerous different developmental lines or streams will flow—such as emotions, needs, self-identity, morals, spiritual realizations, and so on—all proceeding at their own pace, in their own way, with their own dynamic. Thus overall development is absolutely not a linear, sequential, ladder-like affair. It is a fluid flowing of many streams through these basic waves. (Wilber, 2000e, p. 17)

Essentially, whereas individual lines of development do unfold or emerge, in general, in a sequential manner, an individual's overall development is more characterized by nonlinear, fluid, flowing streams and waves; it is not rigidly linear. This is due in large part to the fact that people can—without fundamentally altering their developmental center of gravity—ride different waves (levels) in different circumstances, have various streams (lines) that flow through different waves (not all of their lines are equally developed), have very different personality types that journey through the same basic waves with different emphases, and have different subpersonalities that may also surf different waves (more on this in Chapter 6).

Let us keep in the foreground that the fields of counseling and counseling psychology have founded the practice of their professions upon developmental bases, and the phenomena of human development are exceedingly more dynamic and complex than most traditional theories have suggested (Mahoney 1991; Wilber, 2000e). Not only will clinical cases rarely unfold in as conceptually clear a manner as the logic of stage theories often suggest, but counseling and developmental theories are themselves in the process of developing, and integral theory and integral counseling are attempting to stay abreast of these complex dynamics.

Dangers of Hierarchical Systems

Many social scientists today have strong negative reactions to the notion of hierarchy, primarily because they equate normal, "actualization" hierarchies (which are found everywhere in nature and complex systems—atoms are wholes that are parts of molecules, which are wholes that are parts of cells, which are wholes that are parts of organs, and so forth) with what Wilber has called "pathological" or "domination" hierarchies, in which "one holon assumes agentic dominance to the detriment of all. This holon doesn't assume it is *both* a whole and a part, it assumes it is the whole, period" (2000b, p. 31). Given that the basic structures or waves are actually holons, their organization actually comprises a holarchy, a hierarchy composed of holons.

As I mentioned in Chapter 2, using hierarchical stage models to suggest that others are inferior, or to oppress or marginalize them, is not integral or developmental practice; it is developmental abuse, a form of pathological hierarchy. Moreover, from an integral perspective, a person is not conceived of as being "at" a particular stage of development, although for ease of communication, such discourse is often used. Rather, the entire spectrum of development is a potential, awaiting emergence and unfolding with every human being.

It is also inappropriate to use stage descriptions in a concrete, reifying, reductionistic way. Integral counselors readily admit that it is a rare client who perfectly matches the description of a single stage. On the other hand, the stage component of integral theory serves valuable heuristic functions, and the other components (quadrants, lines, states, types) remind us that how people think, feel, and act varies tremendously as a function not only of their psychological development but also of sociocultural, physical environmental, biological, and other circumstances.

Matching a therapeutic approach to a client's center of gravity is more complex than Table 4.1 suggests. There are dangers in all models, figures, and tables; their logic oversimplifies what are, in fact, highly complex issues. However, integral counseling is not just about implementing a stage conceptualization of human development, even if its spectrum of development is more inclusive than other counseling approaches (many theories of counseling do not even include a developmental model). Integral counselors conceptualize not only with regard to all stages but also with regard to all quadrants, all lines, all types, and all states.

Stages of Change

Although transtheoretical therapy (TTT) (Prochaska & DiClemente, 1982; Prochaska & Norcross, 2003) does not address human development in the same ways that the developmental models thus far described in this chapter do, it provides another metatheoretical scaffolding with which to differentially tailor therapy based upon a given client's "readiness for change." I consider the basic conclusions of the transtheoretical approach an essential part of therapists' education and training.

TTT's three principal components are stages of change, processes of change, and levels of change. In TTT, "stages" refer not to developmental stages (such as stages of cognitive or moral development) but to *stages of change:* stages that people have the potential to pass through in their trajectory of change. In the precontemplation stage, clients do not recognize the need to change or do not desire change. In the contemplation stage, clients begin to recognize the need to change and in some ways consider changing, but still have not made the decision or commitment to make the change. In the preparation stage, clients have reached the conclusion that a change is needed and have committed to making those changes (taking some form of action) in the near future. In the action stage, clients are not only ready and committed to change; they have also invested significant time and energy in reaching their goal. In the maintenance stage, clients have reached their goals and remained at the criterion level for at least 6 months; here, the emphasis is on preventing relapses by consolidating the learning—stressing how they achieved their progress, expecting future difficulties, underscoring the need to continue working with the issue, and so forth.

TTT does not attempt to integrate the single theories of counseling (high level of abstraction), nor does it attempt to integrate the 1,000-plus specific techniques (low level of abstraction). Rather, TTT integrates those *processes of change* (medium level of abstraction) that are observable across different forms of counseling. According to TTT, the primary processes of change are:

1. Consciousness raising: increasing clients' awareness
2. Catharsis/dramatic relief: clients' emotional expression
3. Self-reevaluation: clients' self-assessment
4. Self-liberation: increasing clients' motivation and purposeful choosing
5. Environmental reevaluation: analyzing counterconditioning, stimulus control, contingency control
6. Helping relationships: supporting and encouraging clients' change via care, dependability, acceptance, etc. (Prochaska & DiClemente, 2003)

The key issue here is that the degree of therapeutic success of any given process of change appears to be, at least in part, a function of it fitting with a client's stage of change. For example, "action-oriented therapies may be quite effective with individuals who are in the preparation or action stage. These same programs may be ineffective or detrimental, however, with individuals in the precontemplation or contemplation stage" (Prochaska & Norcross, 2003, p. 525). (For more details on matching stages and processes of change, consult Prochaska & Norcross, 2003, chap. 15.)

In TTT the five *levels of change* are:

1. symptom/situational problems
2. maladaptive cognitions

3. current interpersonal conflicts

4. family/systems conflicts

5. intrapersonal conflicts

According to TTT (and as is also the case with integral counseling), each level is valid and important, yet where to focus varies greatly from client to client and problem to problem. Transtheoretical therapists usually intervene as high up (toward 1) as they can and move down (toward 5) only if intervening at a given level did not achieve the goal. Similar to how the four quadrants mutually influence each other, "the levels of change, it should be emphasized, are not independent or isolated; on the contrary, change at any one level is likely to produce change at other levels" (Prochaska & Norcross, 2003, p. 529).

"In summary, the transtheoretical model sees therapeutic integration as the differential application of the processes of change at specific stages of change according to the identified problem level. In colloquial terms, we have identified the basics of *how* (processes), *when* (stages), and *what* (levels) to change" (Prochaska & Norcross, 2003, p. 530). I view TTT as an approach of immense clinical value, significantly enhancing my work with clients. TTT is a genuinely transtheoretical approach that will help counselors from any single-theory, eclectic, or integrative approach. However, I also believe that it leaves important clinical dimensions either ignored or merely hinted at, especially clients' developmental levels, lines of development, different types of clients, different states of consciousness, and the clients' self-system.

Conclusion

By assessing clients' development, therapists can more fully attune themselves to clients' experiences and how they make meaning, more fully comprehend the nature of the sources of their distress, communicate in such a way that fosters mutual understanding, and more skillfully tailor developmentally sensitive treatment plans that are more likely to meet clients' unique needs. Much of the material in this chapter is born of two articles that Wilber originally published in 1984; I would like to end this chapter with the conclusion he wrote to "The Developmental Spectrum and Psychopathology: Part II, Treatment Modalities":

I would like to be very clear about what this presentation has attempted to do. It has not offered a fixed, conclusive, unalterable model. Although I have at every point attempted to ground it in the theoretical and phenomenological reports of reputable researchers and practitioners, the overall project is obviously metatheoretical and suggestive, and is offered in that spirit. But once one begins to look at the full spectrum of human growth and development, an extraordinarily rich array of material becomes available for metatheoretical work; a variety of connections suggest themselves which were not apparent before; and a wealth of hypotheses for future research become immediately available. Moreover, different analytical, psychological, and spiritual systems, which before seemed largely incompatible or even contradictory, appear closer to the possibility of a mutually enriching synthesis or reconciliation.

This presentation has offered one such full-spectrum approach, more to show the strong possibilities than the final conclusions; if this type of model is useful in reaching better ones, it will have served its purpose. My point, actually, is that given the state of knowledge *already* available to us, it seems ungenerous to the human condition to present any models *less* comprehensive—by which I mean, models that do not take into account both conventional *and* contemplative realms of human growth and development. (1984b, pp. 162–163)

Notes

1. As I have tried to emphasize, integral theory does not suggest that a person's internal experiences or external behaviors homogenously derive from a single, stable developmental structure. Because healthy development involves integrating previous stages into one's current developmental stage, individuals have access to not only their current stage but also their previous ones, and thus they may function, perceive, and exist from several different altitudes or perspectives, even within the same day. Nonetheless, most people will tend to act spontaneously from the most developed meaning-making system or perspective that they have mastered. According to integral theorists, this preferred perspective or "central tendency" from which individuals make meaning is called their developmental "center of gravity" (Cook-Greuter & Soulen, 2007, p. 183), a phrase that Cook-Greuter (2000) originally found in William James' *Varieties of Religious Experience*.
2. All names and other identifying information have been changed to protect the identities of clients who are discussed in examples throughout this book.

3. The deep structures represent the defining underlying, patterned organization of each stage and appear to be cross-cultural, largely invariant, and quasi-universal (Wilber, 1999d). Surface structures, in contrast, are highly culturally influenced and thus are unique to specific types of people, locales, and so forth.

4. Stabilization is usually the first goal of integral psychotherapy. Rather than initially working toward developmental transformation, stabilization involves helping clients become more fortified, steadily balanced, securely supported, and smoothly grounded at their current developmental center of gravity. Integral theory posits that even if a person's ultimate goal is transformation, initially taking the time to stabilize and translate healthily at one's current center of gravity lays the most solid foundations for further development. This is an important point because the goal of integral therapy is not always to "get people developing." Most of the time, a primary goal is to help clients stabilize, with the understanding that this will not only make them healthier at their current altitude but will also likely facilitate future development.

5. Although Wilber has supported this aspect of integral theory with a great deal of professional literature—from psychodynamic and cognitive to existential-humanistic and transpersonal traditions (Masterson, 1981; Kohut, 1971, 1977; Kernberg, 1976; Blanck & Blanck, 1979; Gedo, 1981; Piaget, 1977; Loevinger, 1976; Erikson, 1963, 1968, 1980, 1982; Boss, 1963; Binswanger, 1956; Maslow, 1971; May, 1977; Assagioli, 1988; Walsh & Vaughan, 1993; Scotton, Chinen, & Battista, 1996)—the exact relationship between development and psychogenic pathology remains speculative at this point in time; the nature of Wilber's thesis makes experimental research unethical and other forms of empirical research exceedingly difficult. All theories begin speculatively and remain conjectural—even with numerous corroborating studies—until they are eventually refuted; thus the value of structuring one's theory in form that can be rejected (Popper, 1963). A primary value of Wilber's bold conjecture involves striving to understand the etiology of various psychogenic pathologies; his thesis essentially states that they derive largely from developmental derailments.

5

DEVELOPMENT LINES
AND THE
INTEGRAL PSYCHOGRAPH

With E. Scott Warren, Ph.D. Candidate
University of North Texas
Counseling and Counselor Education Program

A "level of development" is always a "level in a particular line."

(Wilber, 2006, p. 61)

Introduction

Given the lengthy discussion of development in Chapter 4, including both the logic and dynamics of stage models, take a few moments to consider how evenly developed most people are. I suspect you will agree that many of us, and certainly many of our clients, are fairly unevenly developed (Gardner, 1983, 1998; Wilber, 2006; Hy & Loevinger, 1996). Individuals may be highly developed in some ways (cognitively quite aware and intelligent) but poorly developed in others (emotionally clueless about their internal felt sense, especially regarding interpersonal interactions). This notion of uneven development has become widely known in large measure because of the work of Howard Gardner on "multiple intelligences." Gardner has proposed 11 multiple intelligences and has found considerable empirical support for eight of them: linguistic, logico-mathematical, musical, spatial, bodily-kinesthetic, naturalist, interpersonal, and intrapersonal (1983). The three more recently proposed, less well-defined, and more controversial intelligences are spiritual, existential, and moral (Gardner, 1998).

As was mentioned in Chapter 2, lines are the different aspects of our being and functioning that have the potential to develop through the basic structures of development that were delineated in Chapter 4. Wilber (1999d; 2000b) has described and mapped more than 20 different developmental lines, each of which proceeds sequentially, yet quasi-independently, through the basic structures of consciousness. Recall that the lines can and often do develop with different dynamics and at different rates. Hy and Loevinger corroborate Wilber's notions of lines as relatively- or quasi-independent aspects or "strands": "All kinds of development are occurring at the same times. There is no completely error-free method of separating one strand of development from another" (1996, p. 7).

Although specific developmental lines unfold sequentially, overall development is anything but the ladder-like, predictably sequential series of steps that is conveyed by the logic of stage theories of development; it is much more a fluid flowing of many streams through many waves (Wilber, 2000b). "Developmental lines are not really lines in any strict sense. At most, they represent probabilities of behavior—and thus are something like probability clouds more than ruler-straight lines . . . development is a wonderfully organic, streaming, and spiraling affair" (Wilber, 2006, p. 61). As noted in Chapters 2 and 4, Wilber has his reasons for using different terms (*waves, structures, stages*) to refer to developmental levels. In order not to mix metaphors, he speaks of developmental lines proceeding through levels and streams flowing through waves; please bear in mind that streams are another way of conceiving of developmental lines in the same way that waves are another way of conceiving of developmental levels.

Developmental Lines

In addition to being conceived of as different aspects of our being, functioning, or "intelligence," developmental lines can be thought of as different types of responses to many of life's basic questions (see Table 5.1).

Table 5.1   Developmental Lines, Life's Questions, and Researchers

Developmental Line	Life's Question	Researcher
Cognitive	What am I aware of?	Piaget, Kegan, Vygotsky
Self	Of the things that I am aware of, with what do I identify?	Loevinger, Cook-Greuter
Values	Of the things that I am aware of, what matters most to me?	Graves, Beck & Cowan
Moral	Of the things that I am aware of, what should I do?	Kohlberg, Gilligan
Aesthetic	Of the things that I am aware of, what is beautiful to me?	Housen
Spiritual	Of the things that I am aware of, what is of ultimate concern to me?	Fowler, Tillich
Needs	Of the things that I am aware of, what do I need?	Maslow
Kinesthetic	How should I physically do this?	Gardner
Emotional	Of the things that I am aware of, how do I feel about them?	Salovey & Mayer, Solomon, Goleman
Interpersonal	Of the ways that I am aware of, how should I socially relate to others?	Selman, Perry

Adapted from *Integral Spirituality* by Ken Wilber © 2006. Reprinted by arrangement with Shambhala Publications, Inc. Boston, MA, www.shambhala.com

The developmental lines that Wilber most frequently attends to are cognition, self-identity, object relations, morality/ideas of the good, role taking, socioemotional capacity, empathy, worldviews, gender identity, psychosexuality, affect, creativity, aesthetics, altruism, interpersonal awareness, needs, several that can be conceived of as "spiritual" (care, concern, openness, meditative stages, religious faith), values, needs, logico-mathematical competence, communicative competence, modes of space and time, kinesthetic skills, and musical skills (Wilber, 2000, p. 28).

The Cognitive Line and a Few of Its Relationships to Other Lines

We need to be clear with regard to what Wilber means when he refers to cognition and cognitive lines of development. Yes, he posits several cognitive lines. Before getting into those, however, I want to emphasize that by cognition he is *not* referring merely to intelligence, IQ, abstract reasoning abilities, or a Piagetian view of cognitive development, although those may be related in important ways to his general notion of cognition. Usually, and unless he specifies otherwise, Wilber refers to the developmental line of cognition simply as one's capacities for awareness—what individuals are capable of holding in their minds.

Wilber distinguishes three broad classes of lines: cognition, self, and self-related lines. Although the exact relationship of all of the lines is far from known, what is known is that the levels or altitudes of development of one line categorically cannot be assumed to refer to the levels or altitudes of other lines (they are often like apples and oranges); if this were the case, everyone would be very evenly developed and we wouldn't need to differentiate the sundry lines. Loevinger corroborated this notion:

> One alternative [to the notion of a single developmental sequence] is that there are several more or less independently variable dimensions.... [Kohlberg and Selman] believe that there are several related lines of development, cognitive, interpersonal, and moral at a minimum, and that they stand in asymmetrical relation to each other. A given stage of cognitive development is a necessary but not sufficient condition for the corresponding stage of interpersonal development, and the latter stands in the same relation to moral development. (1976, p. 188)

Even though the precise relationships between the developmental lines awaits much empirical research and study, Wilber (2006) has outlined some general contours of the relationships among some of the more salient lines. First, the cognitive line leads the other lines because cognition, broadly defined, constrains what one can be aware of. When Wilber writes that cognition "leads" the other lines, he means (like the above Loevinger quote) that certain levels of cognitive development are necessary but not sufficient for other lines to further develop. Thus, the cognitive line constrains the other lines to a large extent. The self line follows cognition (of the things I can be aware of, with what do I identify?). Wilber argues that the self line (also called self-system line, identity line, or ego line) "follows" cognition because we can't identify with something of which we are unaware. Finally, there are self-related lines that hover around the self-sense or ego (e.g., values: what is meaningful to me?; morals: what should I do/what is just?; needs: what do I need?). The self-related lines tend to follow and develop within the ballpark of the self line because as one's sense of identity develops—which is intimately related to one's modes of meaning-making (Loevinger, 1976; Cook-Greuter & Soulen, 2007)—one's values, needs, and moral decision making tend to follow suit (Wilber, 2000e, pp. 197–217, displays correlations, in chart form, among nearly a hundred different developmental psychologists). The essential notion is that as the cognitive line—broadly defined as awareness—develops, the self-line has the potential but not guarantee for further development. Likewise, as the self-line develops, the self-related lines have the potential but not guarantee for further development.

Different Cognitive Lines

Wilber distinguishes between gross, subtle, and causal cognition. Very briefly, whereas gross cognition takes the external, material, sensorimotor realm as its object of reflection, subtle cognition takes the internal world of thought and altered states of consciousness (including both mental and subtle realms) as its object of reflection. Subtle cognition involves precisely those forms of mental activity that Western cognitive psychologists have tended to ignore, downplay, or dismiss: imagination, creative visions, reverie, hypnotic and hypnogogic states, and transcendental, revelatory, and other noetic states. Causal cognition involves both the root essence of attention itself as well as the capacity to take the "position" of witnessing. Applying the same kind of modeling that he used with cognition, Wilber suggests that the "three great realms—gross, subtle, and causal—are home to three different lines of self, which I generally call ego, soul, and Self (or frontal, deeper psychic, and Witness)" (2000e, p. 125). (For more detailed explications of the different cognitive and self lines, consult Wilber 2000e, pp. 123–127, 255–258.)

How to Assess Developmental Lines

Clients' developmental lines can be assessed in different ways, ranging the spectrum from informal interviews to formal testing. Most therapists, whether integral or not, assess clients' lines relatively informally (Marquis, 2002; Fall, Holden, & Marquis, 2004; Cook-Greuter & Soulen, 2007). In other words, clinical hunches emerge from the responses clients give to various intake forms and therapists' queries, the dilemmas clients bring in to discuss and their reactions to and interpretations of those dilemmas, and therapists' felt sense of clients or countertransferential reactions to them. At the other end of the spectrum are those therapists who administer a battery of psychometrically validated tests to their clients, from the MMPI and WAIS to the WUSCT or SCTi and DIT (Defining Issues Test, a paper-and-pencil test of moral development). Although more involved and detailed case examples will address this in Chapter 7, an introduction to assessing various lines will be presented here.

Which Lines to Assess?

Although opinions about what are the most important handful of lines to assess will vary to some extent as a function of each therapist's theoretical allegiances, I and most of my integral therapist colleagues consider assessing the following lines to be very important, if not critical, to have a good sense of each client's strengths and weaknesses:

- cognition
- self-identity (ego development)
- worldview
- needs/motivation
- values
- spiritual (ultimate concern, care, openness, meditative stages, religious faith)
- moral/ethical/ideas of the good and the good life
- aesthetics
- psychosexuality
- emotional, interpersonal, object relations, role taking, empathy, altruism, and communicative competence (quasi-independent yet lots of overlap)

Of course, the above list is not meant to neglect the importance of clients' strengths or talents in music, art, and other creative endeavors; athletics, dance, or other kinesthetic pursuits; or the satisfaction, fulfillment, and meaning derived from doing one's work well (whether at the office or at home raising children). From many clients' perspectives, being able to "lose themselves" in music, feel a "runner's high," or do meaningful work is a large part of what makes their lives worth living. Those strengths, talents, or capacities should be emphasized, appreciated, and encouraged. Because formal assessment of the above lines must follow the established protocols for their evaluation (i.e., Kohlberg's protocols for assessing moral development or Don Beck's protocols for assessing values development), I will discuss ways to assess these lines informally.

Cognition

Keeping in mind that according to Wilber, the most essential aspects of the cognitive line are capacities for awareness, therapists can get a ballpark sense of clients' cognition by attending to clients' use of language, their responses on the Integral Intake, and different possibilities and perspectives that clients discuss. Regarding language, for example, clients who are not capable of speaking in complex, abstract sentences are likely to think in what Piaget termed concrete operations. Thus, counselors should not speak in intricate metaphors with such clients, but rather speak more concretely and specifically. Regarding the quality of their responses on the Integral Intake, some clients do not understand what certain questions are asking for or respond in very simple, concrete terms, which is also indicative of concrete operational thought. Depending on the population with which you work, many of your clients may be illiterate, in which case a paper-and-pencil assessment is obviously out of the question.

Regarding the issue of possibilities and perspectives, consider two clients. The first speaks mostly in terms of polarities—all-or-nothing statements; there is a right way (his way) and a wrong way (their way)—and he seldom speaks of the many shades of gray that often characterize people and circumstances. This client rarely takes other people's perspectives. In fact, when asked what a person he was in conflict with may have been thinking, his responses are along the lines of "something stupid … he's always wrong," demonstrating that he is not really aware of that person's perspective and other possible ways of construing the world. This client reflects someone who is a concrete thinker at best (he could be either concrete operational or preoperational). The second client speaks with subtle nuances about the myriad aspects of the dilemmas with which she struggles, discussing each issue from numerous angles. When she is asked to describe the perspective of others with whom she differs on specific issues, she presents what appears to be insightful understandings of their views. Although this latter client would probably score higher on an IQ test than the former would, that is not what is most important from an integral perspective. What is most significant is her heightened awareness—of greater possibilities, potentials, and perspectives—without which her possibilities for self- (ego, identity) development and thus sundry lines of self-related development are greatly constrained.

Self-Identity

This is also called the line of self or ego development. Jane Loevinger's work regarding ego development addresses what Wilber refers to as the proximate self, which is intimately experienced as "I." Because this is the developmental line that best gives a measure of a client's developmental center of gravity, it is a particularly significant line, and I will discuss it in depth subsequently in this chapter. As will be discussed in Chapter 6, the proximate self not only navigates and "metabolizes" life's vicissitudes but also proceeds through the fulcra of development by first identifying with a specific wave, then disidentifying with and transcending that wave, and finally including and integrating that wave as it subsequently identifies with the next wave (Wilber, 1999d, p. 15).

Worldview

Worldviews are the different ways that the world appears to people at different waves of development. Although they exist within individuals as a form of their consciousness, worldviews arise and unfold within particular cultures and their local surface features, and thus are a function of "culture" in general: communal meanings, linguistic signs, semantic structures, and various intersubjective contexts and practices (Wilber, 2000e). One's worldview is dependent to some extent upon one's cognition. When one is merely sensorimotor and knows self and world only through sensations and impulses, the corresponding worldview is archaic; when one is preoperational and knows self and world through symbols, the corresponding worldview is magical; when one is concrete-operational and knows self and world through concepts, rules, and roles, the corresponding worldview is mythical; when one is formal-operational and knows self and world through formal reasoning, the corresponding worldview is rational (Gebser, 1985; Piaget, 1977; Wilber, 2000e). The significance of worldviews is demonstrated by the fact that people are not free to see the world any way they want. If an adult is "stuck" in a magical or mythical worldview, he will not be free to conceive of the world rationally; he will tend to devalue cultures that differ from his own. His own thoughts, beliefs, and worldview (UL) are molded by, arise within, and are influenced primarily by the cultural structures (LL) mentioned above. The rational worldview—precisely because it does not unquestioningly accept the stories, beliefs, and perspectives (myths) of its own culture—is the first worldview to emerge that embraces diversity and extends care and compassion to groups and societies that differ from one's own.

Needs/Motivation

According to Wilber (2000e), humans are driven, pulled, or motivated by different levels of need. Similar to Maslow (1970), Wilber conceives of a holarchy of needs, ranging from physical (water, air, food, shelter) and emotional (relationships and exchanges of warmth and care with others, sexual intimacy), to mental (verbal and other symbolic exchanges), and spiritual (experiencing some sort of relationship with something greater than our separate self-sense; some connection to a Source that provides meaning and sanction to us) (Wilber, 2000e). Wilber (1999b, 1999c) goes into far greater detail, however, exploring eight levels of motivation and describing how developmental problems distort the interrelationships and relational exchanges that are necessary to humans' well-being.

Nietzsche (1966) cautioned us not to confuse explanation and motivation (explanation involves the reasons people provide to justify their behavior, whereas motivation involves what is actually the cause or purpose of their behavior). Similarly, Maslow wrote that "these needs are neither necessarily conscious nor unconscious. On the whole, however, in the average person, they are more often unconscious than conscious" (1970, p. 54). When assessing a client's motivations, bear in mind the important distinction between professed motivation and manifest motivation. In other words, the former involves what clients say or report needing; the latter involves what they actually spend their time, attention, money, and energy on.

Values

Clients' responses to questions on the Integral Intake involving what is important and meaningful to them, their most important morals,

cultural activities, and so on provide a good sense of their values (or
at least their expressed values). If, for example, a client reports that
what is most important to him is money, power, and recognition, that
his morality involves avoiding being punished, and that his primary
cultural activities are getting drunk in bars and watching women strip,
we can infer that this person's values are predominantly egocentric.
Conversely, a client who responds that what is most important to him
is doing his duty and upholding the "one true way," that his morality
involves following the dictates of authority (whether scripture, teachers, parents, or the government), and that his primary cultural activities are Bible study and leading a Boy Scout troop, we can infer this
person's values are predominantly sociocentric. Wilber values the work
of Graves (1970), which was popularized and made readily applicable
by the system called spiral dynamics (Beck & Cowan, 1996).

Beck and Cowan (1996) describe the development of eight value
memes (vMEMEs).[1] They also created the Values Test (published by
the National Values Center, P. O. Box 797, Denton, TX 76202). A
vMEME is essentially a value system, and very briefly, vMEMEs
develop as follows (for more information, the reader is encouraged to
consult Beck and Cowan 1996):

1. Automatic/archaic/"instinctual": survival-oriented; biology-driven
2. Animistic/tribalistic/"kin spirits": magical thinking is used to promote a
   sense of safety
3. Egocentric/exploitive/"power gods": control-, power- and dominance-
   oriented; hedonistic and impulsive
4. Absolutistic/conformist/"truth force": meaning- and purpose-oriented;
   there is one right way to be and its righteous, higher authority provides *the*
   code of moral conduct
5. Materialist/achiever/"strive drive": improvement- and achievement-
   oriented; success-driven, opportunistic, and goal-oriented strategies to
   improve and/or beat the competition
6. Relativistic/sensitive/"human bond": egalitarian and humanistically oriented; seeks consensus, belonging, and harmony as well as tolerance and
   acceptance of diversity
7. Systemic/integrative/"flex flow": big-picture-oriented; systemic thinking
   that understands how chaos, complexity, dynamic dialectical development,
   and integrative structures are connected

8. Globalist/holistic/"whole view": Grand-unification-oriented; sees the inter-relationships and synergy of all of life; planetary concerns eclipse narrow group interests

Spiritual

Assessing clients' spirituality and/or religiosity is not always easy, in part because spirituality can be conceptualized in so many different ways. As I have written elsewhere, Wilber acknowledges five different conceptions of spirituality:

1. Spirituality pertains to the highest level of each of the developmental lines.
2. Spirituality is the sum total of the individual's development in all the developmental lines.
3. Spirituality is itself a separate developmental line.
4. Spirituality is an attitude, such as openness or love, that one can have at any developmental level.
5. Spirituality involves peak experiences rather than developmental levels. (Marquis, Holden, & Warren, 2001, p. 226)

Wilber believes that each of those definitions has value and that no single definition exists that incorporates the essential aspects of each of those important perspectives. Wilber also makes the critical distinction between translative/legitimate/exoteric spirituality, on one hand, and transformative/authentic/esoteric spirituality, on the other:

Translative spirituality is the more commonly observed function of religion: *to fortify the self.* Through an *exoteric* system of beliefs and rituals, people are helped to understand and perhaps mini-mize the inherent suffering of the separate self; thus, translative spirituality fosters feelings of security, comfort, consolation, and perhaps protection or fortification. Translative spirituality is *legit-imate* because it provides a certain sense of legitimacy—to one's beliefs about the world and one's place therein ... transformative spirituality constitutes a less commonly observed function of reli-gion: *to deconstruct the self.* Rather than consoling, fortifying, or legitimizing the self, it dismantles, transmutes, transforms, and liberates the self—ultimately from its illusion of separateness—through a series of deaths and rebirths of the self into ever more inclusive developmental waves. Authentic spirituality inquires into legitimate spirituality and concludes that the latter tends to entrench a person in one's current wave of development and, thus, prolong—even if more comfortably—the illusion of separateness that is, ironically, the actual source of suffering. In his glib way, Wilber (2000d) summarized that, in transformative spirituality, "the self is not made content. The self is made toast" (p. 305). (Marquis, Holden, & Warren, 2001, pp. 226–227)

For an excellent discussion of how to differentially assess and respond to clients' healthy and unhealthy spirituality, consult the work of Battista (1996). Further, in 2001 an entire issue of *Counseling and Values* was devoted to spiritual issues in counseling.

Moral

According to Wilber, the line of moral development includes not only how one makes moral decisions (moral judgment) but also who is considered worthy of care, concern, and inclusion in one's decision (moral span); furthermore, it involves issues of the good and what constitutes a life well-lived (Wilber, 2000e). Earlier, I mentioned that the self-related lines "tend to follow and develop within the ballpark of the self line":

Nowhere is the amazing expansion of consciousness more apparent than in the self's identity and its morals.... This expanding identity is directly reflected in moral awareness.... For you will treat as yourself those *with whom you identify*. If you identify only with you, you will treat others narcissistically. If you identify with your friends and family, you will treat them with care. If you identify with your nation, you will treat your countrymen as compatriots. If you identify with all human beings, you will strive to treat all people fairly and compassionately, regardless of race, sex, color, or creed. If your identity expands to embrace the Kosmos, you will treat all sentient beings with respect and kindness, for they are all perfect manifestations of the same radiant Self, which is your very own Self as well. (Wilber, 1999d, p. 548)

In addition, helping clients with their suffering is, at root, an issue of moral engagement: "No matter what mental health practitioners do or say, they have entered the moral sphere" (Miller, 2004, p. 19). Far more than a strictly objective, scientific endeavor, counseling and psychotherapy are ethical and moral enterprises, not in the contemporary sense of judging right and wrong but in the ancient sense of the practical problems regarding what constitutes a life worth living, how to respond to injustices, and how to face and make meaning from suffering (Foster & Black, 2007).

Aesthetics

By "aesthetics," integral helpers are certainly not referring merely to one's sense of aesthetic taste or how well one can critique art. Rather, the line of aesthetics deals with a person's apprehension of beauty; as such, it is one of the preeminent lines of subjectivity: "Beauty is the depth of a holon, or its transparency to Spirit. Art is anything with a frame around it" (Wilber, 2000e, p. 254). Wilber often refers to the four quadrants as the "Big Three" because both right-hand quadrants can be described in objective, third-person language (*it, its*). He supports the significance of the Big Three by pointing out how pervasively these three dimensions have emerged across cultures and time.

> In language: I—UL, we—LL, it/its UR/LR
> In Plato: the Good—LL, the True—UR/LR, the Beautiful—UL
> In Buddhism: Buddha—UL, sangha—LL, dharma—UR/LR
> In Baldwin and Habermas: aesthetic—UL, moral—LL, scientific—UR/LR

Aesthetics refers not only to how refined the client's sense of aesthetics is, but more so to how much beauty the person experiences. Does this person see beauty only in a young person with a specific body type and hair color, or does he see beyond surfaces into the depths and thus see similar beauty in all people, young or old? Does he see beauty in a loved one's graceful dying and in a tragic play? Can you imagine a client whose life is bereft of experiencing beauty reporting a life well-lived? This is the rationale behind inquiring into clients' aesthetic line and helping them experience beauty more deeply and regularly.

Psychosexuality

This was obviously central to Freud's (1971) conception of human nature, but integral therapists are not merely interested in assessing at which of Freud's stages of psychosexual development the client is fixated, although in some instances (usually at the lower ends of the personal or prepersonal stages of development) such assessment may prove helpful. At the other end of the developmental spectrum—with those who are engaged in a noncelibate spiritual practice—integrating sexuality with spirituality is often a great challenge. Deida (1995, 2002a, 2002b) and John (1978) have written extensively on how the same emotional problems that interfere with our sexual lives also interfere with our spiritual development. Psychosexuality—the "emotional-sexual" dimension of life—is not limited exclusively to the genitals but involves body, emotions, mind, soul, and spirit. Thus, attending to clients' psychosexuality is not just about sexual techniques; it is at least equally (more so, I believe) about the intimacy, openness, and sacredness of their emotional-sexual relationships. You may resonate with the notion that if you are in an intimate relationship, your unresolved psychological issues or "baggage" will more likely surface in that context than any other aspect of your life. The type of integrative, heart-opening love practices that Deida recommends are designed to transform those intimacy-limiting neuroses into ecstatic love-bliss:

> For many of the world's greatest wisdom traditions, particularly in their mature phases, sexuality was viewed as an exquisite expression of spirituality—and a path to further spiritual realization. After all, in the ecstatic embrace of sexual love, we are taken far beyond ourselves, released from the cramp of the separate self, delivered at least temporarily in to timeless, spaceless, blissful union with the wondrous beloved: and what better definition of spiritual release is there than that? (Wilber, foreword to Deida, 2002a)

For penetrating insights and practical instructions on self-transcending love in one's relationships, sexual yoga and how the emotional-sexual dimension is involved in spiritual realization, how sex is neither an obligation nor an obstacle to spiritual realization, and specific bodily practices to separate ejaculation and orgasm, thus transforming degenerative orgasms into regenerative ones, consult the work of John (1978), Avabhasa (1993), Deida (1995, 2002a), and Chia and Arava (1996).

Emotional

Because in its broadest sense *emotions* refers not only to emotions per se but also to affect and "feeling-awareness," and because the intersubjective perspective is one of the most common contemporary perspectives from which to explore and understand emotions, I will here briefly address the emotional line together with the lines of object relations, role taking, empathy, altruism, and communicative competence. Although all of those may also be distinct lines in and of themselves, I believe there is more interdependence and overlap among these lines than among the other lines mentioned above.

Despite the fact that emotions can be studied from third-person perspectives such as neuroscience (Damasio, 1999; LeDoux, 1996; Siegel, 2001) and from first-person perspectives such as the phenomenology of emotions (Sartre, 1976, 1998; Gendlin, 1962), many scholars of emotion and affect believe that the most important perspective from which to explore emotions is from second-person interactions (intersubjective field theory; Stolorow, Atwood, & Orange, 2002; Fosha, 2000; Solomon, 2007). The essential idea in this second-person view is that emotions are always about something, and that this something always involves others in the social sphere. Thus, the development and quality of the client's object relations, the client's capacities to take others' perspectives and empathize with them, and how altruistic and communicatively competent the client is play central roles in the quality of the client's interpersonal relations, and thus in her patterns of emotional experience. According to Wilber (2000e), emotions—like all other developmental lines—proceed from prepersonal/preconventional to personal/conventional to suprapersonal/post- and post-postconventional:

- *Prepersonal:* simple reactivity such as pleasure and pain; protoemotions such as fear, rage, and satisfaction; anger, wishing, anxiety, liking, and safety
- *Personal:* joy, love, belongingness, depression, and hate; care, compassion; global justice, worldcentric altruism, and love of all of humanity
- *Suprapersonal:* rapture, awe, love and compassion for all species; love-bliss, ecstasy, and saintly commitment; boddhisattvic compassion, "infinite freedom release," and "one taste" (Wilber, 2000e, p. 198)

Integral Psychograph

Once therapists have a sense of how developed a client's lines currently are, those lines can be displayed as an integral psychograph. One of the ways the lines can be displayed is as a basic bar graph, with each developmental line along the x-axis, with the length of each line/bar

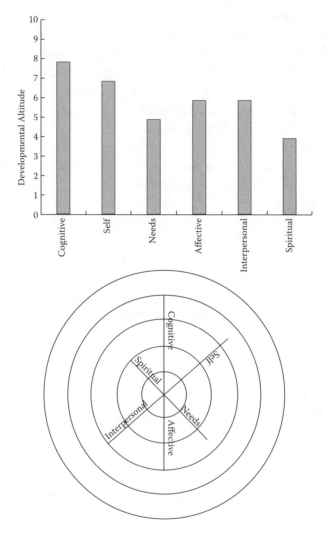

Figure 5.1 Two common ways to depict an integral psychograph. Adapted from *Integral Psychology* by Ken Wilber © 1999d, p. 30-31. Reprinted by arrangement with Shambhala Publications, Inc. Boston, MA, www.shambhala.com

denoting how developed that aspect of the client currently is; the longer the line, the more developed the aspect (see Figure 5.1). Because the various developmental levels or waves are actually holarchical, a client's psychograph can also be displayed as a series of concentric circles, with each larger circle representing a subsequent level or stage of development (this is how I usually display clients' psychographs). As previously mentioned, the longer the line, the more developed that line is (see Figure 5.1).

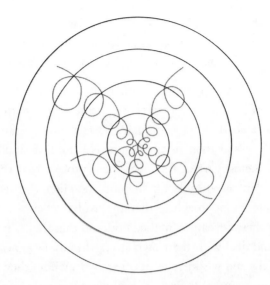

Figure 5.2 Developmental streams dynamically spiralingthrough organic waves. From *Integral Spirituality* by Ken Wilber © 2006, p. 64. Reprinted by arrangement with Shambhala Publications, Inc. Boston, MA, www.shambhala.com

Depending on how psychologically minded a given client is, therapists can explain the idea of developmental levels and lines to that client and ask her to sketch a psychograph depicting, for example, her cognitive, moral, interpersonal, affective, and spiritual lines of development. While she is doing so, the counselor can also sketch a psychograph of the client. Afterward, they can compare the similarities and differences between how the therapist perceives the client and how the client perceives herself, stimulating a discussion of which aspects of the client are implicated in the struggles for which the client is seeking help.

Because Wilber and many other developmentalists believe that developmental *dynamics* (not the order/logic of stages) are far from strictly linear and that developmental lines are often more accurately described as spiraling streams, the dynamics of a client's psychograph across time—as opposed to a client's psychograph as a snapshot in time—are more accurately depicted as shown in Figure 5.2.

Whether therapists include 4 levels or 10 is less important than getting a general sense of the contours of each client's developmental lines. Regardless of where one draws demarcations, most developmentalists agree that the various streams flow through waves, which can be thought of in these general terms:

1. Preconventional: physical/sensorimotor (egocentric)
2. Conventional: concrete operations, rules and roles (sociocentric)
3. Postconventional: more formal and abstract operations (worldcentric)

Many clients have an intuitive hunch that they aren't equally good at all aspects of life, and many of those clients have reported that simply being educated about developmental levels and lines and then seeing our best guess at their psychographs is helpful in and of itself (as opposed to it being part of the assessment process that then leads to a treatment plan responsible for helping the client).[2] This is because part of the integral approach to therapy involves clients' refining their awareness of their developmental contours so that they can more readily identify and deal with their own strengths and weaknesses, as well as the strengths and weaknesses of others with whom they interact. In addition, being aware of their own weaknesses or pathologies in one or more of their lines helps them to cease denying that they are great at everything (many clients, especially initially, externalize their problems and think *they* are perfectly fine and that all of their distress derives from how screwed up the world and everyone else is). Completing and then revising/refining their own psychograph based upon the therapist's feedback and/or the therapist's version of that psychograph helps them recognize the aspects of themselves they need to work on.

To be an integrally informed therapist does not require that each of your lines be maximally developed (I am unaware of any such individual); likewise, that should not be the goal for clients. Rather, understand your and your client's psychograph. If you and/or your client chooses to work on weaker/underdeveloped lines, the purpose of the psychograph will have been fulfilled (Wilber, 2006).

The Line of Ego Development

The activity of being a person is the activity of meaning-making. There is thus no feeling, no experience, no thought, no perception, independent of a meaning-making context in which it *becomes* a feeling, an experience, a thought, a perception, because we *are* the meaning-making context…. "Experience is not what happens to you," Aldous Huxley said, "it's what you *do* with what happens to you" (1972). And the most fundamental thing we do with what happens to us is organize it. We literally make sense. (Kegan, 1982, p. 11, italics in original)

As was previously mentioned, the line of ego development is the single best indicator of a person's developmental center of gravity, and it is thus the best single factor influencing what broad category of treatment (e.g., structure building, uncovering, cognitive-script analysis, introspective, existential) is likely to be most helpful to a given client (Wilber, 1999d). Ego development is inextricably involved with meaning-making. As Kegan noted above, nothing we do as humans is more fundamental than making meaning from our experience.

Loevinger's (1976, 1996) concept of ego development is a broad, holistic, stage model addressing the development of a unitary personality construct throughout the life span. According to Loevinger (1976), ego is a holistic construct representing the fundamental structural unity of personality organization. Ego involves both the person's integrative processes in dealing with diverse intrapersonal and interpersonal experiences and the consequent frame of reference that is used to create self-consistency and meaning. Ego evolves through nine stages of psychological maturity with characteristics ranging from an external approach to oneself and the world (i.e., external sources of reinforcement, lack of insight into oneself, projection of blame) to an increasing internalization of one's experience, interests, and control (i.e., awareness of thoughts, desires, motives; emphasis on self-reliance and competence; autonomy). Ego operates as an overarching master trait, broadly subsuming a number of other developmental sequences, including (1) character development, which incorporates impulse control and moral development as the basis for moral preoccupations and concerns; (2) cognitive style, which incorporates levels of both cognitive complexity and cognitive development; (3) interpersonal style, which addresses one's attitude toward interpersonal relationships and other people, understanding of relationships, and preferred type of relationship; and (4) conscious preoccupations, which involve the dominant themes of a person's thoughts and behavior. Antecedent constructs from the psychological literature include Adler's "style of life" (Ansbacher & Ansbacher, 1956), Sullivan's (1953) "self-system," and Erikson's (1968, 1982) "psychosocial development."

Ego (self-sense or identity) structurally develops through nine distinct stages in a hierarchical, invariantly sequential manner with an inner logic running through the progression. The stages represent a reorganizing of the self-system at each level, resulting in greater: awareness of self and others, flexibility, personal autonomy, and responsibility. Ego is often referred to as a "master trait" of the personality, subsuming various other lines of development including cognitive style, meaning-making, moral development, character development, interpersonal relations, interpersonal integration, impulse control, and conscious preoccupations (Loevinger, 1976; Hy & Loevinger, 1996).

Background

The concept of a unifying structure of character that develops over time probably extends back at least to ancient Greece, if not to Hebrew and Hindu cultures before it (Hy & Loevinger, 1996). Despite common belief in the English-speaking world to the contrary, the concept of ego did not begin with the work of Sigmund Freud. Freud never actually used the term *ego*. Instead, he specifically referred to *das Ich*, literally "the I," a common phrase in ordinary German. Only in the English translation was his concept rendered as the ego, a term, along with similar others such as "self," which was very much in vogue within the general currents of nineteenth-century philosophy (Loevinger, 1976).

For Loevinger (1976), the first approximation of ego that bears resemblance to her use of the term is in the work of Alfred Adler. Adler's characteristic concept, style of life, was used interchangeably with such concepts as self or ego, unity of personality, individuality, and method of facing problems (Loevinger, 1976). Of key importance was Adler's emphasis on the unity and coherence of the personality, actively seeking goals and purpose, in contrast to Freud's conception of the I (ego) as a compromise resulting from the frustration of aggressive and sexual drives (id) by societal mores and values (superego).

Loevinger's (1966, 1976, 1998) contemporary conceptualization of ego represents a "master trait" that serves as a frame of reference for various other personality traits, such as moral development (Kohlberg, 1969), worldview conceptualizations (Perry, 1970), and interpersonal understanding (Selman, 1980). Thus, it appears to be one of the most comprehensive trait constructs in personality psychology.

Ego development represents a developmental characterology of psychological maturation beginning in childhood and extending throughout adult life (Loevinger, 1976). It is similar in structure to other significant developmental processes, such as cognitive or moral development, in that it consists of a series of stages of maturation defined relatively independently of chronological age. Ego development does tend to increase with age fairly uniformly throughout childhood; however, it then proceeds differentially as a function of age during adolescence and adulthood (Loevinger & Wessler, 1970). The age beyond which differential stages occur appears to be approximately 14, after which a wide spread of ego development levels may be found in any given cohort (Hauser, Powers, & Noam, 1991).

As an organismic approach, ego development theory is modeled on living systems as opposed to machines, considers inherent properties and goals, and emphasizes the whole rather than the parts, the relations among the parts, and how the whole gives meaning to the parts (Miller, 2002). Organismic theories presume an active exchange between the self-system and the environment, with the self-system both selecting particular environments and also acting from a repertoire of responses to accommodate itself to those environments (Blasi, 1976).

The self-system's structure provides the framework and horizon of both selectivity and possible forms of response. This concept emphasizes the underlying organizational processes that operate upon the diversity of specific content. Laws and relations of change that are independent of the elements define the structure. Fundamentally, development consists of a change in the basic rules governing the various elements (Blasi, 1976).

Each *stage* represents a probability wave in which thinking and behavior reflect the dominance of a particular structure. Similar to what I wrote in Chapter 4, Loevinger posits that the stage concept consists of five traditional features: (1) stages follow an invariant sequence and no stage may be skipped; (2) each stage derives from the previous stage, incorporates and transforms that stage, and prepares for the next stage; (3) an inner logic accounts for the stages' equilibrium and stability; (4) stages are universal, although individuals may not pass through all of them and/or may progress at different rates; and (5) each stage involves a coming-into-being and a being, with an initial period of transition and a period of achievement (Loevinger, 1976; Miller, 2002).

According to structural developmental theory, the selectivity and flexibility—referred to as "assimilation" and "accommodation" in Piaget's (1926; 1928) terminology—provided by each structure allows for the system's overall stability (Blasi, 1976). The foremost tendency of the system at each stage is to endure and remain the same, preserving the current structural characteristics. However, the system's stability may have limits. Structural tensions may arise as the result of internal processes or environmental pressures, wherein the flexibility of responses becomes inadequate to deal with the stressors of the environment. The result is a disequilibration, in which case the structure must shift in order to accommodate the tension, or the system will disintegrate. In psychological development, the impulse toward structure change is typically influenced by the desire to become more competent, satisfy one's needs more adequately, or grasp the world more fully (Blasi, 1976).

Whereas Loevinger's model is for the most part in agreement with traditional structural systems, it is important to recognize a key exception. Specifically, not all elements of ego development are completely structural to the exclusion of content (Manners & Durkin, 2001). Character development, cognitive style, and interpersonal style all progress in a traditional structural fashion, with each level reorganizing and possessing an inner logic and coherence. The domain of conscious concerns, however, represents changes in both structure and content. The nature of the concerns changes with each subsequent level while also structurally shifting as a function of changes in the other domains. Thus, it is more appropriate to characterize Loevinger's ego development as a quasi-structural theory than a true structural theory.

Loevinger's (1998) conceptualization of ego development arose from her early work in studying the personality patterns of mothers and women in general. She and her colleagues began with a psychometric approach, administering objective test items and then statistically analyzing them in search of personality patterns or traits. Her research group was initially interested in examining women's acceptance of feminine roles. However, after analysis, the largest statistical cluster of items addressed a bipolar trait referred to as "punitiveness versus permissiveness." The characteristics of women who ranked high in punitiveness bore a strong resemblance to the characteristics described in Adorno's model of the authoritarian personality. Consequently, Loevinger (1998) developed a new scale built on these items, called the Authoritarian

Family Ideology. However, through subsequent research (Loevinger, 1998), she discovered that the authoritarian style did not represent so much an extreme of a particular trait as a midpoint in a continuum.

Women at the immature end of the continuum were not marked by authoritarianism, as initially thought, although they possibly would endorse authoritarian items. The researchers found instead that these women were characterized by a chaotic, impulsive, disorganized, and extremely self-centered style of life. From these modes of operation, authoritarianism and conventionality appeared to be a significant improvement. This realization was noteworthy. Instead of attempting to measure bipolar traits, the investigators redefined their variable as a developmental sequence with qualitatively different stages. They elected to adopt the semiprojective sentence completion test (SCT) as a method to validate their interpretation (Loevinger, 1998).

Loevinger and her colleagues (1976) developed an initial 36-item SCT Form 9-62 by adopting items from previous SCTs utilized in other models and by creating new items particular to the researchers' interests. The team adopted initial theoretical guidelines for scoring the tests from the work on interpersonal maturity and interpersonal integration (I-level) done by Sullivan, Grant, & Grant (1957). Loevinger's team developed a rationalized categorical scoring manual, which provided examples of actual answers grouped into theoretically justified categories (Loevinger, 1998). The initial manual was microvalidated using multiple samples from various demographics, with excellent inter-rater and internal consistency reliability (Loevinger, 1998). The final version of the test, now called the Washington University Sentence Completion Test (WUSCT), and the scoring manual were published in 1970. The WUSCT developers revised the items in 1985 and again in 1996, concurrent with their revision of the scoring manual (Loevinger, 1985; Hy & Loevinger, 1996). The current test in use is the WUSCT Form 81 (Hy & Loevinger, 1996). Twelve examples of the 36 sentence stems from the current WUSCT Form 81 are:

1. When I am criticized...
2. Being with other people...
3. The thing I like about myself is...
4. When people are helpless...
5. A wife should...

6. Rules are...

7. I just can't stand people who...

8. I am...

9. My main problem is...

10. If I can't get what I want...

11. My conscience bothers me if...

12. A man should always... *or* A woman should always... (numbers 1–11 are the same for both men and women; number 12 provides the stem for men and women, respectively)

In 1996, the developers reorganized the original five I-levels (interpersonal levels) with three transitional stages into eight E-levels (ego levels). Currently, Loevinger's model consists of nine stages, although, for reasons explained below, one is not addressed by the WUSCT assessment. The following are brief descriptions of each stage adapted from Loevinger (1976, 1998), Hy and Loevinger (1996), and Manners and Durkin (2001).

Presocial/symbiotic (E1): exclusive focus on gratification of immediate needs; strong attachment to caregiver(s); engaged in differentiating self and objects; preverbal and unable to assess via sentence completion method (postulated for theoretical completeness)

Impulsive (E2): emphasis on physical needs and impulses; no sense of psychological causation; demanding; conceptually confused; self and others are understood in simple dichotomies (good/bad, nice/mean, etc.); unable to distinguish emotional and physical malaise

Self-protective (E3): wary; complaining; opportunistic; beginning to be capable of delay for near-immediate advantage; blame assigned to others, circumstances, or a part of themselves for which they are not responsible; preoccupied with staying out of trouble and not getting caught

Conformist (E4): conventional; moralistic; sentimental; identified with group or authority; rules accepted because they are the rules; friendliness and social niceness highly valued; behavior of self and others seen in terms of externals; conceptually simple; cooperative; loyal

Self-aware (E5): increased, although limited, self-awareness and appreciation of multiple perspectives; exceptions for rules are allowable, but only on broad demographic terms; slightly more focused on feelings, problems, and adjustment; banal reflections on life issues such as God, death, and relationships

Conscientious (E6): self-evaluated standards; "ought" differentiated from "is"; motives and consequences more important than rules; intense; responsible; empathic; long-term goals and ideals; rich and differentiated inner life; values achievement; striving for goals; attempts to improve self; thinking beyond personal concerns

Individualistic (E7): sense of personality as a whole or style of life; tolerant of self and others; inner self and outer self are differentiated; values relationships over achievement; awareness of inner conflicts without resolution; particular concern with emotional dependence; awareness of psychological causation and development; role differentiation

Autonomous (E8): recognition of others' need for autonomy; moral dichotomies no longer typical; free from excessive striving and sense of responsibility; high tolerance for ambiguity and recognition of paradox; relationships seen as interdependent rather than dependent/independent; values uniqueness; vivid expression of feelings; self-fulfillment; clear sense of psychological causation; existential rather than hostile humor

Integrated (E9): wise; broadly empathic; full sense of identity; very rare (less than 1% of population in urban areas); differences in descriptions of qualified raters but probably best illustrated by Maslow's concept of the self-actualizing person who is growth-motivated, seeking to understand his/her intrinsic nature and achieve integration

Since its initial development, Loevinger's model has been refined, extended, and validated through an extensive body of research (Loevinger, 1979, 1985, 1998; Manners & Durkin, 2001). Researchers have completed more than 280 studies to explore various aspects of ego development (Cohn, 1991). The most recent comprehensive review of the literature has continued to support the conceptual soundness of the theory (Manners & Durkin, 2001).

Ego Development and Counseling and Psychotherapy

Given the nature of the domains (character development, cognitive style, interpersonal style, conscious preoccupations) that are theorized to be interwoven in the fabric of ego development in Loevinger's model, it would intuitively seem that investigations regarding the construct and its role in the practice of counseling and psychotherapy would be highly relevant. Direct parallels can be drawn with the domains and multiple dimensions of therapeutic practice. For example, character development addresses the development of moral concerns and ethical decision making—a key focus in both the practice of counseling and the content addressed therein (Corey, 2001; Herlihy & Corey, 1996). Cognitive style encompasses cognitive complexity, tolerance of ambiguity, and understanding of psychological causation, all of which potentially have a bearing on a client's manner of relating to distress and meaning-making activities. Finally, interpersonal style captures the nature of relationships, including the understanding of the other and the types of relationships that are sought. Specifically, Loevinger (1976) suggested that this domain captures the development of the capacity for empathy. Carlozzi, Gaa, and Lieberman (1983) explicitly investigated the relationship of ego development level and the capacity for empathy. The results of this study suggest that individuals at lower levels of ego development may be less able to demonstrate empathy.

Instrument and Scoring

The WUSCT is a semiprojective instrument consisting of 36 incomplete sentence stems designed to measure stages of Loevinger's (1976) ego development. Men and women complete alternate forms with slight differences in gendered nouns and pronouns used in the sentence stems. The subject is simply requested to complete the stems without any further instruction. Completion time ranges from about 20 to 30 minutes.

Individual items are scored according to a comprehensive scoring manual (Hy & Loevinger, 1996). The manual provides themes and multiple examples of typical responses to the sentence stems at each of the ego levels. A frequency and ogive score—which describes the distribution curve of frequency distributions—is created for the items in each protocol. Entire protocols are then scored for a total protocol rating of ego level (E-level) via ogive rules. Two trained raters score protocols, with item discrepancies resolved by consensus. Raters are trained via the systematic three-week self-training program specified in *Measuring Ego Development* (Hy & Loevinger, 1996).

Substantial support for the reliability of the WUSCT has been reported. Loevinger and Wessler (1970) initially reported a Cronbach's alpha of .91 using the item sum score with almost identical results found in later studies (Browning, 1987; Loevinger, 1998; Novy & Francis, 1992). High levels of inter-rater reliability have been consistently found in multiple studies across a broad range of populations (Manners & Durkin, 2001). Novy & Francis (1992) reported high and significant correlations for split half reliability where the researchers compared the first and second halves of the items with each other and with the 36-item test itself.

Based on a comprehensive review of the literature, Manners and Durkin (2001) reported broad substantial support for the construct validity of ego development in two primary ways: (1) in terms of the validity of the three central tenets of the theory (the unitary nature of the ego, the ego as an integration of other personality characteristics, the sequence of ego stages) and (2) in terms of the relation to the external criterion of alternative measures. Ego development was also distinct from intelligence and verbal fluency as well as uninfluenced by socioeconomic status (Manners & Durkin, 2001). Despite the strong validity of findings regarding the WUSCT, ego development level is nonetheless a limited representation of the dynamic flow of human experience and behavior. Loevinger (1976) has pointed out that great care should be used when trying to predict particular behavior based on ego development level.

Conclusion

This chapter addressed in more detail the important dimension of developmental lines and how they constitute a client's integral psychograph. Ten of those lines were explored, and the line of ego development—because of its centrality to integral assessment and treatment approach—was described at length. From here, we venture into the territory of types, states, and the self-system.

Notes

1. Knowing what to include in a book such as this one is often a struggle. On one hand, I want to provide information that is practical and clinically useful. I also want to balance that pragmatic side with theoretical rigor and sound corroborating research. The concept of vMEMEs and the work of Beck and Cowan (1996) are an excellent example of something that I want to integrate in an integral conceptualization because they are a good initial attempt to formulate a working metaphor based upon Clare Graves' developmental model of "an open system theory of values" (1970, p. 131); my reluctance to include them stems from their lack of demonstrated psychometric validity and reliability. I decided to include them with the above caveat.

2. Readers who value only psychometrically validated forms of assessment may have trouble with the notion of giving a ballpark estimation or "best guess" regarding a client's developmental lines. In daily practice, most therapists assess and treat cli-

ents primarily on the basis of clinical judgment, not psychometrically established instruments (Miller, 2004; Marquis, 2002). Moreover, the Integral Intake is primarily a form of idiographic assessment. Nonetheless, much of the material in this chapter, especially the forthcoming section on ego development, is in fact assessing clients not in reference to themselves (idiographically), but in reference to normative populations (nomothetically), even if assessed informally based on clinical judgment rather than exclusively with standardized, psychometrically validated tests such as the WUSCT or SCTi.

6

STATES OF CONSCIOUSNESS, PERSONALITY TYPES, AND THE SELF

Introduction

Having discussed both levels/stages and lines of consciousness, we now need to differentiate stages and states of consciousness. Whereas stages of consciousness are conceived of as enduring structures or traits (relatively stable patterns of events in consciousness), *states* of consciousness are more temporary and relatively fleeting.

All States: Different Ways of Being- and Knowing-in-the-World

The two primary categories of states of consciousness are *natural* and *altered*. Most people, including many practicing therapists, are more familiar with natural states of consciousness—waking, dreaming, and deep sleep—than altered states. It is important to distinguish states from stages because *any state of consciousness can arise within any stage/structure of consciousness.* As an example, people dream (which bestows a state of consciousness other than normal wakefulness) whether their stage of ego development is impulsive, conformist, individualistic, or integrated, just as people can remain at a conformist stage of ego development while daily cycling through waking, dreaming, and deep sleep states of consciousness. As mentioned in Chapter 2, many of the world's wisdom traditions posit that wakefulness correlates to our personal ego or everyday self; that the realm of dreams—precisely because our psyche creates it—correlates to the realm of the

131

soul (the original meaning of *psyche* is "soul"); and that the realm of deep dreamless sleep—a content-free domain of formlessness—correlates to the realm of formless, causal spirit (Wilber, 1999d). What is most significant about these spiritual correlates is that they suggest that everyone has (at least temporary) access to the entire spectrum of consciousness—independently of their "stage development"—because everyone regularly accesses waking, dreaming, and deep sleep states of consciousness (provided that they don't have a sleep disorder or neurological impairment).

Altered, or nonordinary, states of consciousness include experiences such as those induced by meditation or other contemplative practices (endogenous states) as well as those induced by drugs or fasting (exogenous states). Likewise, peak or flow experiences—which can occur within people regardless of their stage of development—are often suprapersonal experiences. A very important caveat that was mentioned in Chapter 2 to bear in mind is that *although anyone at any stage of development can temporarily access suprapersonal states of consciousness, the person will tend to interpret those states with the developmental tools she has available.* However, interpretation (in this case of one's states of consciousness) is a function not only of one's developmental status but also of one's quadrants, lines, and type. Thus, how developed a person is relative to cognitive, spiritual, and worldview lines (UL) will greatly constrain or open a clearing for adequate interpretation, just as cultural contexts (LL), neurophysiology (UR), and social systems (LR) set powerful parameters on and strongly influence interpretive frames of reference. In addition, a person's type may powerfully influence how a spiritual experience is interpreted.

Think for a moment of what William James described as tender- and tough-minded personalities. Whereas tender-minded people tend to be reason- and principle-oriented, intellectual (mind-oriented), idealist, religious, "free-willist," and dogmatic, tough-minded people tend to be empirically and fact-oriented, sensational (sense-oriented), irreligious, "deterministic" or fatalistic, and skeptical (1978, p. 13). Despite the fact that few people are "pure" examples of these types, most people do lean more heavily to one side than the other, and I trust that the reader agrees that tender-minded types will tend to interpret profoundly novel experiences in a more spiritual manner than tough-minded types. Obviously, the culture and religious myths with which a person was socialized will almost dictate how certain meta-mental experiences (also called "deity mysticism" or "subtle experiences") are interpreted (refer to Chapter 2 for a description of the meta-mental realm). A Hindu, for instance, will rarely experience an archetypal image of the divine in human form as Jesus, just as a Christian will seldom experience an archetypal image of the divine in human form as Krishna. Nonetheless, within a given cultural context, one's level of ego development is probably the most powerful influence on how one interprets one's experiences.

For the purpose of an example, consider several American Christians whose cultural context has primed their religiospiritual frames of reference toward Jesus Christ. In order to accurately assess and understand these people and their interpretations of their powerful experiences, the first thing we must avoid is the *pre/trans fallacy*.[1] The next thing we need to remain mindful of is how their current centers of gravity will influence how they will tend to interpret their experience. Table 6.1 displays probable—even if highly stylized—examples of how

Table 6.1 Different Interpretations of a Highly Similar Spiritual Experience	
Developmental Stage	**How a Christian Is Likely to Interpret a Subtle/Meta-Mental Experience**
Phantasmic-emotional (magic; egocentric)	Jesus is *my* personal savior and He will miraculously transform the world to meet my whims and desires.
Representational-mind (mythic; ethnocentric)	Jesus is the bringer of the One Eternal Truth. Everyone who believes in the literal interpretation of the Bible will be saved; everyone who does not will eternally burn in hell.
Early formal-reflexive (rational; transition from ethno- to worldcetnric)	Jesus is still conceived of as fully divine, yet he is also seen as a more humanized and believably human being teaching a universal love that allows people to find their salvation through Jesus Christ or other religious and/or spiritual paths.
Late formal-reflexive (pluralistic; worldcentric)	The experience is recognized as being molded by the person's cultural contexts; the God-union—equally present in everyone—could be interpreted as a demythologized rational deism or any of the sundry characteristics of The Postmodern Bible.
Vision-logic (integral; universe-centric)	Differentiating the historical Jesus from Christ-consciousness—which this person recognizes as present to varying degrees in different people—this person integrates her experience with other expressions of Spirit from numerous religious traditions.
Material adapted from Wilber, 2006.	

differently the same experience would be interpreted as a function of a person's developmental center of gravity.

To reiterate the previous point, although people anywhere along the spectrum of development can have peak experiences (temporary states) of any of the suprapersonal stages, whether a given person metabolizes that state into an enduring trait depends on several factors: the frequency and duration of the temporary states, the "distance" between one's center of gravity and the wave from which the experience/state arose, and the degree and persistence of awareness that the person brings to the process of psychospiritual metabolism (e.g., whether the person regularly engages in meditation, contemplative prayer, or some other attentional practice that constitutes a form of "state-training"). Regardless of how compelling or momentous one's peak experiences seem, these states of consciousness are, by definition, transient and temporary. For those who are motivated to convert fleeting peak experiences into enduring traits—what Maslow (1971) referred to as plateau experiences—some form of yogic or contemplative practice (what Wilber calls "state training") appears necessary. Afterall, peak experiences are fleeting, spontaneous, and tend not to be under one's personal control or will; and dreaming and deep sleep states access suprapersonal states in the sleep cycle, but not while one is fully conscious. In contrast, contemplative states of consciousness are capable of accessing suprapersonal realms in a prolonged and deliberate manner (Wilber, 1999d).

Two ideas that were mentioned above (enduring traits and state training) bring up a highly complex theoretical issue that has resulted in Wilber (2006) revising part of integral theory. Although the nature of this book does not afford the space to delve into all of the intricacies of Wilber's thought on this point, I will devote a few pages to the issue of structure-stages and stage-stages (for a more in-depth treatment of this issue, consult Wilber, 2006, pp. 65–94).

Structure-Stages and State-Stages

I have already emphasized that in integral theory, *structure* is another term for levels or stages of consciousness, in contrast to the more transient states of consciousness. However, it must also be remembered that such structures are anything but rigid, fixed, and utterly stable. In fact, these dynamic patterns can appear like whirlwinds. However, even though, by way of an analogy, the different parts of a cell constantly replace and rejuvenate themselves autopoetically (in a self-organizing manner), the cell retains its essential form or pattern, and that basic pattern is its dynamic holistic structure (Wilber, 2006). And, as much of developmental psychology has attested to, basic structures emerge sequentially, hence their fundamental synonymy with developmental stages. However, technically, stages and structures are not identical; there are actually structure-stages (discussed in Chapter 4) and state-stages (which I will briefly discuss in this section). This distinction is necessary in order to more clearly apprehend the nature of spiritual experiences. The next three paragraphs are a theoretical technicality for the sake of clarity and accuracy, not necessarily immediately relevant to the practical work of most therapists, unless they are working with clients who are practicing some sort of meditative or contemplative disciplines.

Before differentiating structure-stages and state-stages, it is pertinent to emphasize that whereas states of consciousness are immediately, phenomenologically experienced by individuals (in the first person), stages of consciousness are not directly experienced but rather are reconstructions of individuals' interiors from a relatively objective, scientific perspective (in the third person). Whereas states of consciousness are explored via the school or discipline of phenomenology (studying the interior of an individual, and viewed from the inside), most stage theories of human development fall into the school of structuralism (studying the interior of an individual, but viewed from the outside). What is significant about this is that *nothing like a structure-stage* (e.g., Piaget's concrete or formal operations, Kohlberg's conventional morality, or Loevinger's impulsive or conscientious levels of ego development) *will ever present itself to your immediate experience or felt awareness*, even though those structures mold and filter your experiences and felt awareness.

You may be wondering: if people can have peak experiences of psychic, subtle, and nondual states of consciousness regardless of their structure-stage of development, what sense does it make to refer to "state-*stages*"? After all, one person's first peak experience can be of the subtle realm, whereas others may get a glimpse of the psychic or nondual before they have a peak experience of the subtle). The significance of state-stages is pertinent to individuals who are involved in contemplative, meditative, and other state-training disciplines. Whereas natural states of consciousness tend not to demonstrate a developmental course (waking, dreaming, and deep sleep occur cyclically, not in a linear unfolding), some states of consciousness can be trained via attention deployment. The best examples are the myriad forms of contemplative prayer and meditation that are core aspects of the world's religions (both Eastern and Western). Research has demonstrated that from Eastern Orthodox Christianity to Patanjali's Yoga Sutras to the Visuddhimagga of Buddhaghosha, trained meditative and contemplative states of consciousness tend to emerge in a sequential manner: gross, psychic, subtle, causal, and nondual (Chirban, Brown, & Engler, cited in Wilber, Engler, & Brown, 1986; Wilber, 2006).

Despite the fact that within the context of state training—through which peak experiences are transmuted into more stabilized plateau experiences—nonordinary states emerge sequentially, people definitely can and do have peak experiences of various state-stages. In sharp contrast, we have no evidence that people can have peak experiences of structure-stages. For example, people characterized by Loevinger's conformist ego development (E4) do not appear to have peak moments of individualistic or autonomous meaning-making capacities (E7 and E8, respectively). Also in contrast to state-stages, structure-stages cannot be skipped. Even though nonordinary states (psychic, subtle, causal, nondual) can be skipped, everyone who thinks with formal operations previously thought with concrete operations and preoperations; no one jumps from preoperations to formal operations without first spending some developmental time in concrete operations.

Relevance of "All States" to Therapy

A relevant question to ask at this point is: how are altered states of consciousness significant in therapy? Recall from Chapter 2 that episodes of anxiety, panic, depression, mania, delirium, and even psychoses are almost always *states* of consciousness. That is to say, most individuals are not permanently anxious, depressed, manic, delirious, or psychotic. Rather, these states of consciousness arise, stay awhile (sometimes far, far too long for the person subject to the state) and pass. This simple but profound realization ("this, too, shall pass") has helped a great many clients, and is a central component of mindfulness-based cognitive therapy for depression (Segal, Williams, & Teasdale, 2002), as well as mindfulness-based therapy for clients with obsessive-compulsive disorder (Schwartz & Begley, 2002), anxiety and a host of other problems. Moreover, even within a given counseling session, clients will likely be more receptive to certain interventions as a function of their state of consciousness. For example, if their minds are racing, clients are less likely to "sit with" and deeply process what they are experiencing in the here-and-now. In such cases, helping a client to become grounded and centered (deep breathing and directing one's attention to one's bodily sensations rather than to one's mental asseverations) may help them make the transition to a state in which they will be more receptive to experiential work. Prime examples of the therapeutic value of altered states of consciousness are prevalent in Ericksonian Hypnosis (Erickson & Rossi, 1981), dream work (Hill, 1996), and Eye Movement Desensitization Reprocessing (Shapiro, 2001).

Carl Rogers also capitalized therapeutically on his own capacity to enter altered states of consciousness while working with clients:

> When I am at my best . . . when I am closest to my inner, intuitive self . . . when perhaps I am in a slightly altered state of consciousness in the relationship, then whatever I do seems to be full of healing. Then simply my *presence* is releasing and helpful . . . when I can relax and be close to the transcendental core of me, then I may behave in strange and impulsive ways in the relationship, ways which I cannot justify rationally, which have nothing to do with my thought processes. But these strange behaviors turn out to be *right*, in some odd way. At those moments it seems that my inner spirit has reached out and touched the inner spirit of the other. Our relationship transcends itself and becomes a part of something larger. Profound growth and healing and energy are present. (1986, pp. 198–199)

Welwood—heavily influenced by both Rogers and contemplative spirituality—has written beautifully about the healing effects of therapists' altered states of unconditional presence, acceptance, and love and laments that although they are perhaps therapists' greatest gift to their clients, therapists' professional training "consists mostly of transmitting knowledge and information. The most important thing—the ability to bring a quality of unbiased presence [an altered state] to experience just as it is—is hardly even mentioned" (2000, p. 144).

With any set of clients and their various presenting problems, their states of consciousness may be either of relatively little consequence or one of the primary determining factors in their successful outcome. Thus, with all the clients you counsel, consider how their sundry states of consciousness may impact both their struggles and their well-being.

Various queries on the Integral Intake (all but one of which fall into the experiential/UL quadrant) inquire into clients' states of consciousness—both disturbing ones and ones that can be a source of relief, strength, and resilience for them:

- How would you describe your general mood/feelings?
- What emotions do you most often feel most strongly?
- Are you aware of recurring images or thoughts (either while awake or in dreams)? Yes/No If yes, please describe.
- Are you *presently* experiencing suicidal thoughts? Yes/No If yes, please describe.
- Describe your leisure time (hobbies/enjoyment).

The clinical relevance of queries regarding clients' moods, feelings, and emotions should be readily apparent to therapists. After all, one of the primary reasons that people seek professional therapeutic help is because of disturbing felt experience. Quickly getting a sense of what a given client's specific patterns of felt experience are will inform the clinician of the nature of the client's problems. Some clients respond very vaguely to these items, which often—though not always—indicates their general lack of awareness of their feelings (as in those who are fairly repressed or overly intellectual) or, in extreme cases, alexithymia (as with those clients who, as children, were chronically deprived of caregivers who allowed them to experience their affective life and failed to learn to recognize, differentiate, and label their various emotions) (Mahoney & Marquis, 2002; Stolorow, Atwood, & Orange, 2002).

Various emotional states of consciousness are also assessed with the checklist on page 4 of the Integral Intake, as well as the "religious and/

or spiritual experiences" item on the developmental problems checklist on page 11. Many people have reported having peak experiences while they are absorbed in activities that they engage in for the sake of the activities themselves (play), as opposed to activities that they engage in for the sake of some alternative end (work). Whether clients' positive states have arisen within the context of religious/spiritual experiences or secular peak experiences or are of a less intense but nonetheless restorative, rejuvenative, and meaningful nature (as in those states that emerge while listening to music, taking a nature walk, playing with a pet or child, knitting, cooking, etc.), such constructive states are often a welcome bulwark against and relief from the more problematic aspects of their lives. Many counseling approaches, from Mahoney's constructive psychotherapy (2003) to Yalom's existential-interpersonal therapy (2002), emphasize the value in encouraging clients to make time for leisure activities that bring joy and meaning to their lives.

The query regarding any recurring images or thoughts that clients have is important because it begins to get clients used to what Aaron Beck has called "the fundamental cognitive probe for identifying automatic thoughts" (Dattilio & Padesky, 1990, p. 29): "At the moment I first realize I am upset, what is going through my mind in the way of thoughts or images?" Of course, for this type of cognitive probe to be maximally helpful, clients must develop their mindfulness so that they realize they are upset as immediately as possible, thus making a more accurate connection between the disturbance and the thought or image that stimulated the upset. I hope the reader has also recognized that heightened mindfulness is, in and of itself, an altered state of consciousness—a state in which even in the midst of depression, anxiety, or physical pain, people report being not nearly as disturbed: they are aware of a feeling they would rather not have, but rather than fighting against it and judging it or themselves negatively, they simply allow it to be as it is and witness it with bare, nonjudgmental attention and thus do not suffer nearly so much from it (Kabat-Zinn, 1994; Segal, Williams, & Teasdale, 2002; Schwartz & Begley, 2002). The importance of the query that asks about the client's *presently* experiencing suicidal thoughts should likewise be obvious. Depending on the client's responses to questions regarding having a suicide plan and the means to carry out that plan, prior suicide attempts, whether they felt relief/embarrassment or disappointment/anger at a failed suicide attempt, and their family's history of suicide, the therapist may need to take immediate action to ensure the client's safety. Other questions to ask yourself when assessing the risk of a client attempting suicide include:

- Does the client have the energy to commit the act?
- How secretive is the client when responding to your queries?
- How willing is the client to problem-solve or consider alternatives to cope with her suffering?
- How willing is the client to seek social support?

Don't forget to trust your intuition and clinical judgment. The client may tell you all the "right" answers even though she plans to kill herself that evening. The Scale for Suicide Ideation and the Beck Depression Inventory are nomothetic assessment instruments that are widely used by therapists working with clients who appear potentially suicidal.

I have geared this section on states of consciousness to reveal more of the fluid and often oscillating complexities of human nature and experience, as well as to demonstrate that not everyone who talks of "altered states" is a substance abuser. In fact, reputable researchers have posited that humans have an innate desire and need for altered states—from children's love of dizziness through adolescents' curious experimenting with substances and adults' fascination with meditation, contemplative prayer, and vision quests (Weil, 1986; Walsh, 1982; Badiner & Grey, 2002).

All Types: Different Ways of Being- and Knowing- and Acting-in-the-World

We have now addressed four of the five primary components of AQAL—quadrants, levels, lines, and states—all of which are relatively universal in nature. In other words, regardless of their culture or gender, all people can be viewed from the four quadrants; all people have the *potential* to develop through the same basic structures of consciousness (even if they do so in very different ways, which *is* the case and is a function of—among other things—their type, soon to be addressed); all people can be described in terms of their lines of development; and all people have access to the same ordinary and nonordinary states of consciousness (even if sociocultural contexts profoundly influence and alter the surface manifestations of those cross-cultural states). Another essential part of the integral model is that of *types*, or personality typologies, which refer to different person's ways of being-, knowing-, and acting-in-the-world. As was mentioned in Chapter 2, in contrast to the often vertical conceptualization of developmental models (although it is preferable to conceive of developmental models as nested, concentric spheres), typologies are conceived of horizontally.

It is all too common to encounter professional literature that poses questions such as "Which is better, autonomy or relationship, work or love, independence or interdependence?" (Ivey, 1986, p. 272). In those three pairs, the first of each is masculine; the latter is feminine. When typologies are included in an integral conceptualization (in the preceding case a simple binary typology of masculine/feminine), a thorny question such as Ivey's fades away in the recognition that neither is better or worse under all circumstances; those polarities (autonomy or relationship, work or love) simply represent different types, each of which passes through developmental stages. For example, work can be egocentric, sociocentric, or worldcentric, just as love manifests itself through those same stages.

Although most typological systems posit that one's type is generally stable over time (if you're feminine, an ESTJ in the Myers-Briggs typology, or an Enneagram type 7 when you're 10, you'll be feminine, an ESTJ, or an Enneagram type 7 when you're 60), aspects of personality certainly can shift, loosen, or otherwise wiggle around. To avoid stereotyping and blaming our actions on our type, we would do well to remember that we are not our type; rather, our type is an aspect of who we are. Nonetheless, we *will* be limited and constrained to some extent by our specific type(s). On the other hand, our limits or wounds are often potential gifts if we are able to make them objects of our awareness, rather than remain embedded in them as subjects. In addition, no one is ever just a single type. That is to say, different types from different systems "mingle" with one another. For example, if a client is an Enneagram type 2, he can be either a feminine 2 or a masculine 2, an introverted 2 or an extroverted 2, and so forth.

Typological systems have emerged across time and cultures, from esoteric philosophical and spiritual traditions (Plato and other ancient Greek systems, Chinese medicine) to numerous folk psychology systems (Native American, Chinese, East Indian). Some of the better-known modern psychological typology systems include the five-factor model (McCrae & Costa, 1996), the Myers-Briggs Type Indicator (Briggs & Myers, 1977), the Enneagram (Riso & Hudson, 1999), Adlerian personality priorities (Fall, Holden, & Marquis, 2004), and tough- and tender-minded personalities (James, 1978). Moreover, gender—principles of masculinity and femininity, not of being biologically male or female—has been conceived of as typological, from Jung (1968) and Keen (1991) to Gilligan (1982), Jordan, Kaplan, Baker Miller, Stever, & Surrey (1991), and Goldberger, Trule, Clinchy, & Belenky (1996). Why are there so many typology systems? First, no single system captures all of the complexities that humans exhibit. Second, at the same time that each typology system offers important insights into the human condition, each system is also limited and partial. The fundamental value of typological systems is to make people more aware of their interiors, as well as to help us and our clients recognize that different types of people do the same things for very different reasons or to accomplish similar goals via very different routes.

To repeat, even though all people can grow through the same basic structures of consciousness, they will do so in very different ways, with very different preferences, tendencies, and dislikes. Moreover, different people will be optimally described by different typological systems. For example, one client may benefit greatly by learning that according to the MBTI she is an ESFP, whereas her husband is an INTJ (this would explain a great deal about the nature of their conflicts, differences in how they make decisions, what they want to do in their leisure time, etc.). Another client may benefit less from an MBTI categorization and find more insight from a gender or Enneagram classification (many women are masculine and many men are feminine, which many clients either don't recognize in themselves or tend to deny and thus fail to integrate that within their identity/self line). As you can see, familiarizing yourself with various typological systems not only is an important component of practicing integral therapy but can be powerfully informative of your client's individualized (idiographic) developmental journey through life.

A Few Caveats About Typing

Although typological (typing) systems offer tremendous benefits, they also have some potential pitfalls. When used properly, understanding different types can facilitate our deeper apprehension of, discernment of, and empathy with others' experience in its uniqueness and difference from our own experience. Improperly using typological systems can lead to stereotyping. Moreover, the population statistics from which many of these systems derive their construct validity do not strictly apply to any given individual. Thus, just because the average MBTI type of INFP is more likely, from a statistical point of view, to find the work of counseling to be more appealing than the average ESTJ, that statistical reality does not mean that a specific person who is an ESTJ won't enjoy being a counselor or that a specific person who is an INFP necessarily will. Finally, even though types are a horizontal construct, and thus no single type has advantages over other types in all contexts, certain cultures and/or subcultures tend to value or privilege some types over others. The United States, for example, tends to value the masculine (gender), the extrovert/sensing/thinking/judging type (ESTJ in MBTI), and Enneagram 3s.

In Chapter 2, I provided an example of how differently masculine boys and feminine girls tend to play, based upon Gilligan's (1982) research. Because many therapists are already familiar with the MBTI, I will here demonstrate the significance of understanding and integrating types into one's conceptualizations through a brief introduction to the Enneagram. Although it is true that all typological systems are partial and have their limits, the vast majority of the integral therapists that I know agree that the Enneagram is the most subtly nuanced, sophisticated, and complex typology system. Nonetheless, despite its popularity as an apparently helpful clinical tool, the psychometric research supporting its validity and reliability is tentative at best (Dameyer, 2001; Sharp, 1994; Gamard, 1986).

The Enneagram

The Enneagram is a dynamic psychospiritual personality typology system that originated in esoteric Sufi teachings (the name *Enneagram* comes from the Greek word for "nine-pointed figure") (Riso & Hudson, 1999, p. 9; Palmer, 1988). Though its origins are not western, George Ivanovich Gurdjieff (a Greek Armenian mystical philosopher) introduced the Enneagram to European thinkers at the beginning of the twentieth century. Subsequently, the Bolivian philosopher Oscar Ichazo and then the Chilean psychiatrist Claudio Naranjo further refined, developed, and expanded the Enneagram system. In 1977, Don Riso added a (vertical) developmental component to what previously had been an exclusively horizontal system and developed an empirically validated instrument that assesses one's Enneagram type (the Riso-Hudson Enneagram Type Indicator, RHETI). Today, the Enneagram correlates significantly with many Western psychotherapeutic systems, such as the MBTI, MMPI T-scores, and perhaps even some *DSM* diagnoses (Palmer, 1988).

Not denying that genetics, culture, and social systems influence one's personality, the Enneagram conceives of one's personality as developing around fundamental patterns of experience that include basic desires, core identifications, strengths (which can degenerate into weaknesses), dominant fears, values, motivations, defenses, and habits. Significantly, the Enneagram posits that beneath one's personality—which is molded and conditioned by experience in this world—one's deepest, most real essence is of a spiritual nature beyond the cramp of the isolated ego. Thus, the ultimate goal of working with the Enneagram is not merely to understand our and others' personalities, but to help people traverse the interior dimensions of their being so that they may free their personalities from what is wounded, fearful, blocked, and conflicted and thus move toward greater self-understanding—realizing more meaning, fulfillment, and spiritual development (Maitri, 2001). For a historical account of the development of the Enneagram—especially its research base and how it became a part of Western psychology and psychiatry—consult Riso & Hudson (1999) and Palmer (1988).

Many Enneagram experts refer to the nine types simply as the numbers 1 through 9, because numbers are value-neutral. Others have provided various names that descriptively convey the various types. To repeat, like all typology systems, each of the nine Enneagram types affords assets and liabilities, even though certain types may seem more successful or desirable in specific contexts (as previously mentioned, U.S. culture particularly values the qualities associated with Enneagram 3s). Table 6.2 displays various characteristics associated with the nine basic Enneagram types.

As involved as Table 6.2 may appear, the Enneagram system is far, far more intricate than what Table 6.2 displays. In addition to the basic types (1–9), there are also triads (thinking, feeling, and instincts), wings, instinctual variants (self-preservation, social, and sexual), and

Table 6.2 Enneagram Types and Characteristics

Enneagram Type (number and name)	Key Characteristics and Strengths	Basic Desires and Core Identifications	Passions and Distortions/ Pitfalls	Unconscious Childhood Messages ("it's not okay to …")	Basic Fears (of being)	Primary Defense	Developmental Jumpstarts (if you bring awareness to the following patterns)
1. Reformer (Perfectionist)	Wise, rational, principled, lives for a higher purpose	Integrity; a sensible person with capacities to discern and evaluate	Repressed anger, resentment; perfectionism	Make mistakes	Bad, evil, corrupt, or defective	Reaction formation	Value-judging yourself and others
2. Helper (Giver)	Compassionate, caring, generous, nurtures self and others	Love; a nurturing being who cares more about others' feelings than one's self	Vainglory-proud of their own virtues; craving to be needed	Have my own needs	Unworthy of others' love	Repression	Valuing others without valuing yourself
3. Achiever (Performer)	Enjoys living, adaptable, ambitious, models for others how to value existence	Self-worth; a self-image of unlimited potential that prompts others' admiration	Vanity, self-deception; chasing after success	Have my own identity and feelings	Worthless or lacking inherent value	Identification	Trying to be someone that is not authentically you
4. Individualist (Tragic romantic)	Intuitive, aesthetic, forgiving, uses all of life for growth and renewal	Autonomous individuality; a sensitive being with strong emotions, esp. feelings of being flawed	Envy, self-absorbed; self-indulgent	Be too happy or too functional	Without personal significance or identity	Introjection	Making negative comparisons

Table 6.2 Enneagram Types and Characteristics (continued)

Enneagram Type (number and name)	Key Characteristics and Strengths	Basic Desires and Core Identifications	Passions and Distortions/ Pitfalls	Unconscious Childhood Messages ("it's not okay to . . .")	Basic Fears (of being)	Primary Defense	Developmental Jumpstarts (if you bring awareness to the following patterns)
5. Investigator (Observer)	Perceptive, innovative, nonjudgmental, contemplates the richness of reality	Competence; an insightful being with detached, objective awareness	Avarice, detached; useless specialization	Be content in the world	Incompetent, useless, or incapable	Isolation	Overinterpreting your experience
6. Loyalist (Devil's Advocate)	Courageous, engaging, responsible, responds to all of life's conditions	Security; a likeable person who perceives a lack of external support	Fear, anxiety, defensive; attached to one's beliefs	Trust myself	Without guidance or support	Projection	Overly relying on external—rather than internal—support
7. Enthusiast (Epicure)	Happy, optimistic, accomplished, celebrates life and shares joy with others	Happiness; an outgoing being who anticipates future positive experiences	Gluttony, impulsive; frenetic escapism	Depend on others for anything	Deprived or stuck in pain	Rationalization	Anticipating your next step rather than enjoying the present

8. Challenger (Boss)	Self-confident, strong, decisive, stands up and acts for their beliefs	Self-protection; a robustly independent being who tenaciously challenges others	Lust (not exclusively sexual), intensely domineering; constantly fighting	Trust anyone or be vulnerable	Harmed or dominated by others	Denial	Trying to control or force your life
9. Peacemaker (Wings)	Serene, kind, reassuring, brings healing and peace into the world	Peace; a stable being who disengages from intense feelings and impulses	Sloth, complacency; stubborn neglectfulness	Assert myself	Alone, fragmented and disconnected from others	Narcotization	Resisting being deeply affected by others and life

Constructed from material in Riso & Hudson, 1999, pp. 18–48.

a "vertical" dimension of development or health that applies to each of the "horizontal" types (Riso & Hudson, 1999, pp. 75, 49–75). Very briefly, the triads are "centers of intelligence" that help pinpoint where fundamental imbalances in personality derive from and how we limit ourselves; the wings help individualize the nine types in that each type can have two subtypes, or wings (there is no such thing as a completely pure type—for example, a person who is a 9 can have either a 1-wing or an 8-wing); and the instinctual variants reveal which of the three basic instincts were most distorted in a given person's childhood, which results in specific patterns of thinking, feeling, and behaving across the entire developmental spectrum of each personality type. Another component of Riso & Hudson's (1999) work is its explicit attention to how each basic type manifests at different levels of development, or degrees of healthy functioning (each type has healthy, average, and unhealthy traits). Together, various developmental levels (vertical) combine with personality types (horizontal) to create a matrix in which any type can exist at any level of development (see Table 6.3).

Table 6.3 does not factor that into account because each of the 9 basic types have both of 2 subtypes (wings), and because each of those 18 subtypes can be characterized by any of the 3 instinctual variants (there are thus 6 variations for each of the 9 types), that there are actually *54 different variations in the Enneagram typology system* (not including the developmental dimension that is included in Table 6.3). Even if we use a very simple developmental scheme of 3 levels, those 54 variations in type combined with the 3 levels yields 162 different variations. As you can see—and in contrast to binary systems such as gender or James' tough- and tender-minded personalities—the Enneagram is amenable to incredibly subtle distinctions, often at a level of detail that most (including me) find overwhelming and no longer clinically helpful (perhaps because they (I) haven't fully mastered an understanding of the Enneagram). In such a case, it is perfectly fine to revert to a more simplified version of it—for example, using just the nine basic types at three different degrees of health or development.

Less-Healthy Types

As mentioned in Chapter 2, the axis II disorders of the *Diagnostic and Statistical Manual of Mental Disorders* (*DSM–IV-TR*) can also be conceptualized as different types. As Table 6.3 revealed, people of each of

Table 6.3   The Nine Basic Enneagram Types Across the Developmental Spectrum

Enneagram Type	Optimally Healthy; Most Developed	→							Least Healthy; Least Developed
1	Wise, accepting	Sensible, reasonable	Principled, responsible	Obligated, driven	Orderly, self-controlled	Critical, judgmental	Inflexible, self-righteous	Contradictory, obsessive	Punitive, condemnatory
2	Unconditionally loving, self-nurturing	Caring, empathic	Giving, supportive	People-pleasing, well-intentioned	Intrusive, possessive	Overbearing, self-important	Manipulative, self-justifying	Coercive, entitled	Burdensome, feels victimized
3	Authentic, inner-directed	Unlimited potential, adaptable	Self-improving, goal-oriented	Success-oriented, overachieving	Expedient, image-conscious	Grandiose, self-promoting	Deceptive, unprincipled	Opportunistic, duplicitous	Relentless, monomaniacal
4	Self-renewing, life-embracing	Introspective, sensitive	Creative, self-revealing	Romanticizing, individualistic	Temperamental, self-absorbed	Decadent, self-indulgent	Alienated, hateful	Clinically depressed, self-rejecting	Life-denying, despairing
5	Visionary, participating	Perceptive, observant	Innovative, focused	Conceptualizing, preparing	Preoccupied, detached	Provocative, extreme	Eccentric, nihilistic	Delirious, horrified	Self-annihilating, seeking oblivion
6	Courageous, self-reliant	Reliable, engaging	Committed, cooperative	Loyal, dutiful	Defensive, ambivalent	Authoritarian, blaming	Unreliable, panicky	Lashing out, paranoid	Self-destructive, self-abasing
7	Joyful, grateful	Enthusiastic, anticipating	Productive, realistic	Consuming, acquisitive	Scattered, distracted	Excessive, self-centered	Escaping, insatiable	Reckless, manic-depressive	Paralyzed, overwhelmed
8	Heroic, self-surrendering	Strong, self-reliant	Self-confident, decisive	Enterprising, pragmatic	Dominating, self-glorifying	Intimidating, confrontational	Dictatorial, ruthless	Terrorizing, megalomaniacal	Destructive, sociopathic
9	Indomitable, dynamically present	Peaceful, unself-conscious	Comforting, unselfish	Agreeable, self-effacing	Complacent, disengaged	Appeasing, resigned	Neglectful, ineffectual	Disoriented, dissociating	Unresponsive, "disappearing"

Constructed from material in Riso & Hudson, 1999. pp. 106–323.

the nine Enneagram types can be anywhere along a continuum from self-actualizing to severely impaired. Palmer (1988) discussed correlations between the unhealthy forms of the Enneagram types and *DSM-III* diagnoses (see Table 6.4). It is important to remember that with the exception of *DSM* categories/types of disorders, no specific type is consistently better or worse than the others in all situations.

Various queries on the Integral Intake (all of which are in the experiential/UL quadrant, with the exception of the developmental checklist on p. 11) inquire into aspects of clients that may provide data helpful in discerning their type.

- How do you make decisions (for example, do you use logic and reason, or do you trust your gut and heart)?

This question addresses the thinking/feeling dimension of the MBTI. It is not that making decisions in one of these ways is always better than the other, but they are *very* different routes toward making choices.

- How do you respond to stressful situations and other problems?

Whereas Enneagram 5s will tend to analyze the situation in as detached a manner as possible, 2s will tend to focus on compassionately nurturing others' well-being. Although this may appear stylized and stereotypical, masculine types (whether male or female) will more often respond to stressful situations by "objectively" analyzing the different dimensions of the problem and then act as soon as possible. In contrast, feminine types (whether male or female) will more often respond to stressful situations by considering how various courses of action will impact their connectedness within various relationships. This query hints at the difference between Kohlberg's and Gilligan's construction of moral reasoning (masculine and feminine, respectively).

- What are the ways in which you care for and comfort yourself when you feel distressed?

Different types of people will respond very differently to this question. Enneagram 8s, for example, tend to be far more self-reliant and self-glorifying, whereas 2s will generally seek comfort in others' love and approval.

Finally, a few of the items in the developmental checklist on p. 11 of the Integral Intake will alert you to potential *DSM* disorders.

Table 6.4 Correlations Between *DSM-III* Diagnoses and Unhealthy Extremes of Enneagram Types

Enneagram Type	1	2	3	4	5	6	7	8	9
DSM-III Diagnosis	Obsessive-compulsive personality disorder (compulsive aspect dominates)	Histrionic and dependent personality disorders	Type A personality; workaholic (no DSM correlation)	Major depressive and bipolar disorders	Schizoid and avoidant personality disorders	Paranoid personality disorder	Narcissistic personality disorder	Antisocial personality disorder	Obsessive-compulsive personality disorder (obsessive aspect dominates)

Adapted from Palmer, 1988, p. 62.

(Obviously, a client checking these items does not automatically suggest that he meets criteria for any disorder; rather, it suggests that you further interview the client regarding whether or not he actually meets criteria for the relevant disorder). For example, if a client checked the "cruelty to animals or people" (at age 7) and upon further inquiry stated that he used to douse neighborhood cats with gasoline and set them on fire, this may be suggestive of a client with antisocial personality disorder. Similarly, clients who check the "self-destructiveness (risky sex . . . excessive risk-taking, etc.)" query are more likely to have a bipolar disorder than clients who do not check that query. Finally, depending on the nature of the social problems that a client specifically has, various *DSM* disorders (from narcissistic personality disorder to social phobia) may be implicated.

I hope it is clear to readers that none of a client's responses to the Integral Intake yields a definitive, cut-and-dry diagnosis, whether *DSM*-, Enneagram-, or developmental-level-related. The Integral Intake is, after all, an idiographic assessment instrument, meaning that its purpose is not to assess a person relative to a normative population but rather to assess the individual's uniqueness as a person. Thus, the important clinical task is not merely to see that a client marked a given question but to then follow up with something along the lines of "Mark, I see on the form here that you marked the self-destructiveness item. Tell me more about what you do that is self-destructive" (and further inquire when those behaviors began, how frequently, what purpose they seem to serve for the client, etc.).

Exploring and studying personality types underscores how multidimensional our conceptualizations of human nature become when we include types in our assessment process. To conclude this section, remember that different types of people prefer different ways of being-, knowing-, and acting-in-the-world and will emphasize and value, as well as dislike and avoid, different dimensions of life. I hope the reader recognizes and appreciates how different clients' struggles and successful courses of therapy may be as a function of the fact that one of them is highly introverted whereas the other is highly extroverted (MBTI); that one of them is intensely feminine whereas the other is intensely masculine (gender); or that one of them tends to bolster his sense of ethical superiority by perfectionistically criticizing self and others whereas the other tends to serve others' needs as a means to obtain love, appreciation, approval, and affection (Enneagram types 1 and 2, respectively).

The Self-System

Even though the self is not one of the five main components of the AQAL model, the self—or more accurately, the self-system—is central to counseling and psychotherapy. As previously mentioned, the self is not so much a thing or noun as it is an action or verb—the dynamic and usually tacit process that holds together the sundry developmental lines, constructing something of a cohesive whole that recursively serves as each person's psychological universe. The self is also the locus of a host of important operations and capacities, such as organization, identification, defenses, metabolism (psychological digestion of one's experiences), will, and navigation (one's journey through the developmental labyrinth). Given that the section in Chapter 5 on the line of ego development was a description of the proximate self, this section on the self-system will introduce the reader to other dimensions of the self, including basic and transitional structures; the distal, proximate, and antecedent selves and their relationships to one another; self-system pathology; repression and five different types of unconsciousness; and subpersonalities. The goal of this section is not to fully explicate all of the detailed depths of an integral view of the self-system; rather, the goal is to pique your interest enough so that you will seek out other primary integral therapy resources that address the self-system more fully (Wilber, 2000e; Ingersoll & Cook-Greuter, 2007).

To begin, integral theory distinguishes between the self-sense (the self as phenomenologically experienced by a person from inside) and the self or self-system (the self as structurally analyzed and conceptualized from outside). As in all cases, integral therapists are mindful of the imperative need to allow first-person views to inform our third-person descriptions and explanations. Some of the best Western psychological descriptions of the self line of development are provided by Kegan (1985), Loevinger (1976), Wilber (2000e), and Ingersoll & Cook-Greuter (2007).

Basic and Transitional Structures

In addition to the functions mentioned above that the self serves (identification, organization, etc.), the self also mediates the basic and transitional structures. Basic structures are those that, once they emerge in development, tend to remain and become incorporated into subsequent stages. Examples of basic structures are motor capacities and Piaget's stages of cognitive development. Transitional structures, in contrast, are those that are replaced, rather than incorporated, with subsequent development. Examples of transitional structures are Kohlberg's stages of moral development and one's worldviews. Wilber suggests that it is the self's identification with a basic structure that generates a corresponding group of transitional structures. Thus, a self that identifies with Wilber's third basic structure, the representational mind, generates or supports a moral stance of obedience and punishment avoidance (Kohlberg), a protective self-sense (Loevinger), and a self-need of safety (Maslow); as the self develops and identifies with the rule/role mind basic structure, a new set of transitional structures is generated, this time consisting of a moral stance of law and order (Kohlberg), a conformist self-sense (Loevinger), and needs for belongingness (Maslow); as the self develops and identifies with the formal-reflexive basic structure, a new set of transitional structures is generated, this time consisting of a moral stance of individual rights (Kohlberg), a conscientious self-sense (Loevinger), and needs for self-esteem (Maslow); and so on (Wilber, 2000c).

Proximate, Distal, and Antecedent Selves

Although constituting the same self-system, the distal, proximate, and antecedent selves are distinct constructs that bear practical consequences for the practice of counseling and psychotherapy. The proximate self is what a person most intimately identifies with; it is what is most near, close, or "proximate" to who you are (Ingersoll & Cook-Greuter, 2007). A great deal of one's proximate self is outside of awareness, not because the person is repressing it but because it is the self-structure in which that person is embedded. Similar to Adler's (cited in Ansbacher & Ansbacher, 1956) schema of apperception, the proximate self is analogous to a pair of clear, transparent lenses through which we are able to see and construe the world without actually seeing the lenses themselves. Analogous to Beck's (1979) cognitive schema, the proximate self consists of organizing structures that mold and otherwise influence experience and perception without the person necessarily being able to articulate what those structures are. To say that a client is embedded in her proximate self is another way of saying that what she calls "I" is mostly a subject of awareness, rather than an object of her awareness.

When aspects of the self that previously were identified with are consistently reflected upon as objects of awareness, they cease being part of the proximate self and become part of the distal self; "distal" refers to having some distance from one's innermost, nearest self (Ingersoll & Cook-Greuter, 2007). Thus, the distal self includes all of those dimensions that were previously identified with by the proximate self and that the proximate self now views not as central to one's identity but rather more like qualities, skills, or parts that someone possesses. For example, years ago I counseled a client who was ordered by the court to attend therapy because of his violent tendencies. When I initially asked him to tell me about himself, the first words he spoke were "I'm a violent man"—as if that was the whole of who he was. Although it took a few months, he would later respond to that same query with *"Part* of who I am is aggressive or violent, but those are really just adjectives that describe the real me, which is more difficult to explain." In this case, what he was previously subject to, identified with, and embedded in— violence—became an object of his awareness with which he no longer exclusively identified. Wilber described the relationship between what is subject and what is object to oneself as a process in which "a *mode* of self becomes merely a *component* of a higher-order self" (1980, p. 81).

Wilber has described the above process in a number of different ways. In addition to the notions that what was subject becomes object and what was the whole becomes a part, he also has said that "what is *identification* becomes *detachment* . . . what is *context* becomes *content*" (1980, p. 81). These dynamics were echoed by Kegan (1982) as the balancing act between subject and object. According to Kegan, development always involves a process of differentiating objects from the subject we are in the process of being and becoming—a process of emerging from prior embeddedness:

> The notion of development as a sequence of internalizations, a favorite conception of psychodynamic thinking, is quite consistent with the Piagetian concept of growth. . . . In fact, something cannot be internalized until we emerge from our embeddedness in it, for it is our embeddedness, our subjectivity, that leads us to

project it onto the world in our constitution of reality. (Kegan,
1982, p. 31)

Kegan further described development as "the evolutionary motion
of differentiation (or emergence from embeddedness) and reintegration
(relation to, rather than embeddedness in, the world)" (Kegan, 1982, p.
39). Kegan also made it clear that although developmental lines such as
cognition and affect clearly develop or evolve, the context in which this
evolutionary motion occurs is that of the self. What has emerged from
embeddedness (what we are in relation to) is the distal self. Whatever
is currently identified with (what one is embedded in) is the proximate
self. Such an evolutionary or developmental conception of the self is
essential to psychotherapy because how a person settles the matter of
what is "self" and what is "other" actually construes the psycho-logic
(the underlying psychological reasons) of that person's meaning-making (Kegan, 1982).

Although therapists of many theoretical orientations may work to
help their clients make some aspect of themselves an object of their
awareness, integral theory appears to provide the most coherent and
comprehensive framework for understanding this aspect of therapy,
thus aiding therapists as they help their clients accomplish it. As was
mentioned in Chapter 4 and discussed immediately above, developing
from one stage to the next involves a process in which what used to be
the subject of one stage becomes an object of the subject of the next
stage. The more consistently a person engages this process (which is at
the heart of meditative and contemplative practices, both Eastern and
Western), the less and less that person will identify with distant parts of
herself, and the closer and closer her proximate self will be to the antecedent self. Each time that a subject ("I," self) becomes an object, a new
and higher subject ("I," self) assumes its place, until all that remains is
the antecedent self (Wilber, 2006).

The antecedent self, in integral theory, is the pure witness or locus
of awareness of the ego, self, or "I." Referred to as the "pure ego" by
James (1890/1950), the "transcendent self" by Fichte (1988), the "witness" by Avabhasa (1985), the "observing self" by Deikman (1983), and
the "I-I" by Maharshi (1985), the antecedent self is the ultimate Subject
of which everything is an object: "the Pure Witness or Pure Self, the
empty opening in which Spirit speaks" (Wilber, 2006, p. 128), whether

that Spirit is the Judeo-Christian God, Allah, Buddha-nature, or the mystery of life itself. As mystics across time and cultural traditions have attested, when we rid ourselves of our mistaken identifications with our false selves (when we recognize that what we thought of as our self/subject is actually just an aspect of our ultimate identity), what remains is the pure Self or Spirit: "the pure Witness that is never a seen object but always the pure Seer" (Wilber, 2006, p. 129). More will be said about clinical applications of the antecedent self and the witness exercise in a moment.

Self-System Pathology: When the Subject/Object Balance Becomes the Subject/Other Dynamic

At this point, it may be helpful to underscore that the statement about the subject becoming an object is a third-person conceptualization of something that occurs within a first-person view. Phenomenologically, a person experiences "what was 'I' has become 'me' (or 'mine')." This is important in order to distinguish healthy from unhealthy development.

In healthy self-development, the first-person "I" becomes the first-person "me" or "mine" (Wilber, 2006). What is most significant about this process is that even though the me/mine (object) is no longer exclusively identified with (it is, in fact, disidentified with), the me/mine/objects are owned. What was subject has become object, but not just any object; it is *my* first-person object, an object of my new subject.

In unhealthy self-development, by way of contrast, the first-person "I" becomes a second-person "you" or third-person "it" (Wilber, 2006). In other words, what was part of "I" has become *other* than I—"you" or "it"—thus the "subject/other" dynamic. Rather than assuming responsibility and ownership for aspects of oneself, the person dissociates from or projects those aspects (shadow elements) onto others or the world at large. Although differentiation and disidentification are essential to healthy development, that is the case only when what has been disidentified with is still owned as an object of oneself, as opposed to an other that is dissociated from or repressed. A great deal of psychological pathologies involve disidentifying with or dissociating from parts of oneself without integrating and assuming ownership of those parts.

To illustrate with an example, consider a client who is having difficulty with his anger. Various meditative techniques—especially what

Wilber (2000a, 2000d) refers to as the "witness exercise"—can foster clients' experiential sense of the antecedent self as a state of consciousness. Because the experience of the antecedent self or witness necessarily involves a perspective of nonattachment, "this state can give the client a feeling of I or self that is free from problems. In this sense the state can provide temporary respite from the suffering that comes from attachment" (Ingersoll & Cook-Greuter, 2007, p. 197). So the therapist instructs the client to disidentify with his anger by saying to himself, "I have anger, but I am not my anger. I am what is aware of my anger. If I can observe my anger arise and fade away, I must be the observer, not what I observe. I am the witness. I have anger, but I am not my anger." When that process proceeds well, the client does indeed realize that he is not exclusively his anger, but equally importantly, he recognizes that the anger that he experiences is *his*—it has emerged from within, and as a part of, his own body-mind. That is part of the importance of the phrase "I have anger" rather than "I am aware of anger." In the latter case, the client could be aware of another's anger (second person) or of dissociated anger overcoming him (as a third-person "it" or "other": "I don't know what happened . . . I was overcome by the anger"); in either case, the anger is viewed as "other" to one's self, and thus is not owned and integrated.

To see how people project their disowned feelings and thoughts onto others or dissociate from them so that they are perceived as third-person "its," recall the client with violent tendencies mentioned above. During one of our sessions, he seemed to be in the process of becoming angry, as evidenced by his tense face and gritted teeth and the fact that he was clenching the arms of his chair so tightly that his knuckles were literally white. When I commented that he appeared angry, he burst out, "Me? I'm not angry, but *you* seem infuriated with me!" (To the best of my self-monitoring/self-awareness capacities, I don't think I was angry; that session was videotaped, and no one in my supervision group who watched it thought I was angry, either.) Moreover, that same client, especially in the beginning of our work together, often spoke not of how "I became angry" but as "being overcome with anger [it] or violent thoughts [its]"—as if they were not part of him, but rather were ego-dystonic to his sense of self (as third-person "its").

As can be seen from this discussion and the example, having a first-person dynamic (such as "*I* am angry") converted into a second-person ("I'm not angry, *you* are!") or third-person ("The anger, *it* just took control of me") dynamic is usually unhealthy. Make note of the "1-2-3" process in the preceding sentence. Because disowning first-person qualities (dissociating from or projecting them onto second persons or third persons) is usually unhealthy, what is therapeutic is the reversal of that dynamic, what Wilber refers to as "the 3-2-1 process of (re)owning the self before transcending it" or more simply as the "3-2-1 process" (2006, p. 136). In its most skeletal form, the 3-2-1 process involves the client's converting the third-person "it" into a second-person "other" or "you" with which he can then have a dialogue, culminating in the client's "owning" or assuming responsibility for previously defended-against material such that he no longer needs to repress it, dissociate from it, or project it. In the case of the angry client, he takes the third-person anger that "overcomes" him, converts that into another (second) person who is angry (whether that is the therapist or anyone else), and then—à la empty chair work or voice dialogue work—has a dialogue with, and as, the second-person "other" who is angry. After some insights into a given client's issues and that which was disowned, projected, and so on, the goal is for the client to reidentify with the other voice (the second person) as part of one's own first person, thus moving from a second-person dialogue to a first-person monologue of ownership. The 3-2-1 process works directly with the repression barrier and the mechanisms of projection and dissociation (1-2-3), resulting in therapeutic ownership (3-2-1) of all aspects of one's being. (For more details on the 3-2-1 process, consult Wilber, 2006.)

To repeat and summarize: healthy self-development transforms "I" into "me" or "mine"; pathological self-development transforms "I" into "you" or "it." Wilber, stressing the ownership piece of this developmental process, wrote that denying ownership of one's impulses, thoughts, and feelings does not lead to healthy disidentification; it leads to denial and dissociation, both of which are often unhealthy. Disidentification is an essential component of the process, but it must occur only *after* the individual has owned her impulses, thoughts, and feelings. Whereas disidentification can lead to growth and liberation, disownership leads to symptoms and an intensification of problems.

Repression

To begin, not all forgetting is repression; there is a continuum of forgetting, with simple inattention at one end and forceful submersion at the
other end. Moreover, repression proper always involves material that is
somehow related to one's self-sense, unconsciously forgetting what was
once identified with, so that the material is now relegated to a place
beneath one's attentional radar. At times, the self can repress material
that it has not yet identified with if that material is becoming close
enough to the self that it could be identified with and such identification entails some sort of perceived danger or threat to the self-system
(thus, only self-related aspects—as opposed to, for example, the cognitive line—are repressed). Likewise, not everything that is forgotten
results in neurotic symptoms; only unconscious material that has been
repressed seeks expression in the form of disguised, symbolic symptoms. One of the values of an AQAL conceptualization of issues such
as this is the recognition that repression occurs only in the self and
self-related lines of development—and usually only when the self has
identified with something that threatens it. Moreover, an integral conceptualization of unconscious psychodynamics reveals not just one form
of unconscious but five qualitatively distinct types of unconscious. (For
more on Wilber's theory of repression, which is grounded in the work of
Freud, Jung, Piaget, Sullivan, and Loevinger, consult Wilber, 1999c).

Five Different Types of Unconsciousness

Many approaches to counseling and psychotherapy commonly assume
that some kind of "unconscious" simply exists. Although there are
certainly differences between how, for example, Freud, Jung, Rogers,
and Perls conceived of the unconscious, Wilber (1980; 1999c) has long
argued that any comprehensive understanding of unconsciousness must
account for not only dynamic factors and structural features but also
developmental or evolutionary issues. For example, although adults who
have learned various rules, roles, and responsibilities may repress guilt
for some action or failure to act, it makes no sense to speak of a two-
year-old as having repressed guilt. Thus, what is in "the" unconscious
is a function of developmental issues; the entirety of what is outside of
consciousness is not merely given from the beginning (Wilber, 1999c).

The following are five different *types* of unconsciousness, not different levels of unconsciousness.

The *ground-unconscious* consists of all of the (basic) deep structures that exist as potentials that may emerge in any given individual's future. These developmental potentials are undifferentiated and enfolded in the ground-unconscious: "All of those structures are unconscious, but they are not repressed because they have not yet entered consciousness. Development or evolution consists of a series of hierarchical transformations, unfoldings, or differentiations of the deep structures out of the ground-unconscious" (Wilber, 1999c, p. 247). Wilber intended a neutral meaning with his choice of the word *ground*—he explicitly does not want the ground-unconscious confused with the "Ground of Being" even though there are dimensions of the ground-unconscious that are "all-encompassing" (Wilber, 1999c, p. 247). The following four types of unconsciousness relate to the ground-unconscious.

The *archaic-unconscious* is "the most primitive and least developed structures of the ground-unconscious" (Wilber, 1999c, p. 249), including alimentary drives, emotional-sexual energies, and mental-phantasmic images. Like the ground-unconscious, the archaic-unconscious is not repressed. Freud realized this fact when he wrote that "it is still true that all that is repressed is *Ucs.* [unconscious], but not all that is *Ucs.* is repressed" (1962, p. 8). Not everything that is unconscious is repressed, because some of the unconscious is simply unconscious from the beginning: "Each single process belongs in the first place to the unconscious psychical system; from this system it can under certain conditions proceed further into the conscious system" (Freud, 1935, p. 260). Wilber agrees with both Freud (1963) and Jung (1963) that this aspect of the unconscious is part of our phylogenetic heritage. To summarize, "the archaic-unconscious is not the product of personal experience; it is initially unconscious but not repressed; it contains the earliest and most primitive structures to unfold from the ground-unconscious . . . largely preverbal" (Wilber, 1999c, p. 249–250).

The *submergent-unconscious* is what most therapists probably think of when they consider the "unconscious"; it consists of material that had previously emerged from the ground-unconscious into an individual's consciousness, only to be submerged beneath that individual's awareness. As such, the submergent-unconscious can entail any and all structures that have emerged—whether individual or collective, prepersonal or personal or suprapersonal. Moreover, the reasons that specific content is in the submergent-unconscious span a continuum of inattention, ranging from simple forgetting to the repression proper (dynamically forceful forgetting) that Freud (1962, 1935, 1963) wrote so much about. Like Jung (1968), Wilber refers to the personal dimension of the submergent-unconscious as the "shadow," and it spans a spectrum ranging from the more developed verbal scripts and injunctions "all the way down to the primal chaos of the unstructured or barely structured *materia prima*, the pleromatic fusion base of the archaic-unconscious" (1999c, p. 251).

The *embedded-unconscious* appears to have puzzled Freud, though he vaguely hinted at it when he wrote that unconsciousness is "a quality which can have many meanings" (1962, p. 8). Freud more directly described the embedded-unconscious when he stressed that "it is certain that much of the ego is itself unconscious" (1967, p. 41) even though, obviously, the ego itself is not repressed: "we can say that the patient's resistance arises from his ego" (Freud, 1967, p. 41). The ego—which Freud wrote in German as *das Ich* (the "I")—is what each of us (each "I") is embedded in. Thus, what is unconscious yet not repressed (the embedded ego) is responsible for "doing the repression." Piaget's (1977) and Beck's (1979) notions of schemas and Adler's (cited in Ansbacher & Ansbacher, 1956) "schema of apperception" provide similar examples of how embedded structures influence, connect, and organize our perceptions and experience without our being conscious of the schemas themselves. Because the embedded-unconscious

> is embedded *as* the self, the self cannot totally or accurately see it . . . It is that aspect of the ground-unconscious which, upon emergence, emerges *as* the self-system and so remains essentially unconscious, possessing the power to send other elements to the repressed-submergent-unconscious. (Wilber, 1999c, p. 254)

In other words, regardless of our developmental stage in life, we cannot directly observe the structures in which we are embedded.

The *emergent-unconscious* refers to those deep structures that have not yet been identified with or realized out of their potentiality at any given point of a person's life course. For example, for a person whose center of gravity hovers around Wilber's representational mind, every basic structure of consciousness beyond the representational mind is part of that person's emergent-unconscious (in this case, the rule/role mind, formal-reflexive, vision-logic, as well as the suprapersonal structure; it may help the reader to consult Table 4.1 on page 82 in Chapter 4). Along these lines, Freud wrote that every mental process

> first exists in an unconscious state or phase, and only develops out of this into a conscious phase, much as a photograph is first a negative and then becomes a picture through the printing of the positive. But not every negative is made into a positive, and it is just as little necessary that every unconscious mental process should convert itself into a conscious one. (1935, p. 260)

Integral therapists are fortunate to operate from such a comprehensive theoretical map that includes not only prepersonal and suprapersonal realms of development but also an emergent-unconscious with developmental potentials awaiting realization by each and all. Thus, even for a client with a center of gravity at vision-logic—someone that most conventional therapists would consider a paragon of mental health and self-actualization—integral therapists recognize several suprapersonal stages of development that rest beyond the strictly personal levels that revolve around an isolated, skin-encapsulated ego (Watts, 1966). Importantly, for people with primarily prepersonal or personal altitudes of development, the suprapersonal realm is not repressed, filtered, or screened out of awareness; the suprapersonal simply has not had the developmental opportunity to unfold. As an analogy, we do not say that a one-year-old is repressing his awareness of language and grammar; neither is he or many adults repressing the suprapersonal—not yet, that is (Wilber, 1999c).

Once people have stabilized at vision-logic, however, their egos/selves are strong enough to repress not only earlier realms (shadow elements deriving from sexual, aggressive, and other body-related impulses) but also the further reaches of human nature; the superconscious can be just as readily sealed off as can be the subconscious. Those aspects of the ground-unconscious that are actually repressed or sealed out of awareness are referred to as the *emergent-repressed-unconscious*. Thus, once it appears that suprapersonal dimensions of a client's self are unconscious not because they are too far in the developmental future but because of actual resistance to them, we may speak of what Maslow (1971), Assagioli (1988), and Wilber (1999c) refer to as *defenses against transcendence,* some of which include rationalization ("Transcendence is a pathological fantasy"); desacralization (Maslow's description of refusing to recognize transcendent values); isolation ("My consciousness and self-awareness are supposed to be contained within my skin"); substitution (attempting to meet one's needs for higher realms with experiences from other realms, as in drugs, sex, adventure, etc.); and death terror ("I'm terrified of dying to my ego—what will be left of me?"). Because many, if not most, conventional therapists do not understand the higher forms of the emergent-unconscious, they have tended to conflate them with the submergent-unconscious. In doing so, they conceptualize the suprapersonal not as the emergence of a higher structure but as the reappearance of a lower one. Paraphrasing Wilber's occasional polemics, they reduce genuine mystical experiences to infantile breast union, God to a teething nipple, and all suprapersonal unitive experiences to prepersonal pleromatic fusion, and in so doing, they congratulate themselves for having explained the Mystery (1999c).

Because no integral discussion of the self-system is complete without addressing the various types of unconscious, this section has served as an introduction to them. Integral therapists believe that most conventional approaches have not adequately differentiated the above types of unconscious dynamics and thus confuse them or consequently reduce suprapersonal potentials to prepersonal fantasies. For more on the different types of unconscious, consult Wilber (1999c, pp. 243–263).

Subpersonalities

In addition to everything above, the self-system also consists of various subpersonalities, which in their benign forms Wilber referred to as "functional self-presentations that navigate particular psychosocial situations" (2000e, p. 101). In other words, a subpersonality is a particular thought-action-feeling-physiology mode that operates in order to cope with certain types of situations. An example that many therapists will recognize is the harsh critic that, when confronted with one's own and/ or others' fallibility, responds with overly judgmental thoughts; with critical words and punitive actions; with angry, superior feelings; and with an aroused and tense physiology. Subpersonalities are often experienced as different "voices" or components of one's internal dialogues (one's conscience, for example, is often conceived of as a subpersonality). As such, one's subpersonalities constitute a subconscious society of selves that the proximate self ideally is aware of and allows expression of as appropriate (Wilber, 2000e).

Some of the more common subpersonalities that have been identified in various psychotherapeutic systems include id, ego, and superego (psychoanalysis); child, parent, and adult ego states (transactional analysis); top dog and underdog (Gestalt therapy); and the critic (Gendlin's focusing). Other, more generic ones include the false self and authentic self, and the achiever and jokester. Subpersonalities frequently revolve around particular archetypal forms and often include social roles such as mother, father, teacher, or hero. Wilber has posited that people can also form subpersonalities associated with the suprapersonal dimensions of their being. Page 11 of the Integral Intake includes a checklist of subpersonalities that clients may identify as problematic in some way.

In general, subpersonalities are pathological only to the degree that they are dissociated from or otherwise screened out of awareness. Thus, many clients will not be able to recognize or "own" their subpersonalities. Rather than owning their subpersonalities as aspects of who they are, people who have repressed or dissociated from their subpersonalities will, when a particular context triggers them, unknowingly act from an embeddedness within their submerged personae. They will thus act, feel, and think from a specific subpersonality without recognizing that they are operating from such. In other words, they may *later* report that something (i.e., their top dog subpersonality) "overcame" them and "took control"—but that is exactly what we would expect them to say, because at that moment their "hidden subject" (the psychological space from which they were operating) was the top dog, a subpersonality they do not identify with but rather dissociate from. Thus, it doesn't feel like them—it feels like something other or alien overcame them—precisely because they have not identified with and integrated that subpersonality within their self-system.

At the severe end of the dissociative spectrum, we encounter dissociative identity disorder (formerly known as multiple personality disorder). More commonly, subpersonalities are submerged or dissociated at mild to moderate levels. Wilber and other personality theorists suggest that most people have about a dozen subpersonalities. Moreover, these subpersonalities can form at any point along the developmental course, and often people have different subpersonalities that do seem to represent different stages of their developmental histories: people can have archaic subpersonalities stemming from the first years of life, magical or mythical subpersonalities that formed in early childhood, and rational subpersonalities that formed in adolescence or later, as well as soul- or transpersonal subpersonalities (Wilber, 2000e).

What appears essential for healthy functioning is the extent to which the self can willfully disidentify with a functional subpersonality, and thus be in control of or master it—to have some measure of choice as to when and how the subpersonality is engaged—rather than merely being the victim of it or being "taken over" by it without one's awareness or against one's will. However, in order to be able to disidentify with a subpersonality within yourself, you first have to be aware of that subpersonality and recognize it as part of who you are, a part that you can disidentify with and transcend, allowing it intentional expression in circumstances that will not be of detriment to you or others. The therapeutic catalyst appears to be clients' awareness and recognition of their subpersonalities, which allows them to convert those "hidden subjects" into "conscious objects" of one's attention, with the goal of integrating them into their overall self-system.

The construct of subpersonalities adds another dimension of complexity to our conceptualization of clients. Not only do the sundry developmental lines emerge relatively independently of each other, the various subpersonalities are also often very "uneven." In other words, even within an individual who is overall very mature, healthy, and "developed," there may exist archaic subpersonalities (such as the child ego state) within that person that are utterly narcissistic and egocentric—as when someone who is usually quite emotionally controlled, empathic, and rational explodes into a temper tantrum. Subpersonalities may take charge and express themselves during a period as short as a few seconds to as long as a few hours. Thus, despite the linear logic of integral theory's developmental model, integral therapists recognize that the actual dynamics of any given person's life trajectory are usually anything but a monolithic, linear progression; rather, they involve a great many ups and downs, regressions, and so forth.

Conclusion

This chapter has concluded the theoretical explication of integral counseling and psychotherapy, addressing states of consciousness, personality types, and the self-system.

These three constructs, in addition to the four quadrants and developmental levels and lines, account for a tremendous amount of commonality among humans. Importantly, however, the almost endless combinations and permutations of these numerous factors as they are creatively expressed by different people in different times and cultures accounts for the diversity of human nature and the uniqueness of each human being. To close this chapter, Wilber has repeatedly emphasized that the psychological structures that have been discussed in his many books, as well as in this book, are not rigid structures but "can better be understood as formative habits of evolution, 'Kosmic memories,' . . . and not pregiven modes into which the world is poured" (2000e, p. 145).

Note

1. According to Wilber (1999c, 1999d), the pre/trans fallacy is a form of category error in which a clinician (or anyone, for that matter) confuses the prepersonal realm with the suprapersonal/transpersonal realm. Because the prepersonal and suprapersonal dimensions are both nonpersonal, those who are not educated and trained to counsel people with suprapersonal issues tend to diagnostically reduce suprapersonal experiences to psychotic (prepersonal) episodes (Freud and many conventional therapists have fallen prey to this error). The converse form of the pre/trans fallacy is to diagnostically elevate psychotic (prepersonal) episodes into suprapersonal experiences (Jung and many transpersonal therapists have been guilty of this error). Grof & Grof (1989) and Scotton, Chinen, & Battista (1996) contain numerous chapters that address issues pertinent to differentially diagnosing pre- and trans-/supra-personal issues in therapy.

7

PUTTING IT ALL TOGETHER

Interpreting Clients' Responses and
Treatment Planning (Case Examples)

Introduction

Chapters 2 through 6 introduced integral theory and its components: all quadrants, all levels, all lines, all states, all types. This chapter will attempt to put all of that material together by examining two cases that span a significant developmental spectrum, one of which involves a fairly high-functioning male, the other of which involves a female client with a borderline personality organization. I intentionally chose two very different clients to demonstrate how integral metatheory provides a framework and justification for working quite differently with different individuals.

This chapter will begin with a brief introduction to issues pertaining to treatment planning. The bulk of the chapter consists of two case examples. In each case, I present the reader with each client's actual completed responses to the Integral Intake. Next, I discuss the initial session and the client's presenting problem(s), my initial AQAL assessment, the client's integral psychograph and *DSM* diagnosis, a case narrative that leads to the initial/tentative treatment plan for that client, interventions and how actual sessions progressed, and a conclusion.

A Brief Primer of Integral Treatment Planning

People seek professional counseling and psychotherapy for many different reasons. Not only do their problems vary, but different people desire drastically different goals, which span a spectrum from immediate symptom relief to general life improvement to profound self-transformation/liberation. These three constructs bear similarity to what Mahoney (1991, 2003) described as problem, pattern, and process levels of therapeutic work. It is important to find out during the first session what clients hope to gain from therapy and how much time and resources they have to devote to those goals. Most clients do not arrive at therapy hoping for self-transformation and deep process work, which is analogous to what Bateson (1972) referred to as "second-order change" (which often involves intensive, long-term self-observation, experimentation, and perseverance, with spiritual disciplines/practices often playing significant roles), but rather hope to solve specific problems and attain some immediate relief from their painful symptoms (such as depression and anxiety). Intermediately, many clients hope for more than mere symptom relief but are not as ambitious as those who want to radically alter their sense of identity; they tend to want general but significant life improvement (increased self-esteem, more intimacy in their relationships, perhaps more meaningful work).

Mahoney's three levels of therapeutic work (problem, pattern, and process) and Bateson's notions of first- and second-order change bear significant relationships to what integral therapists refer to as three degrees of therapeutic focus:

1. *Problem-focused translative work:* tends to be solution-focused and heavily cognitive-behavioral. Part of the cognitive reorganization may involve psychoeducation regarding integral theory and integral life practices (ILPs, discussed below) (Wilber, 2005b); this can often be accomplished in one to eight sessions.

2. *Pattern-focused translative work:* goes beyond working on isolated problems and addresses the underlying patterns and deep structures/schemas that lead to clients continually encountering similar problems in their lives. This often involves more cognitive-emotional work and requires more mindfulness of how core beliefs, thoughts, and so on impact feelings and behaviors. This level of work may require clients to more deeply absorb ideas of integral theory as a way of perceiving self, world, and others differently; it usually takes at least 8 sessions and often 30 or more.

process.

3. *Transformative work* involves persistent, diligent practice of ILPs and moment-to-moment process work/self-transcendence/spiritual practice. Usually takes a minimum of a year or more; more often, it requires several years and then lifelong maintenance work.

Once you have read your client's responses to the Integral Intake, you then develop a (tentative) treatment plan that systematically addresses the issues that you identify as most pressing in the client's AQAL matrix. Although the most critical issues may involves states and types (Chapter 6), it has been my experience that most of the time what draws my clinical attention are quadratic and developmental (levels, lines, self-system) issues. This is the point at which I most often sketch an initial psychograph of the client. I often wait until the third or fourth session, when I have introduced many of my clients to the notions of quadrants, levels, and lines, to ask them to construct a psychograph of themselves (with clients who are seriously disturbed, I do not ask them to do this). If my appraisals are significantly different from their self-assessment, we spend time discussing those differences.

When clients report several or numerous problems, it is often helpful to address a problem with which you are confident that the client will experience quick positive effects; this gives clients tangible, experiential evidence that therapy is helpful, that change is possible, that hope is warranted, and that their active engagement in therapy will be to their benefit (Mahoney, 1991; Garfield, 2003).

As a therapist reflects upon a client's integral psychograph (including developmental levels and lines) and her four-quadrant profile, the therapist then tailors a therapeutic approach most appropriate to that particular client. Again, the two most salient features of this tailoring are quadratic and developmental (Chapters 3, 4, and 5; consult especially Table 4.1 on page 82 of Chapter 4). Additionally, ILPs—practices that honor and nurture the entire human being, from the body, emotions, and mind all the way to soul and spirit as each unfolds in self ("I," UL), culture ("we," LL), and nature ("it" and "its," UR and LR)—often play a significant role in the construction of treatment plans. In essence, regardless of one's level of development, one attempts to be as "all quadrants, all levels" as one can be (Wilber, 2006, p. 26). The basic principle of ILPs is that clients are most likely to experience positive outcomes when they exercise and cultivate as many aspects of their being as possible—a form of therapeutic cross-training, if you will. For many clients, merely thinking differently is insufficient to effect the change they desire (restructuring core schemas involves much more than changing automatic thought patterns). It has been my experience that clients who persistently engage in and practice a personalized ILP regimen achieve their desired goals far more often than those who do not.

Basic Premises of an ILP

Integral therapists often begin co-constructing a client's/Lp by addressing the client's self-system, which can be strengthened by a broad spectrum of practices ranging from physical (weightlifting, jogging, yoga, diet) to emotional (counseling, psychotherapy, qi gong, conscious relationships), mental (reading, study, visualizations, affirmations), and spiritual (meditation, contemplative prayer). Significantly, these waves of existence must be strengthened not only within one's self (UL, UR) but also within cultural and social systems (LL, LR). Thus, community service and advocacy-related activities are encouraged, from volunteering at homeless shelters or hospices to participating in local government to improve school policies, ensure equitable work practices and pay, or increase the availability of mental health services to lower-socioeconomic-status populations. Attending to the LL quadrant also involves clients' working on their (inter)personal relationships in general (whether with bosses and employees, friends, parents, children, or romantic partners) in order to further their own and others' development. Attending to the waves of existence in the LR quadrant also requires that nature is viewed not merely as an instrumental context of our desires and needs but as an essential aspect of our own being and becoming. Thus, actively respecting and (con)serving nature, from recycling and celebrating nature to participating in organizations such as the Nature Conservancy or Sierra Club that work to promote ecological health, simultaneously honors and protects our natural environment. Regardless of the specific exercises or components of one's ILP (and the preceding offers just a few possibilities for an ILP; individuals can create literally endless combinations and permutations of ILPs that are most appropriate to their values, concerns, and proclivities), ILPs attempt to exercise as many as possible of the basic structures of consciousness—from physical and emotional to mental and spiritual (all levels)—in self, culture, and nature (all quadrants). Helpful, and indeed almost essential, to successful, continued engagement with an ILP is some sort of communal support, which can range from a formal group or institution to family and friends who encourage and inspire such practice (Murphy, 1993; Wilber, 2000e).

Four Broad Classes of Treatment Plans

Wilber offered the following examples as broad guidelines:

- A client with borderline pathology, impulsive ego, preconventional morality, and splitting defense mechanism might be offered: structure building therapy, bibliotherapy, weight training, nutritional supplements, pharmacological agents (as required), verbalization and narrative training, and short sessions of a concentration-type meditation (not awareness-training meditation, which tends to dismantle subjective structure, which the borderline does not yet adequately possess).
- A client with anxiety neurosis, phobic elements, conventional morality, repression and displacement defense mechanisms, belongingness needs, and persona self-sense might be offered: uncovering psychotherapy, bioenergetics, script analysis, jogging or biking (or some other individual sport), desensitization, dream analysis/therapy, and vipassana meditation.
- A client with existential depression, postconventional morality, suppression and sublimation defense mechanisms, self-actualization needs, and a centauric self-sense might be offered: existential analysis, dream therapy, a team sport (e.g., volleyball, basketball), bibliotherapy, t'ai chi chuan (or prana circulating therapy), community service, and kundalini yoga.
- A client who has been practicing Zen mediation for several years, but suffers life-goal apathy and depression, deadening of affect, postconventional morality, postformal cognition, self-transcendence needs, and psychic self-sense might be offered: uncovering therapy, combination weight training and jogging, tantric deity-yoga (visualization meditation), tonglen (compassion training), and community service. (Wilber, 2000c, p. 643)

Wilber stressed that the goal for the near future will be for the above types of integral recommendations to "rest on actual clinical evidence and research into the effects of various transformative practices on the major developmental streams . . . not only which practices are indicated for specific occasion, but just as important, which are contraindicated" (2000c, p. 644). As you will soon see in the following case examples, Denise closely approximates the first scenario above, and Gary is in between the second and third scenarios.

Case Example 1: Gary

Gary's Completed Integral Intake

INTEGRAL INTAKE

Andre Marquis, Ph.D.

Assistant Professor of Counseling and Human Development
University of Rochester

Client's Name _____Gary_____Age __25__Date First Seen _____
Home Phone (___)_____(message: Y/N) Work Phone (___)_____(message: Y/N)
Address _____City_____ Zip_____
Date of Birth __February 1981___ Gender (M) Referral Source _____
Emergency Contact: Name _____ Phone (___)_____
**(Please use the back side of this form if you need more space to respond to *any* of
the questions.)**

PRELIMINARY ISSUES AND PREVIOUS THERAPY

What is the primary concern or problem for which you are seeking help?

**I'm feeling a lack of direction—having trouble setting clear goals for myself. I feel
unbalanced in the sense that one area of my life—for example, work—tends to
consume all my energy. I tend to get stressed more easily than normal and I feel a
desire to avoid conflicts or addressing issues.**

What makes it better? What makes it worse?

**My stress level tends to get a bit better (lessens) when I set achievable goals to work
toward. Interpersonal conflicts (argument with partner, coworker) feel almost
paralyzing at times. I have trouble controlling my mental replay of my mistakes.**

Are there any *immediate* challenges or issues that need our attention? Yes/**No** If yes,
please describe.

**I don't think any of my concerns are dire. They seem to have been building for some
time now.**

Have you had previous counseling or psychotherapy? <u>Yes</u>/No From when to when? With whom?

Briefly in college, with graduate students who were working as counselors.

What was your experience of therapy? (What was your previous therapy like?)

I enjoyed talking with an impartial person, didn't feel like I was growing; wasn't ready.

What was most helpful about your therapy?

Speaking with an objective "stranger."

What was least helpful about your therapy?

We met infrequently—I didn't feel a sense of continuity, like we were working toward something.

What did you learn about yourself through your previous therapy?

I learned that I am generally very self-aware. I know from introspection where most issues lie.

What do you expect from me and our work together?

I'd like your help in setting clear goals for my therapy.

EXPERIENCE: Individual-Interior

What are your strengths?

I am intelligent and I enjoy learning new things. I am compassionate and conscientious.

What are your weaknesses?

I have a poor self-image, low self-esteem sometimes. I can be avoidant and passive-aggressive.

How would you describe your general mood/feelings?

My general mood is happy, sometimes overwhelmed. Sometimes I feel disconnected and not extremely hopeful.

What emotions do you most often feel most strongly?

Loneliness, boredom.

What are the ways in which you care for and comfort yourself when you feel distressed?

I listen to music, sometimes overeat, often go for a drive.

How do you deal with strong emotions in yourself?

I try to find outlets: talking or praying or writing about things.

How do you respond to stressful situations and other problems?

I usually either confront something right away, or choose not to deal with it until I am forced to do so.

How do you make decisions (for example, do you use logic and reason, or do you trust your gut and heart)?

A little of both. I rationalize everything. I go over and over possibilities in my mind, often agonizing but ultimately going by gut feeling.

Are you aware of recurring images or thoughts (either while awake or in dreams)? **Yes**/ No If yes, please describe.

In dreams—family members, stages/auditoriums.

Have you *ever* attempted to seriously harm or kill yourself or anyone else? Yes/**No** If yes, please describe.

Violence upsets me.

Are you *presently* experiencing suicidal thoughts? Yes/**No** If yes, please describe.

I sometimes envision car crashes, but I think that's tied more to recognition of my own vulnerability.

Has anyone in your family ever attempted or committed suicide? **Yes**/No If yes, please describe.

My cousin tried to overdose on drugs once. My dad's cousin shot himself.

Have there been any serious illnesses, births, deaths, or other losses or changes in your family that have affected you? **Yes**/No If yes, please describe.

My parents adopted two children just after I left home for college. That was something of an adjustment. My grandfather recently passed away.

What is your earliest memory?

Playing with a top in my grandmother's kitchen on the floor.

What is your happiest memory?

Church services with my grandmother.

What is your most painful memory?

I have many. I'm not sure.

Where in your body do you feel stress (shoulders, back, jaw, etc.)?

Shoulders, neck, jaw.

Do you have ways in which you express yourself creatively and/or artistically? **Yes**/No
  If yes, please describe.
I write sometimes. I used to play piano but don't have that outlet anymore.

Describe your leisure time (hobbies/enjoyment).
**I feel like I waste a lot of time. I like to read and do so sometimes. I shop
occasionally never for anything in particular—just like to be around people.**

Have you ever been a victim of, or witnessed, verbal, emotional, physical, and/or sexual
  abuse? If yes, please describe.
**I have been in emotionally/physically abusive relationships in the past. Sometimes
I feel that I was seriously abused in the past but no clear memory.**

In general, how satisfied are you with your life?
Not at all   1   2   3   4   **5**   6   7   Very

In general, how do you feel about yourself (self-esteem)?
Very bad   1   2   3   **4**   5   6   7   Very good

In general, how much control do you feel you have over your life and how you feel?
None at all   1   2   3   4   **5**   6   7   A lot

Please mark any of the following emotions that you often feel:

_____ angry

_____ sad

___x___ lonely

_____ afraid

_____ anxious/worried

_____ shameful/guilty

_____ jealous

_____ happy

_____ grateful/thankful

___x___ sexual/erotic

_____ excited

_____ energetic

_____ hopeful

_____ relaxed/peaceful

_____ other emotions you often feel:

_____

BEHAVIOR: Individual-Exterior

Please list any medications you are presently taking (dosage/amount and what the medication is for).

None

Do you have a primary care physician? **Yes**/No   If yes, who is it? **Dr. Jane Doe, M.D.**
Height **6' 1"** _____ Weight__**220**lbs.

When was your last physical?

3 months ago.

Were there any noteworthy results (diseases, blood pressure, cholesterol, etc.)?
The doctor encouraged me to watch my diet and monitor cholesterol.

Have you ever suffered a head injury or other serious injury? Yes/**No**   If yes, please describe.

What other significant medical problems have you experienced or are you experiencing now?
I have headaches frequently.

Please mark any of the following behaviors or bodily feelings that are true of you:

_____ drink too much

_____ use illegal and/or mind-altering drugs

__x__ eat too much

_____ eat too little

__x__ neglect friends and family

__x__ neglect self and your own needs

_____ difficulty being kind and loving to yourself

_____ act in ways that end up hurting yourself or others

_____ lose your temper

_____ seem to *not* have control over some behaviors

_____ think about suicide

__x__ have difficulty concentrating

__x__ spend more money than you can afford to

_____ crying

_____ any other behaviors you would like me to know about?

___x___   headaches

_____   menstrual problems

_____   dizziness

_____   heart tremors

_____   jitters

_____   sexual preoccupations

_____   tingling/numbness

___x___   excessive tiredness

_____   hear or see things not actually there

_____   blackouts

_____   do you have any other bodily pains or difficulties? Yes/No If yes,
what are they?

In general, how would you rate your physical health?

Very unhealthy   1   2   3   4   **5**   6   7   Very healthy

Describe your current sleeping patterns (When do you sleep? How many hours per 24 hours? Do you sleep straight through or do you wake up during sleep time?).
I fall asleep around 1 a.m., get up at 8 a.m.; 7 hours, restless sleep.

Do you feel rested upon waking? Yes/**No**

Describe your usual eating habits (types of food, and how much).
Simple prep foods: sandwiches, snack foods . . . not usually in great quantities—I generally stop eating when I feel full.

Do you take vitamins and other nutritional supplements? **Yes**/No If yes, please describe.
Occasionally take a multivitamin.

Describe your drug and alcohol use (both past and present).
Drank too much in college, don't drink much anymore (less than one drink/week); experimented with ex—never any other drug (tried Extasy [sic] 3 times in 2004).

Do you engage in some form of exercise (aerobic and/or strength building)? Yes/**No** If yes, please describe.

Do you have any communication impairments (sight, hearing, speech)? Yes/**No** If yes, please describe.

CULTURE: Collective-Interior

Describe your relationships, including friends, family, and coworkers.
I'm comfortable with and enjoy my coworkers. My family is far away. I talk with Mom about once a week, Dad once a month, and my sister Kathryn about once or twice a week. I am closest to Kathryn. Mom and Dad have issues with my homosexuality. Friends—I've been a little estranged, but I'm coming back.

What is important and meaningful to you (what matters the most to you)?
Spirituality is important to me; serving/helping others is important.

In general, how satisfied are you with your friendships and other relationships?
Not at all   1   2   3   4   **5**   6   7   Very

In general, how comfortable are you in social situations?
Not at all   1   2   3   4   **5**   6   7   Very

In general, how satisfied are you with your religion/spirituality?
Not at all   1   2   3   **4**   5   6   7   Very

Which emotions were encouraged or commonly expressed in your family of origin (family you grew up with)?
Anger, frustration, happiness, embarrassment.

Which emotions were discouraged or not allowed in your family of origin?
Disappointment, boredom, sexuality.

What emotions are most comfortable for you now?
Frustration, happiness, peacefulness.

What emotions are most uncomfortable for you now?
Embarrassment, guilt.

How do you identify yourself ethnically? How important is your ethnic culture to you?
White Anglo-Saxon; Appalachian.

How did your family of origin express love and care?
Words, physical (hugging)—never felt quite comfortable.

How does your current family express love and care?
Words and physically.

How did your family of origin express disapproval?
Words. In a way that induces feelings of guilt/disappointment/shame.

How does your current family express disapproval?
Words. In a way that is healthy and constructive.

Describe your romantic/love relationships, if any.
Just ended a 5-month relationship that felt stifling, trapping, controlling, not trusting.

Describe your sex life. How satisfied are you with your sex life?
I don't have sex often (less than 1x per week), though I masturbate daily.

Have you ever been a victim of any form of prejudice or discrimination (racial, gender, etc.) or felt that you were disadvantaged in terms of power and privilege in society? Yes/No If yes, please describe.
[This question wasn't on the Integral Intake at the time I counseled Gary.]

SOCIAL SYSTEMS: Collective-Exterior

Describe your current *physical* home environment. (For example, describe the layout of your home and other general conditions, such as privacy, whether it is well-lighted, whether you have A/C and, heating, etc.)
I rent a room in a 4-bedroom house. It is large, well lighted, and physically comfortable. Common areas are very dirty because of 3 dogs.

Describe your neighborhood. (Is it safe/dangerous, nice/unpleasant, quiet/loud, etc.?)
I get along well with roommates. Jason is loud, controlling, obnoxious; Mark is quiet; Craig is never home; Kevin is wonderful.

Describe your current social home environment. (How would an outside observer describe how you get along with those who live with you?)
Average suburb . . . seems safe generally though my car has been robbed twice.

Describe your work environment (include coworkers and supervisors who directly affect you).
My supervisor is very hard to work with—lacks interpersonal skills; inconsistent management style. My subordinates are fun, idealistic.

Do you have a romantic partner? Yes/**No** Have you been married before? Yes/No If yes, please describe.
Recently broken up.

Are you currently involved in a custody dispute? Yes/**No** If yes, please describe.

Have you had any involvement with the legal system (incarceration, probation, etc.)? Yes/No If yes, please describe.
[This question wasn't on the Integral Intake at the time I counseled Gary.]

What aspects of your life are stressful to you? Please describe.
**Romantic relationships; work; family. I would prefer to talk about these . . . too
much to write.**

What sort of support system do you have (friends, family, or religious community who
help you in times of need)?
I have a few very good friends I can count on; one sister I can depend on.

List your family of origin (family you grew up with), beginning with the oldest,
include parents and yourself.

Name	Age	Gender	Relationship to you (include "step-," "half-," etc.)
Mom, Lesli	**49**	**F**	**Mom**
Dad, Steve	**50**	**M**	**Dad**
Jessica	**27**	**F**	**Sister (biological)**
Stephanie	**24**	**F**	**Sister (biological)**
Melinda	**5**	**F**	**Sister (adopted)**
Julie	**7**	**F**	**Sister (adopted)**

What is your educational background?
B.A. international studies [*midwestern*] state university.

What is your occupation? **Resource developer.**
 How satisfied are you with the type of work you do?
Not at all   1   2   3   **4**   5   6   7   Very

What is your yearly income? **$ 30,000** per year. How satisfied are you with your
standard of living?
Not at all   1   2   3   4   **5**   6   7   Very

Describe any family history of mental illness. **Depression heavy on Mom's side.**

List your current family or all the people you currently live with (begin with the oldest
person and include yourself).

Name	Age	Gender	Relationship to you (include "step-," "half-," etc.)
Jason	**47**	**M**	**Roommate**
Mark	**42**	**M**	**Roommate**
Craig	**35**	**M**	**Roommate**
Kevin	**30**	**M**	**Roommate**

Are you involved with any organizations? Yes/**No** If yes, please describe.

Do you participate in any volunteer work? Yes/**No** if yes, please describe.

Please mark any of the following that you experienced difficulty or problems with. Also indicate to the right of the problem in the parentheses (   ) your approximate age when the difficulty or problem occurred:

[This checklist wasn't on the Integral Intake at the time I counseled Gary]

_____ nursing and/or eating (   )

_____ toilet training (   )

_____ crawling or walking (   )

_____ talking (   )

_____ nail biting or other nervous habits (   )

_____ going to school/separating from caregivers (   )

_____ cruelty to animals or people (   )

_____ serious illnesses or injuries (   )

_____ academic problems (   )

_____ social problems (   )

_____ moves or other family stresses (   )

_____ abuse (emotional, physical, or sexual) (   )

_____ any problems with sexual maturation (   )

_____ being made fun of or joked about at school, home, or elsewhere (   )

_____ self-destructiveness (risky sex, eating problems, drug use, excessive risk-taking, etc.) (   )

_____ fitting into social groups (   )

_____ standing up for what you believe in when it differs from your peers' views (   )

_____ making important decisions, especially when they differ from social norms (   )

_____ any existential dilemmas (   )

_____ any religious and/or spiritual experiences (these could be completely positive) (   )

The following is a list of various parts, aspects, or subpersonalities that many people notice within themselves in certain situations, but not in others. Please mark any of the following that you have experienced difficulty or problems with. Often, it is only after the fact that we notice that we were behaving, thinking, or feeling in a problematic manner. Also, please indicate to the right of the problem the situation or context in which you noticed this part of yourself.

[This checklist wasn't on the Integral Intake at the time I counseled Gary.]

_____ irresponsible child _____

_____ critical parent _____

_____ dominating "top dog" _____

_____ prone-to-fail "underdog" _____

_____ overly harsh judge or critic _____

_____ false or phony self _____

_____ unworthy, not-good-enough self _____

_____ grandiose, better-than-everyone-else self _____

_____ other, please describe _____

Is there anything else you want me to know about? (use the back of the page if you need to).

[Gary left this blank.]

Initial Session and Presenting Problem(s)

Gary, a single, gay 25-year-old Caucasian male, contacted a community clinic after being referred through his managed care network.[1] Upon initially meeting with me, Gary complained first and foremost of lacking direction in life, having difficulty establishing clear goals, and "feeling unbalanced" in his life. He also expressed struggling with multiple demands at work as well as feeling frustrated with aspects of his romantic relationships, specifically his most recent, which had just ended. He also described occasionally feeling uncomfortable around straight men. Gary reported that his concerns were "nothing serious or critical" but that they had intensified after his recent breakup and included experiencing mild depression, anxiety, social isolation/loneliness, and poor self-esteem. Gary also expressed concern with his lack of a social network and issues with his career.

In the initial session, Gary disclosed that he was college-educated with an undergraduate degree in international studies and currently employed as a resource developer for a nonprofit organization that assists in the relocation of international refugees. He expressed finding great meaning in his helping of refugees. However, he also reported difficulties with his supervisor along with feeling "stressed, overworked, and underpaid." He talked of possibly considering a change in his position or career but did not know what direction to take.

In terms of his previous therapy experience, Gary reported having briefly met with a counselor in training while in college and that while he enjoyed speaking with an "objective" party, he felt that the meetings became stagnant. In addition, he felt that their irregular meeting schedule interfered with developing a clear sense of continuity. Finally, he expressed that he sought a neutral "sounding board" from me as his counselor and that he hoped to establish some clear goals for his therapy. I was quite encouraged by Gary's willingness to take an active role in his counseling process. It seemed from the outset that Gary was clear about being an engaged collaborator in achieving the changes he sought.

Through the intake session, Gary responded clearly and directly, with affect generally appropriate to the content he was discussing. I quickly felt comfortable with him and enjoyed the descriptive metaphors and allusions he would use when describing his concerns. Occasionally, he would appear nervous (more fidgeting and laughter and less eye contact) when discussing his romantic relationships. His range of affect appeared appropriate, although it did not appear that he was strongly moved when speaking about any of his problems. He was active and engaged throughout the intake session and cooperative in answering each of my questions. Gary was able to elaborate upon his responses without much additional prompting.

In the course of the first session, I conveyed the policies and procedures of the clinic and provided a basic outline of the counseling process. My main focus at this point was to develop rapport through empathic mirroring while inviting Gary to elaborate further regarding his concerns. At this initial stage, I was largely centered on empathically understanding Gary, getting a sense of his primary concerns, obtaining relevant personal history, cultivating the therapeutic relationship, and beginning to develop collaborative goal setting. At the conclusion of the first session, a regular meeting time was established and Gary agreed to complete the Integral Intake before the next scheduled appointment.

Initial AQAL Assessment, Integral Psychograph, and DSM Diagnosis

Based on his language and vocabulary as well as his insight regarding his concerns, Gary appeared to possess above-average intelligence and well-developed judgment and abstract thinking skills. Gary was fully oriented during the interview session, with his attention and concentration appearing normal. There was no evidence of a thought disorder, and he specifically denied any suicidal or violent ideation. The following is a basic, initial developmental and quadratic assessment of Gary, his integral psychograph, and DSM diagnosis.

Ego developmental level (Loevinger): between E-6 (conscientious) and E-7 (individualistic) (at intake)[2]

Developmental center of gravity (Wilber): between formal-reflexive and vision-logic

Most relevant quadratic issues (both problems and strengths/resources):

Experience: Individual-Interior (UL)

- depressed mood
- anxiety
- poor self-image and self-esteem
- boredom
- highly intelligent, self-reflective, and self-aware
- ability to learn and enjoy new activities
- compassionate, conscientious
- able to care for himself via taking drives, writing, reading, praying, and listening to music

Behavior: Individual-Exterior (UR)

- difficulties sleeping
- frequent headaches
- no medications
- slightly overweight but overall quite healthy
- no physical exercise

Culture: Collective-Interior (LL)

- "feeling paralyzed" in the midst of interpersonal conflict; often avoiding conflict or acting passive-aggressively
- loneliness
- recent ending of a romantic relationship
- history of being in abusive relationships, but pride in extricating himself from them
- difficulties with his supervisor
- supportive family, but they denied his homosexuality
- spirituality is important to him, but he is dissatisfied with his spiritual community

Social Systems: Collective-Exterior (LR)

- one of his cousins attempted suicide; another cousin committed suicide

- likely history of undiagnosed depression on his mother's side of the family
- mostly positive relations with his four roommates
- content with his living conditions

Gary's psychograph (on a scale of 1–10) (at intake)

Cognitive	8
Self	7
Needs	3
Affective	6
Interpersonal	4
Spiritual	7

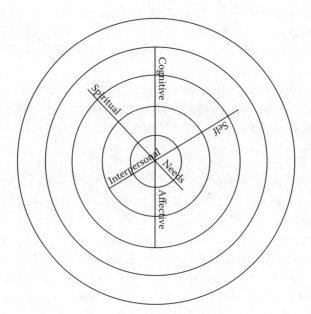

DSM Diagnosis

Axis I:	309.28 Adjustment disorder with mixed anxiety and depressed mood, V62.2 Occupational problem
Axis II:	V71.09 No diagnosis
Axis III:	None
Axis IV:	Problems related to social environment; occupational problems
Axis V:	GAF=60 (at intake)

Case Narrative

Overall, Gary's responses on the Integral Intake were comprehensive, descriptive, and lengthy, all congruent with his initial presentation. He displayed a broad vocabulary and was articulate in describing his concerns, both in person and with the Integral Intake. His responses in the "Preliminary Issues and Previous Therapy" section generally aligned with his descriptions provided in his intake session. However, there was one item that warranted attention and elaboration in the follow-up meetings: "feeling paralyzed" in interpersonal situations involving conflict. Upon review in the second session, Gary disclosed to me that this typically involved anxiety and fear in situations where he needed to assert his own feelings or needs, most often surfacing in his romantic relationship and with his work supervisor. I made note of this disclosure in terms of its potential transference implications for the therapeutic relationship. Again, in his written answers, Gary emphasized his desire for clear therapeutic goals, which I felt could be used in building a rationale for his developing an ILP. We thus quickly and collaboratively established goals, which are mentioned in the initial treatment plan section.

Experience: Individual–Interior (UL)

With regard to the UL, Gary listed and elaborated upon a number of significant strengths, including his intelligence, ability and enjoyment of learning new skills or activities, his compassion, and his conscientiousness. He indicated struggling with his self-image and, while not questioning his sexual identity as a gay man, having difficulty with his appearance and with feeling attractive to other men. He also mentioned that he often avoided conflict with others and acted in what he thought were passive-aggressive ways. I again noted this response for possible implications for the therapeutic relationship.[3] This response and further elaboration in session illustrated Gary's capacity for reflection, self-observation, and self-awareness—a skill I hoped to build upon throughout the course of his therapy.

Gary described his overall mood as rather down since his recent breakup and frequently punctuated with periods of anxiety, feeling overwhelmed, deep loneliness, and boredom. He did *not* report, however, feeling down or anxious most of nearly every day; the afore-mentioned unpleasant affects thus reflect relatively temporary—even if highly unpleasant—states of consciousness, which we would subsequently address in therapy. Gary also listed several means of self-care, including writing, prayer, taking drives, and listening to music. I made note of his self-caring capacities and resources and anticipated that they could be encouraged and engaged throughout the course of treatment.

Through the Integral Intake, it was disclosed that one of Gary's cousins had attempted suicide through a drug overdose as a teenager and that a second cousin had committed suicide by shooting himself. We discussed these events and their impact on Gary, and I closely monitored him for any potential suicidal ideation over the course of treatment to ensure that he was not a risk to himself. He did indicate that he believed that there were a number of family members on his mother's side who suffered from undiagnosed depression. My impression, based on my observation and Gary's responses, was that he did not represent a risk to himself, nor did he qualify for a diagnosis of depression. My *DSM-IV-TR* diagnosis at this point indicated an adjustment disorder with mixed anxiety and depressed mood, brought about by the recent termination of his relationship.

Gary indicated that he was only moderately satisfied with his life and his self-esteem and felt only moderately in control of his life. He endorsed feeling lonely, anxious, and erotic as his most common emotions, congruent with his description at his intake. He reported that he experienced stress and tension most often in his shoulders, neck, and jaw.

Behavior: Individual-Exterior (UR)

With regard to the UR, Gary indicated that he was currently taking no medications and that he had received a physical exam in the last three months in which he was encouraged to watch his cholesterol and modify his diet. While he reported having headaches frequently, they were not attributed to an underlying medical condition, and were assumed to result from stress. At 6' 1" and 220 pounds, he was slightly overweight. There were no other reported medical concerns.

Through the Integral Intake, Gary disclosed difficulty falling asleep and reported waking multiple times throughout the night. He also reported an irregular sleep schedule. In our follow-up session, Gary revealed that he had experienced difficulty with sleep since his college years, but that it, too, had intensified as a result of his recent breakup.

Gary reported that he ate too much, as a means of coping with stress. He also discussed occasionally neglecting his friends and family as well as often neglecting himself and his own needs, and spending more money than he could afford to. Upon further inquiry, his spending did not appear to be extravagant and gave me no cause to be suspicious of a manic episode. Likewise, his difficulties in concentrating were not severe. He reported that he considered himself moderately healthy, endorsed no forms of exercise, and reported often consuming "simple preparation" foods. While admitting to "drinking too much in college," he currently reported drinking alcohol less than once a week, which was further confirmed in session. He disclosed using MDMA (Ecstasy) three times in the past, but reported not using it within the last two years and experienced no desire to do so. No communication impairments were noted or reported. I assessed that Gary's eating and exercise habits would be one area that we could immediately improve upon.

Culture: Collective-Interior (LL)

With regard to the LL, Gary reported being very close to and supported by his family, although they resided far away in another state. He reported speaking with siblings more often than with his parents, although he still spoke with his mother at least once each week. He discussed difficulty with his family regarding his sexual orientation; they essentially denied the fact that he was homosexual. When questioned about this issue, Gary tended to laugh and mock his family. He claimed that although he wished that they could accept him as he is, he understood their conservative religious views and felt that he still benefited from the relationship in other ways. He reported getting along well with his coworkers and supervisees, but also stated continued difficulties with his supervisor. He expressed having few close friends in the local area and that he often felt estranged and lonely.

Gary reported in a number of his responses on the Integral Intake that spirituality was important to him. He was raised in a southern, conservative Christian home with a father who was a minister, but he gradually had moved away from his parents' beliefs, largely as a result of his sexual identity. Gary identified as a Christian and expressed that his spirituality was very much a part of his daily life through regular prayer, scriptural readings, and acts of assistance, kindness, and tolerance. He also expressed feeling moderately dissatisfied with his spirituality. Upon questioning, he explained this as resulting from a lack of a spiritual community in the area and feeling homesick for some of his friends from his church in his hometown. He also emphasized seeking a spiritual community that was less conservative than the one in which he was raised. Gary accentuated the importance to him of tolerance, compassion, and understanding the needs of others as opposed to endorsing a specific doctrine. Gary responded that his spirituality involved a belief in "a personal God with whom one has a relationship and that our relationships with others should reflect the divine." He became more animated when he discussed how angry he was at the hypocrisy of so many of the Christians he encountered on a daily basis. He espoused honesty, compassion, and love as his most important moral values. Many of these elements became further apparent throughout the sessions with Gary as virtues that he attempted to cultivate and express in action. I conceptualized this as a key strength, in that I felt that Gary was actively attempting to live his spirituality in an authentic, transformative fashion and that his interests and values could be utilized to facilitate his development.

Gary discussed his sexuality quite openly. He appeared very comfortable with his identity as a gay man and stated that this had become very clear to him at a young age. He responded that he had come to the conclusion rather uneventfully, save the fact that he wished his parents could be more understanding. He indicated that sexuality was an "important dimension of a relationship, but that it was not the most important." He indicated that he typically had sex within a monogamous relationship, although it was typically less than once per week. He did report that he fantasized about men frequently and masturbated daily. He disclosed no sexual impairments. My impression of Gary in session was congruent with his responses that his sexual identity was not a source of distress for him.

Gary also indicated that he had been in emotionally and physically abusive relationships in the past. He described one of his former, and by his estimate most significant, romantic relationships as tumultuous

and conflict-ridden and that it would occasionally, but regularly, escalate to a degree of physical violence in which he was the recipient. He
reported that his most recent relationship, although conflicted at times,
lacked any violent altercations. Gary indicated that his efforts to extri-
cate himself from his earlier violent relationship were a source of pride
for him and that he had been vigilant to avoid entering into such a
relationship again. I made a note of his being proud of that, in case any
of his self-defeating and/or masochistic tendencies emerged in other
relationships that he described.

Social Systems: Collective-Exterior (LR)

With regard to the LR, Gary reported living somewhat comfortably in
a rented room in a four-bedroom house with three other male roommates. He expressed getting along well with most of them and described
his environs as an "average suburb." He indicated that although he felt
it was "generally safe," he did have some concern, as his car had been
broken into twice. Upon review, he did express desiring more time for
himself and hoping to move at some point. Gary indicated that he felt
that his home was satisfactory in terms of amenities. Finally, he denied
participating in any organizations or with any volunteer work other
than his professional work resettling international refugees.

Initial (Tentative) Treatment Plan

Having reviewed Gary's responses to the Integral Intake with him and
having discussed his life, his strengths, and his struggles, Gary and I
began to collaboratively establish therapeutic goals. Our initial list of
goals included:

- Practice relaxation skills (for both his sleep disturbances and anxious
  states)
- Begin an exercise regimen as part of a solution for mood and stress levels
  (sleep and headaches)
- Increase social interactions
- Improve his interpersonal skills, including assertiveness training
- Examine his thought patterns, history, and how our relationship unfolds
  to learn more about his depressed and anxious feelings

As previously mentioned, when clients report numerous problems
or goals, it is beneficial to address a problem or goal with which clients

are likely to experience positive effects quickly because this provides tangible, experiential evidence that therapy is helpful, that change is possible, and that their active engagement in therapy will benefit them. Thus, at the same time that we began to address his depressed mood, we also began tackling issues that I surmised would produce positive effects more quickly, which will soon be discussed.

With the above information, I began developing a treatment plan. Based on his responses from the intake, supplemented with information gained in the clinical interviews, I approximated that Gary was operating generally from a formal-reflexive level of development, with some indications of occasional early vision-logic (this corresponds to the ego development assessment of E-6 to E-7). Gary was principally concerned with self-evaluated standards and the effects of his actions on others, with motives and consequences being more important than the rules themselves. He also was very concerned about relationships and emotional dependence issues. Throughout our sessions, he tended to generally display adaptive defenses of anticipation, humor, self-observation, and sublimation with occasional bad faith as well as isolation of affect and intellectualization. In accordance with the spectrum of development, pathology, and treatment (see Chapter 4), I adopted the general therapeutic approach of introspection and experiential, existential inquiry as broad compasses with which to work with Gary during the course of our sessions. I felt that he was quite psychologically minded and would be capable of determining the content of the sessions and would likely benefit most from an attuned counselor who mirrored and interpreted his concerns authentically. While I did recognize a number of behavioral and social elements that I wanted to address as components of an integral approach (very few clients have "even" developmental lines), I deemed that Gary would benefit most in counseling from an empathic, experiential, and authentically engaged relationship, through which he could explore himself and his concerns, rather than a counseling approach that was more specifically behavioral or directive. It is important to remember that treatment plans represent a set of general principles to inform and address clients' concerns, rather than specific interventions that will "cure" them of a reified mental illness (Mahoney, 2003; Marquis, 2006). The following suggestions represented possibilities for Gary to choose to address given his presentation, rather than a specific, preprogrammed order to our sessions:

Upper Left Quadrant

1. Encourage experimenting with yoga classes for relaxation, exercise, and any communal or spiritual benefits
2. Therapeutic journaling to explore and assess his thoughts, feelings, and behaviors
3. Introspective, experiential psychotherapy to explore concerns of depression, anxiety, self-esteem, and self-image, as well as his goals and aspirations
4. Facilitate client's introduction to contemplative practices within his spiritual tradition

Upper Right Quadrant

1. Assess and modify diet
2. Modify sleep patterns to achieve 8 hours of restful sleep per night
3. Develop a regular exercise regimen
4. Instruction in and rehearsal of systematic relaxation scripts/techniques to counteract anxiety symptoms
5. If depressive symptoms do not subside within 4 weeks or there is any indication of suicidal or violent ideation, refer to psychiatrist for evaluation for antidepressant medication

Lower Left Quadrant

1. Address concerns with romantic relationships and friendships
2. Encourage client to develop volunteer work with a charity organization of his choice in order to encourage interaction with others and decenter self
3. Encourage client to develop his membership in social organizations such as church, community agencies, etc.

Lower Right Quadrant

1. Address concerns with career and workplace environment

Interventions and Sessions

At the outset of counseling, I introduced the basic tenets of an integral approach and the possibility of contextualizing our work within the various quadrants in the form of an integral life practice. I encouraged Gary to think about our in-session time as largely devoted to his interior, subjective, and intersubjective psychological concerns, while also suggesting that he attempt to address growth in the other quadrants outside of session that we could then monitor (e.g., more socializing, participating in social organizations, confronting his supervisors or others when he feels disrespected or devalued). Gary was quite receptive to utilizing his time during the week in order to address other areas of his development, in hopes of facilitating his overall growth and well-being.

Given his responses with the Integral Intake, my first immediate suggestion was to modify some elements of the UR, specifically concerning Gary's diet and exercise. I encouraged Gary to consult with a nutritionist to develop a healthy eating plan and attempt to develop an exercise regimen suitable to his schedule. He was not inclined to consult a nutritionist, so I recommended Weil's *8 Weeks to Optimum Health* (1998) and *Eating Well for Optimum Health* (2001). We discussed various possibilities that Weil addressed in those books, and Gary determined that he could initiate walking in the evenings four times per week, with the possibility of running as his cardiovascular endurance improved. Over the course of Gary's counseling, he was generally able to maintain his exercise routine, and it proved to be quite beneficial; he reported that he felt that his self-esteem increased due to his weight loss—in addition to having an outlet through which to address stress and negative feelings. Following more encouragement from me and Weil's books, he also agreed to modify his diet, eating fewer processed foods, preparing full meals more frequently, and consuming lower-fat, lower-sugar, and higher-protein foods.

Another area of UR concern was Gary's sleep patterns. I suggested that he cease drinking coffee in the evenings and attempt to establish a regular sleep routine. Gary was open to this and agreed that his irregular rest probably negatively affected his mood. He expressed that while he enjoyed using caffeine and that it helped when working late hours, the overall cost in terms of his sleep was too great. He agreed that he would attempt to cut back gradually, with the goal of eventually having coffee only in the mornings (I told him that he could do 60–90 seconds of calisthenics whenever he noticed himself dozing off while working in the evenings, which works quite well). I also educated Gary regarding the value of consistent sleep hygiene and encouraged him to establish specific times for sleep (including waking up at the same time even if he went to bed later than usual). If he has been in bed without falling asleep for more than 20 minutes, he should get up and do something else until he feels very sleepy. He should also exercise regularly but not late in the day (he switched his walks to his noon break); keep his bedroom dark and quiet (or use a white noise machine), and practice his relaxation skills (both deep breathing and progressive muscle relaxation). While not consistent over the entire course of treatment, Gary was generally able to apply many of these suggestions, and he found that his sleep did improve substantially.

In conjunction with addressing Gary's sleep hygiene and routine, I suggested that Gary listen to a relaxation script on CD and to practice relaxing regularly at home. The script addressed both diaphragmatic breathing and progressive muscle relaxation, which Gary received well. Our goal was for Gary to develop skills so that he could counteract his feelings of anxiety as well as to cultivate a method to help him relax before falling asleep. At the outset, Gary struggled to make time to listen to the CD regularly, largely due to his active work schedule. After a few weeks, however, he did find that it assisted him not only in inducing sleep when he was having difficulty but, perhaps more important, it significantly enhanced his ability to self-soothe when he was in an anxious or depressed state. By the sixth session, he reported that he was consistently sleeping through the night for seven to eight hours and waking up feeling rested.

From the LL, I encouraged Gary to consider volunteering or otherwise working with an organization along with attempting to seek out more social support through joining a church that was in alignment with his spiritual orientation. While I agreed that his family was a strong source of support for him, they were also hundreds of miles away, and I suggested that Gary could benefit from a more immediate social network. As a result, Gary began visiting various churches and eventually settled on one that was predominantly made up of members of the local gay and lesbian community. He quickly made a home for himself there and began reaching out to meet new friends. In addition, he took up volunteering for a local radio station and helping out with their pledge drive. These efforts were well received and facilitated Gary's becoming less internally focused, as well as his reaping the experiential rewards of helping others.

In addition to the UR and LL interventions, a considerable amount of Gary's sessions were spent addressing how his psychological history had affected his relationships. Through the middle phase of counseling, Gary began to address the impact that his father's absence—largely due to his extensive charity and missionary work—had upon Gary's relationships with other men. Gary uncovered that he tended to relate to most heterosexual men as if they were unpredictable and inconsistent, and he usually kept his guard up. We also discussed how he enacted this pattern in his initial relationship with me. In our early work, Gary reacted with great intensity over a session I was forced to cancel with little notice. In the following session, Gary had little to say beyond a mechanical recount of his week. When I made a here-and-now comment (Yalom, 2002) that he seemed distant and that I didn't feel as connected with him as in previous sessions, and wondered out loud about the possibility that it might be related to my canceling of our session and how that could have reminded him his father's characteristic lack of concern about him, Gary resonated highly with my interpretation, and we were able to explore the issue at length and fruitfully. Working through such interpretations, Gary became increasingly more trusting and confident in our relationship. Further, Gary's feelings appeared to generalize beyond the consulting room, with his eventually developing a satisfying friendship with a straight male colleague at work.

Gary and I also addressed how his family's emphasis on helping others had made it difficult to speak up for his own needs. As religious leaders in their small community, Gary's parents were very active and concentrated extensively on helping and assisting others. However, a side effect of this attitude was the idea that expressing one's own desires was considered selfish, shameful, and worthy of reproach. This internalization of "others' needs are more important than mine" appeared to influence Gary's tendency to remain in unsatisfying relationships or situations. Similar to the notion mentioned in Chapter 3 that excessive attention to the UR can lead to narcissism and that excessive preoccupation with the LR can lead to conformity, it appeared in this case that excessive charity (LR) can potentially result in insufficiently attending to one's own psychological needs (UL). Gary struggled with defending himself when verbally confronted by his supervisor and often would satisfy his partner by spending time together when Gary actually preferred being alone. By the middle phase of our work together, Gary became increasingly competent at identifying these patterns and gradually began asserting his own wishes without being overwhelmed by a sense of shame or selfishness.

Much of the aforementioned work regarding Gary's relationships (LL) intertwined with UL concerns, which was the primary focus of our in-session work. Many of Gary's self-esteem and body image concerns affected his relationships. In our meetings, we began to explore the origins of these ideas—which Gary felt largely emerged from his sisters' early concern about their own weight and tendency to ridicule him as a child—and how those ideas continued to impact him presently. Discussing his body image openly was a struggle at the outset for Gary, particularly with my being a male therapist. However, in time, he was able to cultivate a more accepting and gentle attitude toward himself. I instructed him about the difference between self-esteem and self-compassion (Neff, 2003a, 2003b) and, given that he recognized his compassion for others as a personal strength of his, I encouraged his directing some of his compassion toward himself. I occasionally noticed his self-disparaging comments in session, such as referring to himself as fat and unattractive, which I would gently confront, pointing out how harsh and critical he sounded—reminiscent of his sisters. He was often receptive and could reframe his experience once it was brought to his awareness. As with most of my clients, I had previously encouraged a practice of mindfulness, which eventually dovetailed very nicely with the contemplative practices that I suggested he read about and begin practicing. Both of these interventions (mindfulness and self-compassion) ultimately proved very helpful to Gary.

Another tool that Gary found effective was imagery. One idea he utilized was to imagine himself as a small child and restructure his negative self-talk as if he were a loving, encouraging, concerned parent. Over the course of treatment, he became more mindful of his critical internalizations and was able to modify them into statements and self-attitudes that were more compassionate, warm, and gentle. I had already emphasized the importance of cultivating these attitudes through consistent, regular, engaged, and attentive practice. What I told Gary was something along the lines of: "What we tell ourselves (self-talk) is critical to our processes of change and our awareness of what *is*. The success of cognitive-restructuring interventions depends in large measure upon your creating and strengthening patterns of thinking that will serve your well-being. However, before you can replace dysfunctional thoughts with functional ones, you must be aware of those dysfunctional thoughts. Thus, training in mindfulness or other attentional processes such as the centering prayer you practice is a helpful component to the cognitive methods we're now working with. After all, you cannot change negative self-talk if you are not first aware of it." This is empirically corroborated by research by Segal, Williams, and Teasdale (2002)—who demonstrated that integrating mindfulness meditation with cognitive therapy increases the latter's efficacy, particularly its long-term effectiveness and the prevention of relapse—and work by Schwartz and Begley (2002), who demonstrated the efficacy of mindfulness-based interventions with people diagnosed with obsessive-compulsive disorder.

As the instigating issue that brought him to counseling, Gary and I spent much time addressing his romantic relationships. During our work together, his partner had resumed contact and they went through a number of repeated and conflict-ridden oscillations. Once he became involved with his partner again, Gary would experience him as excessively needy, demanding, and smothering, which increasingly frustrated Gary and usually resulted in Gary's emotional withdrawal. Eventually, Gary would become exhausted with the perceived demands of his partner and they would stop seeing each other for a time. Once alone, Gary would grow lonely and anxious in his free time, which would eventually lead to his receiving his partner when he again reached out for Gary.

In our sessions, Gary became aware of this pattern and of the draining emotional toll it was taking on him. He explored the implications of their fluctuating interchanges as well as to what degree this man represented the ideals of what he wanted in a partner and in a relationship. He gradually developed a conviction that he did not share his partner's desire for constant attention and that he longed for more independence. However, his ability to remove himself from the relationship proved difficult, and throughout the course of treatment they continued to see each other periodically.

In addition to his concerns with his body image, self-esteem, and relationships, our sessions also addressed Gary's concern for deeper meaning and direction in his life. Gary revealed that he had kept a journal on and off for many years, and I encouraged him to continue doing so as a way to monitor his experience and note his concerns, struggles, joys, setbacks, and victories, as well as any effects (or lack thereof) of our work together. I suggested that he deeply consider and reflect upon the questions "Who am I?" and "How should I live?" in his writings, both of which he found evocative. Through his explorations, Gary became increasingly aware of his desire for a spiritual center or "hub" around which the rest of his life would revolve. These discussions further galvanized his willingness to take responsibility for his life situation. Raised within a conservative Christian church, Gary was unaware of Christianity's rich contemplative tradition. I thus recommended several books for Gary to read that we could subsequently discuss together (bibliotherapy): *Open Mind, Open Heart: The Contemplative Dimension of the Gospel* (Keating, 1986), *A Listening Heart: The Art of Contemplative Living* (Steindl-Rast, 1983), and *Gratefulness, the Heart of Prayer* (Steindl-Rast, 1984). Gary devoured these books and quickly and enthusiastically began practicing centering prayer, which he said he instantly felt held tremendous potential for him, something that he had felt was previously missing from his faith. He also experienced immediate benefits from practicing being grateful. Now that his capacity for mindfulness was increasing, as soon as he would notice negative thought patterns (such as "It totally sucks what an ass my supervisor is" or "I am so unattractive because I'm overweight") he would counteract them by being grateful for all of the gifts in his life (such as "my work is important and meaningful and I enjoy many of my colleagues" and "I may not be as buff as I would like, but I am fundamentally healthy, and I am thankful for that").

Addressing the LR, Gary struggled with his career position, and we attempted to explore his concerns. While he found deep meaning with his work in terms of the help he provided the refugees, the toll of his office culture and politics repeatedly wore on him. He felt that he was taken for granted and that his efforts to constructively address his supervisor were generally ignored (we did some role-plays and role reversals, which had some positive effects, but not enough to effect the change he desired with his boss). We continued to process his concerns, with my remaining open, empathic, and reflecting his underlying affect, and he eventually became more assured of his dissatisfaction regarding work; he soon developed the resourcefulness to seek out another position. One key exercise that was helpful for Gary was my suggestion that he compose his own epitaph as a way of focusing his intention (Yalom, 2002). Considering how he would want his life's project to be viewed at its end seemed to allow Gary to focus his energies toward moving out of his current job and finding something that was more satisfying for him. Once the decision was made, he prepared his resume and quickly obtained a number of offers; he chose to accept a temporary contract as a fund-raiser for an inner-city youth program.

Conclusion of Case 1

The complete course of Gary's counseling lasted just over ten months and consisted of regular weekly sessions. Toward the end of our work, as Gary found that he had less to address in session, we transitioned to meeting every other week. As I do with all of my clients, I emphasized the critical importance of *maintenance* work. In the maintenance stage—the 5th and final stage of change in the transtheoretical approach of Prochaska and DiClemente (1982, 2003)—clients have reached their goals. At this point, the emphasis is on preventing relapses by consolidating their learning (stressing *how* they achieved their progress and to expect future difficulties; stressing the need to continue working with their issues; that just because they have reached their goals does not mean they do not have to do any more therapeutic work). Successful maintenance (of one's progress) depends, in part, upon continual self- and environmental-assessment and the conscious realization that the work one is doing is helping one be the type of person he or she desires to be.

Ironically, Gary's decision to change jobs—one of his main goals for seeking counseling—also eventually brought about the end of our sessions. This was due to his loss of mental health benefits with the insurance plan at his newly accepted employment (a very real LR issue). Although such issues can often be problematic in this age of managed care, we both agreed that Gary had achieved many of his goals and that he felt comfortable trying things "on his own." Gary indicated he had benefited from our sessions and that he intended to continue with his integral life practice. I received a follow-up e-mail a few months later that indicated that he was doing quite well, content in his new job, and, having finally terminated his relationship with his former partner, enjoying his jogging and daily practice of centering prayer.

Unfortunately, not all therapy proceeds as smoothly and successfully as Gary's case, as we'll see in the next case example.

Case Example 2: Denise
Denise's Completed Integral Intake

INTEGRAL INTAKE

Andre Marquis, Ph.D.
Assistant Professor of Counseling and Human Development
University of Rochester

Client's Name _____Denise_____Age_31___Date First Seen _____
Home Phone (___)_____(message: Y/N) Work Phone (___)_____(message: Y/N)
Address _____City_____ Zip_____
Date of Birth __September 1973___ Gender (M/F) Referral Source _____
Emergency Contact: Name _____ Phone (___)_____
(Please use the back side of this form if you need more space to respond to *any* of the questions.)

PRELIMINARY ISSUES AND PREVIOUS THERAPY

What is the primary concern or problem for which you are seeking help?
My mother has cancer, relationship issues, childhood issues, personality issues.

What makes it better? What makes it worse?
I'm pretty good if I don't have too many fires burning. I can ignore old events and be happy.

Are there any *immediate* challenges or issues that need our attention? **Yes**/No If yes, please describe.
My mother's cancer and the decisions I need to make.

Have you had previous counseling or psychotherapy? **Yes**/No From when to when? With whom?
John Smith, David Johnson, and John & Jane Doe and two more that I can't remember.

What was your experience of therapy? (What was your previous therapy like?)
John & Jane Doe, "Christian" counseling—very damaging, other therapy always interrupted.

What was most helpful about your therapy?
Validation and being able to purge.

What was least helpful about your therapy?
Not enough time to really solve problems.

What did you learn about yourself through your previous therapy?
I am codependent; parents are alcoholic.

What do you expect from me and our work together?
Just make more progress on my ability to reason, rationalize, and solve problems.

EXPERIENCE: Individual-Interior

What are your strengths?
Very organized, kind, generous, loving, nurturing, patient, friendly.

What are your weaknesses?
Poor self esteem, constant second-guessing, sometimes anger—not so much anymore, fear, worry too much about what others think, don't really like being alone.

How would you describe your general mood/feelings?
Very happy or very anxious.

What emotions do you most often feel most strongly?
Extreme joy or feeling of coming out of my skin when facing a loss or when my "hands are tied" or my decisions taken away.

What are the ways in which you care for and comfort your self when you feel distressed?
Go to the gym.

How do you deal with strong emotions in yourself?
I don't know.

How do you respond to stressful situations and other problems?
Cry, detach if possible.

How do you make decisions (for example, do you use logic and reason, or do you trust your gut and heart)?
Both—I try to use logic most of the time.

Are you aware of recurring images or thoughts (either while awake or in dreams)? **Yes/** No If yes, please describe.
Thoughts that I'm bad or have done something wrong, fear of death, dwell on getting older and uglier.

Have you *ever* attempted to seriously harm or kill yourself or anyone else? **Yes**/No If yes, please describe.
Myself several times in high school. History of cutting myself; would never hurt anyone else.

Are you *presently* experiencing suicidal thoughts? Yes/**No** If yes, please describe.
Not suicidal thoughts, but sometimes I wish I could just die and get it over with.

Has anyone in your family ever attempted or committed suicide? **Yes**/No If yes, please describe.
My maternal grandfather shot himself.

Have there been any serious illnesses, births, deaths, or other losses or changes in your family that have affected you? Yes/No If yes, please describe.
Just normal things—loss of pets, grandparents, my mother's cancer, parents' alcoholism.

What is your earliest memory?
I don't remember much. I question if I only know things or stories I've been told. I can't really remember any event that someone else hasn't told me a story of.

What is your happiest memory?
I don't know. Can tell you many good things but don't know the happiest.

What is your most painful memory?
I don't know—I can tell you many painful things, but I don't know the most painful.

Where in your body do you feel stress (shoulders, back, jaw, etc.)?
Shoulders, jaw, get headaches.

Do you have ways in which you express yourself creatively and/or artistically? **Yes**/No If yes, please describe.
Painting, writing poetry. But I can't create from my own mind.

Describe your leisure time (hobbies/enjoyment).
Reading, exercise, painting, poetry, movies, riding bikes, cooking, my cat.

Have you ever been a victim of, or witnessed, verbal, emotional, physical, and/or sexual abuse? If yes, please describe.
Yes—see John Smith's (former therapist) file.

In general, how satisfied are you with your life?

Not at all   1   2   **3**   **4**   5   6   7   Very

In general, how do you feel about yourself (self-esteem)?

Very bad   1   **2**   **3**   4   5   6   7   Very good

In general, how much control do you feel you have over your life and how you feel?

None at all   1   2   3   **4**   **5**   6   7   A lot

Please mark any of the following emotions that you often feel:

   _x_   angry **only with triggers**

   _x_   sad

   _x_   lonely

   _x_   afraid

   _x_   anxious/worried

   _x_   shameful/guilty

   _____   jealous

   _x_   happy

   _____   grateful/thankful

   _x_   sexual/erotic

   _x_   excited

   _____   energetic

   _x_   hopeful

   _____   relaxed/peaceful

   _____   other emotions you often feel:

BEHAVIOR: Individual-Exterior

Please list any medications you are presently taking (dosage/amount and what the medication is for).

None

Do you have a primary care physician? **Yes**/No. If yes, who is it? **Dr. "Jane Doe"**

Height   **?**   Weight   **118** lbs.

When was your last physical?

last year

Were there any noteworthy results (diseases, blood pressure, cholesterol, etc.)?
No

Have you ever suffered a head injury or other serious injury? Yes/**No** If yes, please
describe.

What other significant medical problems have you experienced or are you
experiencing now?
Headaches, stomach problems in the past.

Please mark any of the following behaviors or bodily feelings that are true of you:

_____ drink too much

_____ use illegal and/or mind-altering drugs

_____ eat too much

_____ eat too little

__x__ neglect friends and family

__x__ neglect self and your own needs

__x__ difficulty being kind and loving to yourself

__x__ act in ways that end up hurting yourself or others

__x__ lose your temper

__x__ seem to *not* have control over some behaviors

__x__ think about suicide

__x__ have difficulty concentrating

__x__ spend more money than you can afford to

__x__ crying

_____ any other behaviors you would like me to know about?

__x__ headaches

_____ menstrual problems

__x__ dizziness

__x__ heart tremors

__x__ jitters

_____ sexual preoccupations

_____ tingling/numbness

_____ excessive tiredness

_____ hear or see things not actually there

_____ blackouts

_____ do you have any other bodily pains or difficulties? Yes/No. If yes, what
are they? _____

In general, how would you rate your physical health?

Very unhealthy   1   2   3   4   5   **<u>6</u>**   7   Very healthy

Describe your current sleeping patterns (When do you sleep? How many hours per 24 hours? Do you sleep straight through or do you wake up during sleep time?).
Wake up several times 4–6 hours.

Do you feel rested upon waking? Yes/**<u>No</u>**

Describe your usual eating habits (types of food, and how much).
Probably not enough calories. Try to eat very healthy choices.

Do you take vitamins and other nutritional supplements? **<u>Yes</u>**/No If yes, please describe.
Yes—multivitamins.

Describe your drug and alcohol use (both past and present).
Past drug use—coke, crack, pot. Never been much of a drinker.

Do you engage in some form of exercise (aerobic and/or strength building)? **<u>Yes</u>**/No If yes, please describe.
Yoga, cardio—walking, biking, and free weights.

Do you have any communication impairments (sight, hearing, speech)? Yes/**<u>No</u>** If yes, please describe.

CULTURE: Collective-Interior

Describe your relationships, including friends, family, and coworkers.
[Denise left this blank, which is clinically revealing.]

What is important and meaningful to you (what matters the most to you)?
Having a partner in life. Contentment in my job, comfortable home, friends and family, peace.

In general, how satisfied are you with your friendships and other relationships?

Not at all   1   2   **<u>3</u>**   4   5   6   7   Very

In general, how comfortable are you in social situations?

Not at all   1   2   **<u>3</u>**   4   5   6   7   Very

In general, how satisfied are you with your religion/spirituality?

Not at all   1   2   3   4   **<u>5</u>**   6   7   Very

Which emotions were encouraged or commonly expressed in your family of origin
(family you grew up with)?
Anger.

Which emotions were discouraged or not allowed in your family of origin?
My anger.

What emotions are most comfortable for you now?   **?**

What emotions are most uncomfortable for you now?
[Denise wrote "None" then marked a line through it and wrote "?"]

How do you identify yourself ethnically? How important is your ethnic culture to you?
**I am Caucasian-American, don't really have a culture, but I love studying other
cultures, Indian, Lebanon [*sic*], etc.**

How did your family of origin express love and care?
Don't know.

How does your current family express love and care?
I don't have a current family.

How did your family of origin express disapproval?
Anger, yelling, grounding, fighting, throwing or breaking things.

How does your current family express disapproval?
[Denise drew a line through this, indicating "N/A."]

Describe your romantic/love relationships, if any.
In a new romantic relationship.

Describe your sex life. How satisfied are you with your sex life?
Very.

What beliefs do you have about sex? How important to you are those beliefs?
**No one should push their partner to do things that they don't want to do.
Everything is ok as long as both parties are ok.**

Do you have a religious/spiritual affiliation and/or practice? <u>Yes</u>/No If yes, please
describe.
I believe in God, not religion.

What beliefs do you have about religion/spirituality? How important to you are those
beliefs?
[Denise left this blank.]

What are some of your most important morals? How important to you are those morals?

Honesty, compassion, responsibility.

Describe any political or civic involvement in which you participate.

Not much—we are so insignificant what we vote really doesn't matter. I do vote in the presidential elections.

Describe any environmental activities in which you participate (recycling, conserving, carpooling, etc.).

[Denise left this blank.]

Are you involved with any cultural activities or institutions? Yes/**No** If yes, please describe.

Have you ever been a victim of any form of prejudice or discrimination (racial, gender, etc.) or felt that you were disadvantaged in terms of power and privilege in society? Yes/No If yes, please describe.

[This question wasn't on the Integral Intake at the time I counseled Denise.]

SOCIAL SYSTEMS: Collective-Exterior

Describe your current *physical* home environment. (For example, describe the layout of your home and other general conditions, such as privacy, whether it is well-lighted, whether you have A/C and, heating, etc.)

2-bedroom apartment with all the comforts; nicely decorated; not well lit; not such a great neighborhood.

Describe your neighborhood. (Is it safe/**dangerous,** nice/**unpleasant**, quiet/loud, etc.?)
Somewhat.

Describe your current social home environment. (How would an outside observer describe how you get along with those who live with you?)

[Denise left this blank.]

Describe your work environment (include coworkers and supervisors who directly affect you).

[Denise left this blank.]

Do you have a romantic partner? **Yes**/No Have you been married before? **Yes**/No If yes, please describe. **Divorced.**

Are you currently involved in a custody dispute? Yes/**No** If yes, please describe.

Have you had any involvement with the legal system (incarceration, probation, etc.)? Yes/No If yes, please describe.
[This question wasn't on the Integral Intake at the time I counseled Denise.]

What aspects of your life are stressful to you? Please describe.
[Denise left this blank.]

What sort of support system do you have (friends, family, or religious community who help you in times of need)?
Not much of one.

List your family of origin (family you grew up with), beginning with the oldest, include parents and yourself.

Name	Age	Gender	Relationship to you (include "step-," "half-," etc.)

[Denise left this blank.]

What is your educational background?
Graduated high school, some college.

What is your occupation? **<u>Accounts payable</u>** How satisfied are you with the type of work you do?
Not at all   1   2   3   <u>4</u>   5   <u>6</u>   7   Very

What is your yearly income? **<u>$32,000</u>** per year. How satisfied are you with your standard of living?
Not at all   1   2   3   <u>4</u>   5   6   7   Very

Describe any family history of mental illness.
[Denise left this blank.]

List your current family or all the people you currently live with (begin with the oldest person and include yourself).

Name	Age Gender Relationship to you (include "step-," "half-," etc.)

Live alone.

Are you involved with any organizations? Yes/**<u>No</u>** If yes, please describe. **<u>No</u>**

Do you participate in any volunteer work? Yes/No if yes, please describe.
When I can—spirit committee @ [*sic*] work. I do some of the cancer runs/walks.

Please mark any of the following that you experienced difficulty or problems with. Also indicate to the right of the problem in the parentheses ( ) your approximate age when the difficulty or problem occurred:

[This checklist wasn't on the Integral Intake at the time I counseled Denise.]

_____ nursing and/or eating ( )
_____ toilet training ( )
_____ crawling or walking ( )
_____ talking ( )
_____ nail biting or other nervous habits ( )
_____ going to school/separating from caregivers ( )
_____ cruelty to animals or people ( )
_____ serious illnesses or injuries ( )
_____ academic problems ( )
_____ social problems ( )
_____ moves or other family stresses ( )
_____ abuse (emotional, physical, or sexual) ( )
_____ any problems with sexual maturation ( )
_____ being made fun of or joked about at school, home, or elsewhere ( )
_____ self-destructiveness (risky sex, eating problems, drug use, excessive risk-taking, etc.) ( )
_____ fitting into social groups ( )
_____ standing up for what you believe in when it differs from your peers' views ( )
_____ making important decisions, especially when they differ from social norms ( )
_____ any existential dilemmas ( )
_____ any religious and/or spiritual experiences (these could be completely positive) ( )

The following is a list of various parts, aspects, or subpersonalities that many people notice within themselves in certain situations, but not in others. Please mark any of the following that you have experienced difficulty or problems with. Often, it is only after the fact that we notice that we were behaving, thinking, or feeling in a problematic manner. Also, please indicate to the right of the problem the situation or context in which you noticed this part of yourself.

[This checklist wasn't on the Integral Intake at the time I counseled Denise.]

_____ irresponsible child _____
_____ critical parent _____
_____ dominating "top dog" _____

_____ prone-to-fail "underdog" _____

_____ overly harsh judge or critic _____

_____ false or phony self _____

_____ unworthy, not-good-enough self _____

_____ grandiose, better-than-everyone-else self _____

_____ other, please describe _____

Is there anything else you want me to know about? (use the back of the page if you
   need to).
[Denise left this blank.]

Initial Session and Presenting Problem(s)

Denise, a single, 31-year-old Caucasian female, employed in the
accounts payable department of a pharmaceutical company, was referred
to a community counseling clinic by her employee assistance program
(EAP). During the first session, Denise expressed difficulty with anxiety and stress that she said resulted from her recent decision to end a
two-year intimate relationship with a man, for whom she had worked
as a secretary in his chiropractic practice. According to her, she had
financially supported her former partner in establishing his business as
well as assisted him in purchasing a home. When her partner terminated the relationship, he reportedly refused to honor any of the financial debts and terminated Denise from her job. At this point, Denise
reported difficulty concentrating, depressed mood, and lack of interest
in activities. In addition, she also reported feelings of inadequacy due
to learning of her ex-husband's recent marriage. Moreover, she was dissatisfied and anxious about her new intimate relationship.

Near the beginning of the initial session, I had told Denise something like: "This first session is really a two-way interview. I'm trying to
understand who you are, the nature of your struggles, and get a sense
of whether or not I think I can be helpful to you. At the same time,
you should be testing the water to get a sense of your comfort with
me, and whether or not you have a sense of optimism that our work
together could be fruitful." As usual, my initial therapeutic goal was to
develop rapport through empathic mirroring while inviting Denise to
share more of her struggles and concerns. I was primarily interested in
empathically understanding Denise, getting a sense of her fundamental
issues, obtaining relevant personal history, cultivating the therapeutic
relationship, and beginning to develop collaborative goal setting.

What stood out the most to me from the first session was her style of responding, which seemed to reflect concrete, dichotomous thinking and alluded to the defense mechanisms of splitting and denial. When I questioned her about some of her past relationships, Denise indicated that she preferred to "ignore old events and be happy." Upon further questioning, she emphatically stated that "I don't *have* any old friends, okay!?" (Although no single answer to a single question necessarily indicates a given diagnosis, I always suspect a diagnosis of borderline personality disorder when I hear that someone has zero long-term friendships, unless there are understandable, extenuating circumstances.) With this in mind (plus what appeared to be her pattern of beginning new romantic relationships almost immediately after a previous one ended), I asked Denise if she currently, or in the recent past, had had any thoughts of killing or harming herself; she specifically denied such.

Denise reported having sought counseling with six previous mental health professionals and specified her two courses of religious counseling as "very damaging." She elaborated on this by describing her religious counselors as judgmental, critical, and inducing guilt and shame in her. Denise reported that her other courses of therapy were not very helpful and either blamed the therapists or, in two instances in which she said the therapists were wonderful, blamed an insufficient amount of time "to really solve problems." Her reported benefits from counseling were feeling validated, being given the opportunity "to purge" (emotionally), learning from her therapist that she was codependent, and learning that her parents were alcoholics. When I asked her what she would most like to accomplish from therapy with me, she emphasized her desire to make progress on her ability to solve all of her problems (no specific goal was stated).

Denise did not appear comfortable in the session, and I felt uneasy as well. Although her anger and negativity (dissatisfaction with most of her life) seemed appropriate given the content of what she spoke about, her emotional swings in the first session (she would appear cautiously guarded one moment and then deeply emotionally disclosing the next) and the intensity with which she stated that she didn't have any long-term friendships resulted in my acting more from my "professional counselor" role than the authentic humanist that Gary (from case example 1) encountered. (Denise was the first client I worked with that I diagnosed with borderline personality disorder, though I had studied about, and observed colleagues of mine work with, such clients and their psychodynamics.)

Toward the end of the session, I asked her how she felt about our working together; she replied that she would like to give it a try—that I seemed as though I could be helpful. I conveyed the policies and procedures of the clinic and provided a basic outline of the counseling process. At the conclusion of the first session, we established a regular meeting time, and Denise agreed to complete the Integral Intake before our next scheduled appointment.

Initial AQAL Assessment, Integral Psychograph, and DSM Diagnosis

Based on her presentation in session, Denise appeared to be of average intelligence. She generally presented as alert, engaged, and attentive. Her capacity for abstract thought was limited and she tended to focus on concrete, simplified, and specific events. Denise appeared to have difficulty with any abstract concepts that we discussed in the sessions. Her level of judgment appeared moderately impaired, with her being easily misled and taken advantage of by others, difficulty anticipating others' reactions to her behavior, and distorted (unusual and highly idiosyncratic) interpretations of events and their meanings. In the sessions, she presented as fully oriented to person, place, and time. Denise's memory appeared normal with regard to recent events, but she experienced poor recall of events in childhood and adolescence. Denise displayed limited insight into the psychological nature of her condition, most often tending to blame others and her circumstances for her problems. There was no evidence of a thought disorder.

Affective observations included an intense and volatile range of affect, including fear, anger, frustration, sadness, and elation on a few occasions. Her general mood appeared dysphoric and irritable. Denise often appeared anxious and frustrated in session, as evidenced by fidgeting and pressured speech. Denise was usually resistant to further discussions of emotionally uncomfortable material. Denise appeared very uncomfortable with the role of emotional processing and exploration in counseling, stating she felt "out of control" when doing so. She expressed that she had difficulty sharing her feelings with others and reported trying to "hold things in" and "think logically" when upset. Denise used some emotional language in her descriptions of events, but she tended to focus on concrete details of situations.

Denise's responses on the Integral Intake were largely congruent with her initial presentation: in response to the query, "How do you deal with strong emotions in yourself?" she wrote, "I don't know"; in response to the query, "How would you describe your general mood/feelings?" she wrote, "Very happy or very anxious"; and in response to the query, "What emotions do you most often feel most strongly?" she wrote, "Extreme joy or feeling of coming out of my skin." The polar extremes of her emotions and her reported inability to deal with them (she cries and detaches "if possible" in response to stress) are strongly suggestive of borderline personality organization (Kernberg, 1980; Greenberg & Mitchell, 1983; Wilber, 1999d). The following is a basic, initial developmental and quadratic assessment of Denise, her integral psychograph, and *DSM* diagnosis.

Ego developmental level (Loevinger): between E-2 (impulsive) and E3 (self-protective) (at intake)[4]

Developmental center of gravity (Wilber): representational mind and *early* rule/role mind; phantasmic-emotional (when triggered)[5]

Most relevant quadratic issues (both problems and strengths/resources):

Experience: Individual-Interior (UL)
- Inner instability/swinging from emotional extremes, with which she copes by trying to "detach if possible"
- Depression
- Anxiety
- Lack of psychological insight
- Uncomfortable processing/reflecting upon her emotional reactions
- Poor self-esteem, afraid of being alone
- Self-reportedly "organized, kind, generous, loving, nurturing, and friendly"

Behavior: Individual-Exterior (UR)
- multiple suicide attempts
- history of self-mutilation: cutting her arms with glass, razors, and knives
- insomnia
- hobbies of reading, exercise, painting, poetry, movies, and cooking

Culture: Collective-Interior (LL)

- dissatisfied with past and current intimate relationships
- lack of social support group and no long-term friendships
- poor track record with six previous therapists

Social Systems: Collective-Exterior (LR)

- she was sexually molested by a family friend when she was 4
- she was raped by a coworker when she was 18
- mother recently diagnosed with cancer
- only child of alcoholic parents who were erratic and inconsistent
- she married when she was 25; after three years of hostile conflicts and his infidelity, they divorced when she was 28

Denise's psychograph (on a scale of 1–10) (at intake)

Cognitive	5
Self	3
Needs	3
Affective	2
Interpersonal	2
Spiritual	2

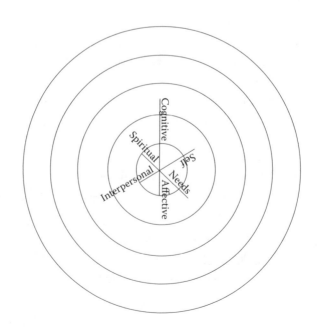

DSM Diagnosis

Axis I:	296.32 Major depressive disorder, recurrent, moderate
Axis II:	301.83 Borderline personality disorder
Axis III:	None
Axis IV:	Problems with primary support group; problems related to social environment
Axis V:	GAF=45 (at intake)

Case Narrative

Experience: Individual-Interior (UL)

With regard to the UL, Denise indicated that her strengths included "being organized, kind, generous, loving, nurturing, and friendly." She described her weaknesses extensively as "poor self-esteem, worry, concern with the thoughts of others, and fear of being alone." Denise reported extreme variance in her emotions ranging from feeling very happy and elated to very anxious and depressed. Denise's ability to regulate her affect seemed considerably undeveloped, as manifested by her inability to describe how she deals with her strong emotions as well as reporting that she detached when placed in stressful situations. Denise disclosed a number of relevant disturbing images, including "thoughts that I'm bad or have done something wrong, fear of death, and dwelling on getting older and uglier." Both in the initial session and in follow-up sessions, Denise appeared to minimize her circumstances as "normal things," despite describing her history of abuse, self-harm, and her parents' alcoholism.

Denise appeared to have difficulty remembering the majority of her childhood and adolescence. On the Integral Intake, Denise responded that she could not recall a specific happiest or most painful memory but that she had many of both. Upon follow-up in session, Denise failed to recall any specific pleasant memories from her childhood and spoke about the issue in vague terms. Denise was subsequently able to recall a number of painful childhood memories in specific detail, primarily around her parents' drinking and repetitive arguments.

Based on the information obtained from the Integral Intake and in session, Denise appeared to operate much of the time from a developmental level of early rule/role mind, but with significant evidence of borderline pathology emerging from general fixations at the phantasmic/emotional level. This was indicated by Denise's frequent use of major image-distorting defenses of splitting, idealization and devaluation, and projective identification. Denise also displayed action-level defenses of acting out, passive aggression, and denial. Consonant with her general level of pathology, she displayed an impulsive self-sense, as well as early conventional morality, as evidenced by rigid rules and expectations of herself and others; she often appeared engulfed or overwhelmed by her emotional environment. Denise endorsed symptoms in alignment with a *DSM-IV-TR* diagnosis of a major depressive disorder, moderate, and also met the symptom criteria for borderline personality disorder.

Denise reported experiencing stress in her shoulders and jaw as well as regularly getting headaches. She expressed herself creatively through writing poetry and painting but stated that she was incapable of "creating things from her own mind." In session, she reported that she felt she lacked imagination and creativity and simply recycled others' work. Denise listed a number of hobbies including reading, exercise, painting, poetry, movies, and cooking. She expressed that she still experienced pleasure with these activities but that her leisure time had been limited due to work obligations and dealing with her mother's illness.

Behavior: Individual-Exterior (UR)

With regard to the UR, Denise was of a petite build and average height. Her speech was often overly critical of herself and others, accusatory, and overly dramatic. Denise's speech productivity was normal, and her voice quality became quite shrill when she was upset or agitated. Denise would occasionally twist her hair when speaking and gesture with her hands when discussing emotional material. She expressed a normal range of vocabulary and pronunciations. No motor, auditory, or speech deficits were noted.

Denise reported having a recent physical within the last year with no noteworthy results. She said she took a multivitamin regularly but no medications. Denise expressed a number of relevant behaviors, including neglecting herself as well as friends and family, difficulty being kind to herself, losing her temper, difficulty concentrating, and crying. She also reported that when her anxiety was at its worst (which had escalated since she became aware of her mother's diagnosis), she sometimes experienced dizziness, accelerated heart rate, and jitters. Although her symptoms resembled those of a panic attack, her experience seemed subclinical in intensity, and she agreed that the intensity of her worry and discomfort seemed to be less panic than intense worry.

Although Denise reported difficulty with initial, middle, and terminal insomnia—averaging only 4–6 hours of sleep per night, according to her—she and I agreed that her sleeping difficulties did not cause enough impairment in her occupational, social, and other dimensions of her life to warrant a *DSM* diagnosis of primary insomnia. She further expressed concern with her weight: that she probably did not eat enough given that she exercised every day, including yoga, walking, biking, and weightlifting. Denise reported that she currently drank only very rarely but that she had used marijuana, cocaine, and crack cocaine extensively during her teenage years.

Culture: Collective-Interior (LL)

With regard to the LL, Denise expressed that she was always "kind of shy and anxious" and had difficulty developing and maintaining friendships throughout her life. She reported being sexually molested by a family friend at age 4, which she had not disclosed until adulthood. Denise's maternal grandfather committed suicide when she was in the seventh grade, amidst rumors of having sexually abused both Denise and her mother. Denise reported no clear recollection of being molested by her grandfather.

Denise had one serious romantic relationship in high school, which she described as "passionate and intense." She explained that they fought regularly and that their disagreements would often escalate to shouting at and pushing each other, but that "the makeup sex was incredible." That relationship lasted almost two years. From age 16 to 20, Denise regularly engaged in self-mutilation, cutting her arms with glass, razors, and knives. She also attempted suicide at least five times by various means, including overdosing on prescription pain medication and cutting her wrists. She was never hospitalized. At age 17, Denise's mother disappeared for two days and was later found after being arrested for driving under the influence of alcohol. That same year, following a casual sexual encounter, Denise had an abortion after accidentally becoming pregnant. Later that same year, Denise was raped by a coworker, which she never reported to the authorities. From age 18 to 20, Denise abused cocaine on a regular basis and also developed chlamydia, which was successfully treated with antibiotics.

Denise married at age 25 after dating a man for only 4 months. She reported that their relationship was wonderful at first but that he became increasingly withdrawn and critical after 6 months together. Denise disclosed that the last 2 years of the relationship were marked by repeated conflicts, hostility, and absence and infidelity on her husband's part. They eventually divorced when she was 28, but continued to reside together for another 8 months while her husband completed school. Her ex-husband recently remarried, which Denise reported as a significant stressor.

Denise failed to describe her relationships on the Integral Intake (she left blank the query "Describe your relationships, including friends, family, and coworkers"; such omissions are often clinically very illuminating). At session follow-up, she reported that she felt that all of her relationships were difficult in some way and that she lacked anyone with whom she felt particularly close, including her current romantic partner. She expressed that it had been hard for her to make and maintain relationships throughout her life and that she often felt exploited and manipulated by others. Overall, Denise expressed feeling quite dissatisfied with her relationships and experienced considerable discomfort in social situations. Nonetheless, what she reported as most important to her was having a partner in life, contentment in her job, friends and family, and peace.

Denise disclosed that the anger of others was the most commonly expressed emotion in her family of origin; with her anger as the emotion most discouraged. Currently, she had difficulty expressing or discussing which emotions were comfortable or uncomfortable for her, stating that she did not understand my questions—that "they are just feelings." Although she described in detail how she was forced to perform acts of sodomy and bondage with her previous partner, in which she felt degraded and humiliated, she reported feeling very sexually satisfied in her current relationship. Denise reported little or no interest in spirituality, politics, the environment, or cultural activities and listed her important morals as honesty, compassion, and responsibility.

Social Systems: Collective-Exterior (LR)

With regard to the LR, Denise reported being raised by both of her parents, who are still married. Denise described her parents as alcoholic, erratic, and inconsistent. Denise has no siblings. Denise reported not remembering much of her early childhood, but what she did remember, she recalled as conflicted and argumentative. She stated that her parents would drink excessively in the home most nights and that there were many episodes in which one or both parents would disappear for hours or more at a time.

On the Integral Intake, Denise avoided listing the members of her family of origin. During follow-up in session, she reported that she had been confused and had presumed the question referred to her current household. She was then capable of listing the members of her family of origin (which consisted of only her parents). Denise emphasized that she lacked a support system with no close friendships and estrangement from her family. She indicated that her mother's recent cancer diagnosis had instigated the most contact she had experienced with her family in years. Beyond her parents' reported alcoholism, Denise indicated no family history of diagnosed mental illness. She reported being involved in no organizations and only minimally involved in volunteer work.

Denise had successfully completed high school as well as a few courses at a local community college, but she eventually dropped out and has not completed a degree. Since then, Denise has been employed in various low-wage retail, service industry, and administrative positions. She has been at her current job for 9 months, which she reported was "boring and unsatisfying." Denise reported residing in a lower-cost two-bedroom apartment with typical middle-class amenities and appropriate conditions. She expressed that it was decorated to her liking and that she was largely satisfied with it. She did state some concern with the safety of the neighborhood and noted that the area was not very well lit, but she did not feel that it represented an immediate danger.

Initial (Tentative) Treatment Plan

In accordance with the spectrum of development, pathology, and treatment (see Table 4.1 on page 82 in Chapter 4), I adopted the general therapeutic approach of structure-building psychotherapy as the form of treatment to address Denise's primary concerns. As the table alludes to, the borderline and narcissistic disorders that derive from developmental derailments during the phantasmic/emotional stage are, after Kohut, disorders of the self (Kohut & Wolf, 1978). The major task in this approach is to strengthen the ego/self (build ego/self structure) so that the client no longer needs to resort to primitive defenses (splitting, projective identification, defensive idealization and devaluation, etc.) because once her self structure is strong enough, she will then be capable of higher-level defense mechanisms; in other words, she will be capable of creating the repression barrier itself (Kohut & Wolf, 1978; also mentioned in Chapter 6). In this process, various split-off or part-object relations are integrated into whole-object relations via empathic interpretation and analysis of transference (Kernberg, 1980; Kohut, 1977, 1984; Stolorow, Brandchaft, & Atwood, 1987; Stolorow, Atwood, & Orange, 2002). Thus, as the client's self develops, not only is her internal experience more coherent, stable, and organized, but she will also be able to esteem herself, decrease her impulsive acting out, and regulate her affective experience more adaptively.

This process is both experiential (using immediacy to bring attention to the here-and-now interactions between client and therapist) and analytic (examining the here-and-now experiences as well as how the client experienced and internalized the primary objects/caregivers in her early childhood and how her internalized representations of her early selfobjects persist in her current psychological organization of experience, greatly influencing the nature of her current experience) (Kohut, 1984; McWilliams, 1994; Greenberg & Mitchell, 1983). Clients with disorders of the self will enact a selfobject transference in which "the specific needs that had remained unresponded to by the specific faulty interactions between the nascent self and the selfobjects of early life" are reactivated (Kohut & Wolf, 1978, p. 414). As I have written elsewhere about treating clients with disorders of the self, the basic therapeutic process, or the fundamental treatment plan, involves

> (a) reactivation of the client's need(s) (selfobject transference), (b) nonfulfillment of some of the client's needs by the counselor (optimal frustration/empathic failure), and (c) reestablishment of the empathic bond between client (self) and counselor (selfobject). *This sequence must occur many, many times throughout the course of therapy.* (Fall, Holden, & Marquis, 2004, p. 88; for more details of this process, see chap. 3 of Fall et al., 2004; see also Mahoney & Marquis, 2002, pp. 802–811)

Critical to the therapeutic process are the therapist's interpretations of what transpires between the client and therapist, but more important than the objective accuracy of the interpretation is the therapist's sustained empathic attunement to the client's experience, especially when the client experiences being judged or misunderstood; these "optimal empathic failures"—when processed by therapist and client—potentially facilitate the client's transmuting internalizations in which she increasingly fulfills self-system functions for herself that she (previously demanded) the therapist or other selfobjects provide. In the midst of optimal empathic failures, therapists ideally (1) nondefensively acknowledge their roles/errors that impacted the client's negative experience, (2) remain empathically attuned and thus apprehend how the apparently disproportionate intensity of the client's reaction reflects the traumatic residue from previous experiences in the client's life (transference), and (3) when the disruption/perturbation in the relationship has been mended (reestablishment of the self-selfobject bond), to empathically provide an interpretation regarding how to understand what just transpired between the therapist and client. Significantly, Kohut emphasized that curative factor in the therapeutic process is sustained empathic attunement (understanding phase); interpretations (explanatory phase) are secondary: "It bears stressing that the analyst's essential activities in each of [these phases], not only the first one are based on empathy" (1984, p. 176). By empathically recognizing a disruption in the therapeutic bond, a potential retraumatization can be transformed into a "development-enhancing structure building optimal frustration" (Kohut, 1984, p. 207).

In contrast to Gary (case example 1), who expressed a desire for clear, specific goals, I estimated in the initial session that therapy with Denise was going to be difficult and that positive effects would likely derive slowly, from long-term work. My primary goals at this point were developmental:

- to help Denise develop enough self structure to enact more adaptive defense mechanisms
- to increase her affect regulation abilities
- to increase her capacities to self-soothe and esteem herself
- achieve the three points above so that she will be more likely to establish and sustain long-term relationships

Denise and I would work toward the above goals primarily via the alternating sequence of experiencing and analyzing that was described above. Specific interventions that would most likely be used included:

Upper Left Quadrant

1. Self-observation and self-monitoring, which she records in the Daily Record of Dysfunctional Thoughts (see below; on p. 226–227)
2. Psychodynamic psychotherapy (Kernberg, 1980; Kohut, 1984; McWilliams, 1994; Greenberg & Mitchell, 1983) to explore concerns of depression, anxiety, self-esteem, and self-image
3. Therapeutic journaling to explore and assess client's thoughts, feelings, and behaviors
4. Self-soothing and affect regulations via (in part) her hobbies and relaxation exercises (see below)
5. More affirming, positive self-talk

Upper Right Quadrant

1. Daily Record of Dysfunctional Thoughts (Beck, 1979)
2. Modify sleep patterns to achieve 8 hours of restful sleep per night
3. Instruction in and rehearsal of systematic relaxation scripts/techniques to counteract anxiety symptoms
4. Referral to psychiatrist for evaluation for antidepressant medication

Lower Left Quadrant

1. Empathically interpreting what transpires between the client and myself
2. Address concerns with her romantic and other relationships

Lower Right Quadrant

1. A likely potential: a no-suicide contract
2. Expressing unfinished business with her mother
3. Address concerns with career and workplace environment
4. Social skills training

Therapy sessions each week were established with very structured and stable parameters, including meeting time, meeting length, plans for vacations or breaks, fee payment, and so on. With such clients, the importance of a clear, formal contract is paramount in that it attempts to stabilize their chaotic inner world. Further, Denise's potentially negative reaction to the structure of the contract may serve as a vehicle for later processing.

Interventions and Sessions

The early counseling sessions largely centered on developing a secure and stable therapeutic relationship through the communication of empathy, counselor congruence, and unconditional positive regard. At the outset of counseling, Denise appeared mildly suspicious and expressed concern with working with a male counselor. She stated that she had reservations about working with a male because most of the men in her life had not been trustworthy. Denise agreed to continue with the option of a referral if her comfort level did not increase. By the fourth session, she expressed being more at ease with me and stated that she felt that she could trust me. Typically, Denise was nervous and unfocused in the beginning of sessions and maintained a low level of anxiety throughout the course of the session. Following the initial discomfort at the outset of counseling, rapport was established and maintained to varying degrees throughout the course of therapy.

Despite her consistent complaints regarding her partner's lack of commitment, Denise was generally resistant to confrontations and interpretations about her choice to remain in such an unsatisfying relationship in which she felt exploited and used. Denise often appeared uncomfortable when we explored or processed her emotions, especially when we directly attended to her immediate experience of, and with, me. Denise was moderately to significantly resistant to a number of my interpretations of her immediate experience of the counseling session, stating that I was "being critical and don't want her to be happy" (more about this will be discussed subsequently). In general, she appeared to have difficulty with the less structured elements of the sessions and expressed that she wanted "answers about how to make herself different." In counseling, Denise occasionally lost her temper, refused to process immediate emotional reactions, and blamed me ("You don't want me to be happy"), threatening to terminate her treatment several times. In order to accommodate her wishes and requests for assisting her to solve her problems and her clear preference for concrete strategies, I began instructing her in several behavioral and cognitive strategies: systematic relaxation, sleep hygiene, behavioral rehearsal and role-playing specifically centering on her concerns in her romantic relationship and with her colleagues at work, daily monitoring of dysfunctional thoughts, and decatastrophizing. Denise was generally responsive to these more concrete interventions and developed an initial skill at recognizing and modifying her maladaptive cognitions in certain contexts.

Regarding the relaxation skills, I educated Denise about slow, deep, diaphragmatic breathing; I explained that we cannot be simultaneously relaxed and anxious, and that anxiety is a function of physiology, behavior, and thoughts. I capitalized on her desire for problem-solving skills by emphasizing the scientific research supporting progressive relaxation, guiding her through it in one session and providing her with a CD that had several guided relaxation scripts on it for her to practice at home. As usual, I emphasized the importance of daily practice (not waiting until circumstances are bad to try these skills) and that the power of the skills increases with consistent practice. Fortunately, she was able to experience the positive effects of my guided relaxation with her, and several times in our work together, when she became disturbed in session and refused to process the immediate moment, I facilitated her relaxing and soothing herself. Each time this happened in session, I would try to take less and less of a guide role and encourage her to relax and soothe herself, with my providing cues as needed. Regarding the sleep hygiene, I gave highly similar instructions as those that I described to Gary on pages 195–196 of this chapter.

Regarding Beck's (1979, p. 403) Daily Record of Dysfunctional Thoughts, I supplied Denise with several pages of the form and instructed her to complete the five columns of that form upon experiencing an unpleasant emotion, recording:

- the situation (the event that precipitated the unpleasant emotion)
- the specific emotion and its intensity (on a scale of 1–100)
- the automatic thoughts that coincided with the unpleasant emotion and her belief in those thoughts (on a scale of 1–100)
- a rational response to the automatic thoughts and her belief in that rational response (on a scale of 1–100)
- the outcome (rating for a second time her belief in the automatic thoughts and specifying and rating subsequent emotions, both on a scale of 1–100)

I instructed her to keep the forms with her at home and work and to fill out the form whenever she noticed herself upset. I told her to do so as consistently as possible and to bring the forms with her to each session for us to work with together. Overall, she enjoyed this intervention more than any others and reported considerable insight into her thought patterns. Here is an example of one of her "rows" in her Daily Record of Dysfunctional Thoughts :

- the situation: "my boyfriend went out with his friends instead of doing what I wanted us to do"
- the specific emotion and intensity: "rage, betrayal, fear (90)"
- the automatic thoughts and intensity: "he's cheating on me or he's going to leave me (90)"
- a rational response to the automatic thoughts and her belief in that rational response: "maybe he just needs some 'guy time' and that we will be happy together (50)"
- the outcome: "my automatic thoughts make things a lot worse (75); still unhappy but feel better than before (75)"

As addressed earlier, Denise generally reacted more positively to action-oriented and solution-focused suggestions for her concerns and often implored me to tell her specifically what she should do. When her petitions were redirected to her and her own autonomy, she would often become childlike and pleading. Denise was capable, at times, of rehearsing communication techniques such as using "I" statements and responding with her feelings, and she reported utilizing them to some success within her romantic relationship. Her maintenance of a thought record enabled her to learn to recognize a number of pathogenic beliefs, such as "I have to be perfect," "Everyone thinks I'm unattractive," and "If I don't please my partner consistently, the relationship will fail." She reported some benefit from implementing the cognitive techniques of thought stopping and hypothesis testing. However, she would often question herself and her conclusions, seeking support, encouragement, and validation from me.

I continued to try to balance what I deemed most likely to be of ultimate service to her development (less concrete, more immediate Kohutian work) with her preference for cognitive-behavioral work. Operating from the perspective that if therapists can't satisfy their clients enough to keep them coming to therapy, they won't be able to help them, I spent most of the time in the first seven sessions being very cognitive-behavioral with Denise. Following the seven sessions that were provided by her EAP, Denise elected to terminate counseling, saying that her stopping therapy was due to her lack of financial resources. She reported some relief from her depressed mood but displayed little or no insight regarding her choice of romantic partners who tended to mistreat or take advantage of her. Fortunately, in the process of terminating, we were able to find a solution to her financial situation, involving both our clinic's sliding scale and using her insurance to cover most of the counseling fees. At this point, Denise took two weeks off from work and our sessions and visited her mother.

Upon returning, Denise's depression and anxiety had intensified, as her concerns focused on her mother and her advanced stomach cancer, which was expected to be terminal. She reported deep sadness, crying regularly, anxiety that verged on panic attacks, poor concentration, and very little joy in her life. As if she wasn't going through enough, her boyfriend broke up with her while she was visiting her mother; she reported him saying he didn't want to be tied down, he couldn't take her mood swings, and she was "too high-maintenance." I viewed her reaction to the breakup as a sign of her improvement. Despite a great deal of sadness and anger, she appeared to be handling it well. There were no suicide threats, and she was even able to soothe herself, saying, "He didn't treat me right anyway . . . I can find someone better than him . . . I need to focus on my mom now anyway . . . He didn't even seem to care that my mom is dying!" I both praised and encouraged her for responding in such a healthy way to the breakup. Denise reported that her primary goal at this point was deciding whether to move back to care for her mom (who lived 8 hours away). After a few weeks, she decided not to move back home.

In response to her mother's condition, in addition to empathy and support, I discussed the stages of grief with her, as well as the dying process. Denise identified feelings related to the pending loss and what issues she wanted to address with her mother before her death. Denise also elected to bring pictures and mementos of her mother to session and discuss their meaning for her.

With the psychosocial stresses of her mother's dying and the end of her romantic relationship, I was increasingly concerned about Denise's safety. She consented to sign a no-suicide contract, and I suggested that she see a psychiatrist about medications to help her with her anxiety and depression. Denise was initially resistant to seeing a psychiatrist, but after I persuaded her about the potential benefits of psychotropic medications, she complied. The psychiatrist was in agreement with my diagnoses and established a daily dosage of Effexor XR 350 mg. (I find it indispensable to have a good reference source—such as the *Physician's Desk Reference*—to consult when I am counseling clients who are taking prescription medications, so that I am mindful of any possible side effects that they may experience.) In this case, Denise did develop initial side effects of mild constipation and nausea, but these were manageable given the benefit obtained from the medication. As the Effexor apparently began to demonstrate its positive effects regarding the intensity of her depressed mood, Denise also reported less insomnia as well; this latter effect was unexpected, because a common side effect of Effexor is insomnia (Ingersoll & Rak, 2006).

Denise was also encouraged to continue her current exercise regimen, specifically her cardiovascular training. She continued to engage in both cycling and jogging over the course of treatment, reporting that it helped keep her mind off things and feel she was doing something good for herself. I praised her for taking such initiative, for knowing what she could do to make herself feel better, and for caring enough about herself to actually do it. Denise also initiated attending a yoga class that included concentrative meditations; she reported that this was very relaxing and soothing.

At her yoga classes, Denise met another man, with whom she elected to move in after knowing him only a few weeks. When I confronted her about the possible implications of this choice and the similarity with other relationships that had ended unsuccessfully, Denise quickly became angry and threatened to terminate counseling. When her reaction itself was examined, she only became more frustrated and responded that no one wanted her to be happy. I continued to be as empathically attuned to her as I could be, which was often excruciating for me. The interchange went something like:

Client (upbeat and excited): What I am excited to tell you is that David and I have decided to move in together and I'm so happy . . . I mean, it just makes so much sense . . . he's only working part-time and could use the extra income and together we could have a bigger place . . . plus he's just been great lately and we've been getting along so well. I mean, I really think this could go somewhere . . . that's if the two cats can get along.

Counselor: Yes, I know the cats are important to you, but tell me . . . you seem really elated about the possibilities with him, but I'm wondering if this feeling or situation might remind you of anything else.

Cl (puzzled, confused): What do you mean? I'm just happy for once.

Co: I know, I see your excitement all over your face and in your tone of voice, and I'm delighted that you are so happy—you seem genuinely elated. I'm also curious, however, if you have any sense that what's going on here may resemble anything you've experienced before.

Cl (still puzzled): Well . . . I guess not . . . I can't think of anything. . . .

Co: Is it possible that it could be similar to the excitement you had after meeting Jim when you had been so sad after a previous breakup? . . . You seemed to think that that could really go somewhere, too. I also remember your talking about the beginning of another relationship you have had in somewhat the same way. I recall you saying how much faith you had in that as well, so much that you were willing to give him the money for his practice and his home—

Cl (becoming angry and interrupting me): But this isn't like that! David is different . . . I know he really cares about me.

Co: How do you know that after only three weeks?

Cl: Well . . . (stutters) . . . he's asked me to move in, for one. And we actually go on dates that I enjoy.

Co: You also mentioned that he really needs the money . . . and you told me earlier how you were paying for most of your evenings out . . . even to the degree that you had trouble paying some of your bills this month.

Cl (more angry and heated): What are you talking about? Why do you say those things? David cares for me and he wants us to be together! Why do you have to make so much of things when I'm feeling so good? It's like you don't want me to be happy!

Co: It may very well be true that David cares for you . . . my efforts here are to point out what seems to be a pattern in your relationships with men. It seems to me that you idealize them very quickly and tend to think that there may be more going on than the guy is experiencing. I just wonder if this could be similar to previous relationships you've had and how it might turn out for you. I'm concerned that you may allow yourself to become vulnerable to someone who may not deeply have your best interests in mind.

Cl: It's not true! You don't really care for me and you always spoil things when I'm excited about something! You just criticize! I don't know why I come here if this is how I'm treated! Maybe I should just stop. . . .

Co: I can see how very hurt and upset you are with me over what I've said. . . .

Cl (sarcastically): Hell yes, I'm upset . . . I'm more than upset . . . I'm pissed!

Co: I know . . . You're angry that you came here excited about your relationship and I've suggested that you consider it from another perspective—

Cl (interrupting): No! It's just that you don't want me to really be happy . . . just like everyone else!

Co: Everyone else?

Cl: Yes, my parents, my friends, even my past stupid therapists, it's all the same . . .

Co: I realize that it must feel that way to you—that nobody wants to support you or share in your excitement. It must feel terribly disappointing to want to share your excitement with me and how I reply suggests that maybe you should be a bit more cautious with the relationship rather than rush into things. . . . I also wonder how much of your father's criticism and anger might have influenced you to see me in such a way.

Cl (a little less angry): What?

Co: I'm curious how my responses today seem similar to "everyone else's." You have often spoken of how when your father was around he was drunk and very critical of you—I wonder how that might affect the way you perceive me. . . . I hope you understand that I *do* care for you and I think, if you stop for a minute, you will recall that I've said many things that you didn't perceive as criticism. I'm not sure it's accurate to say that's *all* that I do . . . that is the very reason that I thought you could look at your decision from another perspective . . . I just don't know if your decision to move in with David so quickly

will actually get you the results you want . . . and I am concerned about your getting hurt again. *[Obviously, I am being
far more directive with her than I would be with clients who were
not struggling with such profound problems; I am trying to help
her see that she is acting impulsively and to learn ways of analyzing situations before jumping into things such as this so quickly.]*

Cl: Well . . . you might be right about my dad . . . he was an ass . . . but
even so, I really think David is different and I'm going ahead
with this. . . .

Co: I respect your making your own decisions. I would simply encourage you to not rush into things and to try to be as aware as
possible as the relationship develops . . . we sometimes have
a tendency to repeat the same situations in our relationships
despite our efforts to do otherwise.

Cl: Yeah . . . you've said that before. I guess we'll see. . . .

In this case, Denise wasn't able to recognize her pattern with her
romantic partners, but she was able—partially—to step outside of her
anger with me and acknowledge that *some* of how she was reacting to
me was a function of her relationship with her father. I viewed that as
significant progress and communicated that to Denise. Especially significant was the fact that she was initially highly angry with me, accus-
ing me of not wanting her to be happy, but with sustained empathic
attunement, she was able to remain in psychological contact with me
while retaining me as a whole-object: someone who both cares about
her and pisses her off at the same time.

While the primary focus of Denise's sessions addressed her internal
subjective processes, she also desired more and better relationships in
general. Specifically, I regularly encouraged Denise to attempt to develop
new relationships with her colleagues at work. However, she continued
to experience difficulties in this area and was unable to establish meaningful relationships beyond her romantic partner. Congruent with her
borderline personality organization, her relationships were often erratic
and unstable and marred by her tendency to oscillate between idealizing and devaluing others (which in part accounted for her pattern of
falling in love often, only to have the relationships quickly deteriorate).
However, consistent with a self-psychology (Kohutian) perspective, I

tended to view her symptomatic behavior as her best efforts to avoid unbearable emotions and to regain a sense of self-comfort, self-cohesion, and self-worth. Framing clients' maladaptive behaviors in this way allows therapists to view such behaviors not merely as pathological but as their best attempts to meet the needs of their underdeveloped self, which is an indicator that the self's developmental process is still under way and capable of being fostered (Kohut, 1984).

Denise was often highly suspicious of others' intentions, and she often interpreted apparently neutral interactions as exploitative or critical. A number of sessions were spent addressing e-mails from coworkers and her partner to which she reacted by feeling slighted or insulted. Despite efforts to modify Denise's impressions, she was often resistant, perceiving others—and at times me—as "out to get her." I was the target of many of Denise's idealizations and devaluations. It is not easy to be on the receiving end of "You just don't care about me!" "You don't want me to be happy!" and "Why doesn't anyone want to help me?"—especially given how hard I was working to help her. In the midst of her devaluing accusations, I did my best to remain centered (both feet on the floor and slow, deep breaths) and to remember Kohut's admonitions regarding the challenges of working with clients with borderline structural organization (all severe personality disorders can represent a borderline personality organization):

> Only the analyst's continuing sincere acceptance of the patient's reproaches as (psychologically) realistic, followed by a prolonged (and ultimately successful) attempt to look into himself and remove the inner barriers that stand in the way of his empathic grasp of the patient, ultimately have a chance to turn the tide. (Kohut, 1984, p. 182)

For Kohut, nondefensively providing empathic understanding and owning one's (at times) real role in reenacting some aspects of the client's painful experience is central to psychotherapy. He stressed that "if some of my colleagues will say at this juncture that this is not analysis—so be it. My inclination is to respond with the old adage that they should get out of the kitchen if they cannot stand the heat" (Kohut, 1984, p. 183). As anyone who has ever worked with clients with borderline personality organization knows, the therapy can be hot indeed.

Fortunately, when therapists are perceived as accepting, attuned, and helpful in articulating and regulating their affect, clients' emotional blocks often diminish some, as they allow some of the disavowed parts of themselves to reemerge for the renewed developmental opportunities that part of them recognizes as available to them in therapy (Mahoney and Marquis, 2002). This is the arena in which

> the therapist's "affective competence"—the capacity to handle, "deal with," metabolize, and facilitate one's own and others' affective (relational) experience becomes paramount (Fosha, 2000). Unless the therapist is able to empathically know the client's experience of impending fear or danger—which results in the client's felt need to enlist resistance—analysis of resistance will be therapeutically useless. Consequently, the client's feeling understood in a moment of great fear (re)establishes the selfobject bond—creating the image of an object (the therapist) that is *not* a repetition of the client's past parental imagoes. (Mahoney & Marquis, 2002, p. 808)

Due to the severity and complexity of Denise's developmental dynamics and concerns, the only direct interventions regarding the LR (social systems) perspective was to explore her mother's life and death. Denise initially reported feeling in some way responsible for her mother's illness and guilty for residing so far away. In order to address her feelings, Denise composed a number of poems about her mother that she brought to sessions along with photographs and other significant objects. Further, she engaged in a tearful discussion with me regarding their relationship, attempting to come to terms with her experiences of neglect and also cultivate compassion for her mother's situation. Denise reported significant emotional relief and insight regarding her responsibility for her mother's illness from the supportive nature of these sessions.

A few sessions later, I further encouraged her to express any unfinished business to her mom while she still could. Denise replied that she didn't want to get too emotional with her mom. I replied: "Denise, as painful as this may be for you, imagine that your mom died today, that she is no longer here for you to talk to. As painful as that is, what do you think you would most regret not having told her? This could be

that you love her, that you're angry at her for not nurturing and protecting you more . . . it could be anything." This was apparently too much
for Denise. In the midst of my spiel, Denise decompensated, sobbing
deeply for minutes. I simply empathized with her, offered supportive
statements, and reminded her to practice her self-soothing skills: to
breathe deeply and slowly, to self-talk positively ("As painful and scary
as this is, I will make it through my mom's death"), and to esteem
herself for her nurturing, loving qualities (how much Denise still cared
for her mother despite all the harm she had done to Denise as a child).
Although Denise had improved her affect-regulating skills and in a
few minutes had regained her composure, I think—in retrospect—that
my encouraging her to address her mother's dying in such a direct way
(which is completely appropriate with clients with more ego strength)
may have been developmentally inappropriate.

Conclusion of Case 2

The following week, after an altercation with her boyfriend, she locked
herself in a bathroom and took an overdose of Effexor. Her boyfriend
called 911, and she was taken to a community psychiatric hospital. Following an initial observation, Denise was taken before the court and
deemed a risk to herself and was mandated to remain in the psychiatric
facility. This was reportedly a very traumatic and overwhelming experience for Denise, with a number of calls placed to me to address her
situation. Within the facility, Denise received psychoeducational group
counseling along with individual sessions with another counselor, and
she was put on additional medications, including Seroquel and Xanax.
After one week she was released and began individual sessions with me
at a frequency of twice per week. Denise was extremely upset regarding
the treatment she had received in the hospital, and displayed little or no
insight into the nature of her actions, proclaiming that she hadn't really
meant to do it and that she didn't deserve treatment like that. Denise
was compliant with four more sessions of counseling and then abruptly
elected to terminate because she decided to relocate in order to care
for her mother. I suggested that Denise continue treatment in her new
locale and provided appropriate referrals. Following termination and
of this writing, there has been no further contact. I counseled Denise
for 22 sessions over a period of 6 months. The 50-minute sessions were

held weekly with the exception of two weeks during which Denise was seen twice.

Unlike counseling Gary, this case did not end happily. Despite some growth and modest improvement over the course of therapy, it was disappointing that she terminated so quickly after her suicide attempt. Like some of her other courses of therapy, it appears that not enough time was available to make as much progress as we had hoped. According to Kernberg (2005), the average amount of therapy required to significantly help clients with severe borderline disorders is 3 to 5 years with two sessions each week. Although Denise represented a milder form of borderline personality organization, the time we had together still seems far too brief. Nonetheless, the treatment plan and interventions that I used with Denise are representative of an integral approach to a client such as Denise.

Conclusion

I counseled both of these clients five years ago (as a tenure-track assistant professor, my time in the past years has been devoted to research, publishing, and teaching). Much of my thinking has changed in the intervening years, and although I have reconstructed our work together from case presentations I gave in my supervision groups, I have surely forgotten some significant details of my work with Gary and Denise.

As you saw, my work with these two clients was very different. Denise's developmental center of gravity was, in many regards, phantasmic-emotional, which reflected her borderline personality organization. My primary goal for her (which was not fully realized) was for her to develop enough of a self or ego so that she could better regulate her affect, esteem herself, and utilize repression as a defense mechanism, rather than splitting, denial, and so forth. This primary goal was in stark contrast to the goals that Gary and I established and worked toward, which were a function of his having a significantly more developed center of gravity. Despite some of Gary's struggles with self-esteem, he had developed a solid, personal sense of self (between formal-reflexive and vision-logic). Thus we worked on his relaxation and assertiveness skills and explored what was meaningful to him, in order to help him establish clearer life goals that he could pursue and so that he could generally feel more balanced in his living.

To summarize and conclude this chapter, integral treatment plans are designed, first and foremost, as a function of each client's most salient developmental and quadratic features. Although it is not meant to be implemented as a rigid rule, the spectrum of development, pathology, and treatment (Table 4.1, page 82) offers the principal scaffolding for the general therapeutic approach used with each client. Next, integral therapists scan for noteworthy quadratic features that likely are implicated in—or are exacerbating—the client's struggles, for example, any environmental stressors, social oppression, or lack of access to economic, medical, or educational systems (LR); any ethnic/religious/political beliefs and other relevant cultural meaning-making systems (LL); any medical conditions, observable behaviors, or patterns of diet, exercise, or drug and alcohol use (UR); and any noteworthy patterns in the client's self-experience, from empty feelings of depression to chronic worrying or panic attacks (UL). In the process of assessing each client's development, issues pertaining to specific developmental lines are often addressed, especially with clients whose center of gravity is beyond phantasmic-emotional and whose development appears quite uneven (see Chapter 5). Therapeutic attention to clients' states of consciousness is sometimes central; at other times it is peripheral. Helping clients develop mindfulness of their anxious or depressed states, or assuming the witness perspective for those states, often provides great relief from that suffering. Precisely how each therapist works with clients' personality types is more idiosyncratic, partly due to how many different typological systems are available to therapists.

Many courses of treatment do not attend to every dimension of integral therapy (all quadrants, all levels, all lines, all states, all types) because of time restraints or other pragmatic constraints (I didn't work with the dimension of types in either of these cases). Integral therapists do, however, use the AQAL framework to help them scan for as many potentially relevant factors as possible in each client's problems, as well as for specific interventions that may address those problems—for example, mindfulness, basic centering techniques, and awareness/consciousness raising (UL); relaxation training, cognitive restructuring,[6] and (referrals for) pharmacotherapy (UR); role-plays, empty chair work, analysis of transference, and the therapeutic relationship itself (LL); and exposure therapy, genogram analysis, and social liberation (LR).

In essence, integral treatment planning involves using the AQAL framework to complement, rather than fundamentally change, how you already assess, plan, and carry out treatment. In other words, by scanning each client's AQAL matrix (quadrants, levels, lines, states, types), you may observe relevant features of a client's living that will add to the type of therapy you already provide. You can retain your therapeutic preferences, for integral therapy recognizes value and merit in all of the traditional therapeutic approaches. What AQAL treatment planning does is to contextualize clients, their struggles, and our traditional therapeutic practices within a larger, more embracing, framework.

Notes

1. All names and other identifying characteristics have been altered to protect the identities of clients involved.
2. Although I counseled Gary prior to my training in ego development assessment, in retrospect, I believe Gary's center of gravity probably hovered between E-6 (conscientious) and E-7 (Individualistic) (see page 127 in Chapter 5).
3. Although my primary guiding (meta)theoretical framework is integral, I also draw heavily from psychodynamic approaches and thus am alert to clients' cyclical maladaptive patterns (CMPs) and how they play out in the therapeutic relationship (Levenson, 1995). One of the beauties of integral metatheory is that it provides a parsimonious conceptual scaffolding while allowing each practitioner tremendous personal freedom. While I am heavily experiential and psychodynamic, other integral therapists are heavily cognitive-behavioral, transpersonal, Gestalt, and so forth.
4. As with Gary (case example 1), I counseled Denise prior to my training in ego development assessment; in retrospect, however, I believe Denise's center of gravity probably hovered primarily between E-2 (impulsive) and E-3 (self-protective) (see page 126 in Chapter 5).
5. Denise's case demonstrates that some people aren't "at" just one stage but, rather, vary considerably as a function of contexts and environmental stressors. Even though most people's being and functioning do not derive from a single developmental stage, most do have a center of gravity characterized by the qualities of a single stage of development. Denise, like many people with borderline characteristics, was less stable and more "all over the place" than most people.
6. Recall from note 1 in Chapter 3 that cognitive interventions are categorized as UR interventions because the cognitive approach strives to be as objective and empirical as possible, which is a way of "gaining distance from" one's thoughts—as from the outside/exterior looking in—so that one is not so involved with the matter that one cannot see one's thoughts as they "really are," which is what "objectivity" is all about.

8
RESEARCH

Past and Future Developments

In the first chapter, I made a case for the need for integral assessment. This chapter describes a research study—my doctoral dissertation—that evaluated the existing theoretically grounded idiographic intake instruments. Because a detailed description of that research study is "in press" in The *Journal of Mental Health Counseling*, this chapter's description of the study will be far briefer—merely providing an overview of the study, the results, and conclusions. Marquis & Holden, (in press) will provide all the details needed to replicate the study I performed, including all data analyses and statistical procedures. This chapter also discusses changes made to the Integral Intake in response to my dissertation data, as well as some plans for future research on the Integral Intake.

A thorough review of professional literature revealed a surprising lack of reported research regarding the relative utility of the few published idiographic initial assessment instruments. Such research, however, could contribute to more efficient and effective service to counseling clients and, thus, warranted attention. In an attempt to fill this research void in the professional counseling literature, I explored how counseling and psychotherapy experts evaluated the Integral Intake (II) in comparison to the two published (at the time of my dissertation) theoretically grounded, idiographic initial assessment instruments: the Multimodal Life History Inventory (MLHI) and the Adlerian Life-Style Introductory Interview (LSII). "Experts" were defined as professors of counseling or psychology and licensed practitioners who have been practicing as counselors or psychologists for at least five years.

Purpose of Study

The purpose of the study was twofold. First, I wanted to explore whether or not there were differences—and if so, what those differences were—in how expert therapists evaluated the II, the LSII, and the MLHI. Participants ranked and rated the inventories relative to how comprehensive, helpful, and efficient the instruments are in assessing eight dimensions of clients: thoughts, feelings, behaviors, culture, spirituality, physical aspects, environments, as well as what is most meaningful to clients. Second, I wanted to receive feedback and suggestions from the participants regarding how to improve the Integral Intake. On the evaluation form that participants completed, *helpfulness, comprehensiveness,* and *efficiency* were defined as follows:

> *Helpfulness*: how clinically useful the inventory is to the clinician relative to understanding clients, their most pressing issues, and optimal courses of treatment.
>
> *Comprehensiveness*: how thoroughly each instrument assesses the client. Comprehensiveness consists of two components, breadth and depth. Whereas depth involves the extent to which a specific domain is investigated, breadth involves the extent to which the numerous domains that comprise the client are investigated. Regarding eight dimensions that seem essential to understanding a person's mental health—thoughts, emotions, behaviors, physical aspects of the person, physical aspects of the person's environment, culture, spirituality, and meaning—I was inquiring relative to deep comprehensiveness. In the question addressing overall comprehensiveness, I was more concerned with the inventories' comparative breadth, not depth.
>
> *Efficiency*: how productive the time required to complete the inventory is. It is a function of the amount of time required to yield a given degree of comprehensiveness—something approximating the amount of comprehensiveness divided by the amount of time required to complete the inventory. In other words, was any of the time required to complete the inventory wasteful or unnecessary? This dimension is relevant to issues of client fatigue and the likelihood of clients completing an inventory.

Research Questions and Hypotheses

Three research questions and 22 hypotheses were tested. The first question involved how participants' evaluations differed regarding the overall helpfulness of the three different initial assessment inventories. The second question involved how participants' reactions differed regarding its comprehensiveness, relative both to each of the aforementioned eight dimensions and to the three inventories overall. The third question involved how participants' evaluations differed regarding the efficiency with which the three inventories assessed the eight client dimensions enumerated in hypotheses 2–9 and 13–20. The research hypotheses were as follows (hypotheses 12–22 are the same as 1–11 except that they refer to ratings, whereas 1–11 refer to rankings; in all cases 3 is best and 1 is worst):

1. On the dimension of *overall helpfulness,* participants will rank the inventories as follows: II (3), MI (2), and LI (1).

2. On the dimension of the *client's thoughts,* participants will rank the inventories as follows: MI (3), II (2), and LI (1).

3. On the dimension of the *client's emotions,* participants will rank the inventories as follows: MI (3), II (2), and LI (1).

4. On the dimension of the *client's behaviors,* participants will rank the inventories as follows: MI (3), II (2), and LI (1).

5. On the dimension of *physical aspects of the client,* participants will rank the inventories as follows: MI (3), II (2), and LI (1).

6. On the dimension of *physical aspects of the client's environment,* participants will rank the inventories as follows: II (3), MI (2), and LI (1).

7. On the dimension of the *client's culture,* participants will rank the inventories as follows: II (3), MI (2), and LI (1).

8. On the dimension of the *client's spirituality,* participants will rank the inventories as follows: II (3), MI (2), and LI (1).

9. On the dimension of *what is most meaningful to the client,* participants will rank the inventories as follows: II (3), MI (2), and LI (1).

10. On the dimension of the *overall comprehensiveness* of the inventories, participants will rank the inventories as follows: II (3), MI (2), and LI (1).

11. On the dimension of the *overall efficiency* with which the inventories assess the various dimensions, participants will rank the inventories as follows: II (3), MI (2), and LI (1).

12. On the dimension of *overall helpfulness*, participants will rate the inventories as follows: II (3), MI (2), and LI (1).

13. On the dimension of the *client's thoughts*, participants will rate the inventories as follows: MI (3), II (2), and LI (1).

14. On the dimension of the *client's emotions*, participants will rate the inventories as follows: MI (3), II (2), and LI (1).

15. On the dimension of the *client's behaviors*, participants will rate the inventories as follows: MI (3), II (2), and LI (1).

16. On the dimension of *physical aspects of the client*, participants will rate the inventories as follows: MI (3), II (2), and LI (1).

17. On the dimension of *physical aspects of the client's environment*, participants will rate the inventories as follows: II (3), MI (2), and LI (1).

18. On the dimension of the *client's culture*, participants will rate the inventories as follows: II (3), MI (2), and LI (1).

19. On the dimension of the *client's spirituality*, participants will rate the inventories as follows: II (3), MI (2), and LI (1).

20. On the dimension of *what is most meaningful to the client*, participants will rate the inventories as follows: II (3), MI (2), and LI (1).

21. On the dimension of the *overall comprehensiveness* of the inventories, participants will rate the inventories as follows: II (3), MI (2), and LI (1).

22. On the dimension of the *overall efficiency* with which the inventories assess the various dimensions, participants will rate the inventories as follows: II (3), MI (2), and LI (1).

Methods and Procedures

Development of the Integral Intake and the Evaluation Form

I had created the Integral Intake years prior to my dissertation research because I was dissatisfied with the intake instruments that had been used in the clinics in which I counseled. For the purpose of the study, I developed the Evaluation Form (EF). The EF consisted of four parts. The first part addressed demographic information. The second part was a qualitative assessment consisting of six open-ended questions designed to gather participants' initial and, thus, minimally biased subjective evaluations of the inventories. The third part was a quantitative assessment in which participants first ranked each inventory on 11 dimensions and then rated each inventory on those same dimensions. Part 4 consisted of an open-ended "Anything else?" question designed to gather additionsl qualititive data. Using both quantitative and qualitative measures is a type of methodological triangulation, an attempt to eliminate biases that may ensue from an exclusive reliance on a single method of data collection (Gall, Borg, & Gall, 1996).

Procedures

I assembled packets consisting of informed consent forms, instructions, the three inventories, the EF, and a postage-paid return envelope. Next, I distributed the packets to the recruited participants. Participants were instructed to read through—not fill out—each of the three inventories and then complete the EF. The order in which the participants read through the inventories was controlled and rotated. The six ordinal permutations were II, LI, MI; II, MI, LI; MI, LI, II; MI, II, LI; LI, II, MI; and LI, MI, II. Each time I mailed or handed out the packets, the three inventories were rotated so that each permutation was equally represented. Instructions and brief introductions to each of the three inventories that the participants read before reading the actual inventories were included in the packets.

Analyses

I entered data from the EF into a computer and analyzed it using SPSS for MS Windows Release 10.1. Reliability of the quantitative portion of the EF was established through the examination of its internal consistency via Cronbach's alpha. For the purpose of this study, a Cronbach's alpha of .80 or higher was considered reliable, .65–.79 marginally reliable, and .64 or lower unreliable. The Cronbach's alpha was derived by analyzing all responses to all 11 items for each inventory, separately for the rankings and the ratings. Results of this analysis appear in Table 8.1.

As shown in Table 8.1, internal consistency reliability for the three inventories ranged from .85 to .97. As a result, the EF was deemed a reliable source with which to evaluate the three inventories.

The dimensions of the EF with which participants were asked to rank and rate the three inventories were culled from the counseling literature to reflect those aspects of clients that are most commonly assessed in initial sessions (whether via intake forms or interviews) by mental health counselors from a variety of theoretical perspectives. As such, the eight client dimensions—thoughts, emotions, behaviors, physical aspects, culture, environmental systems, spirituality, and what is most meaningful to each client—were intended to represent common

Table 8.1 Internal Consistency Reliability Analysis of the EF

Section of EF	Inventory	Alpha
A (Rankings)	II	.88
A (Rankings)	LI	.90
A (Rankings)	MI	.85
B (Ratings)	II	.97
B (Ratings)	LI	.93
B (Ratings)	MI	.93

constructs of clients that are significant in understanding them and their distress, as well as the dimensions that counselors most often address in their treatment plans. The three instrument dimensions—overall helpfulness, comprehensiveness, and efficiency—were, likewise, constructs that are frequently encountered in intake assessment literature; counselors who use intake instruments want an instrument that is both comprehensive but not too long—one that is "efficient" and clinically helpful.

To test the research hypotheses that involved rankings, I calculated mean rankings of each of the three inventories on each dimension. Using these means, I determined the rank orderings of the inventories on each dimension.

To test the statistical significance of difference in rankings, I ran a Friedman test on each of the 11 dimensions of Section A of the EF. Also known as the Friedman two-way analysis of variance, this statistic is founded upon the rationale that if the different groups (in this case, the three inventories) do not differ with regard to the criterion variables (in this case, the 11 dimensions), then the participants' rankings should be random and, therefore, not exhibit statistically significant differences (Siegel, 1956).

After determining whether or not participants ranked the three inventories differently on each dimension, I ran a post hoc Wilcoxon signed-rank test on each pair of inventories (II-LI, II-MI, LI-MI) to determine between which mean rankings the differences existed.

To test the research hypotheses that involved ratings, I calculated mean ratings of each of the three inventories on each dimension. Using these means, I determined the rating orderings of the inventories on each dimension.

To test the statistical significance of difference in ratings, I then ran a one-way repeated measures ANOVA on the ratings for each of the 11 dimensions of the EF. After determining whether or not participants rated the three inventories differently on each dimension, I then ran an ANOVA paired samples test on each pair of inventories (II-LI, II-MI, LI-MI) to determine between which mean ratings the differences existed.

In this study I used research/directional hypotheses rather than null/nondirectional hypotheses because I believed that I had a strong sense of how each inventory addressed each of the 11 dimensions. Although I stated the hypotheses in directional/one-tailed terms, as opposed to null hypotheses, I nonetheless ran the above statistical tests in two-tailed fashion. I did this for two reasons. First, running two-tailed analyses allows for the discernment of differences even when those differences are in a direction that was not hypothesized. In other words, if I had run one-tailed tests and differences existed contrary to my hypotheses, those differences would have gone unnoticed, which is far from ideal research practice. Second, two-tailed tests are considered more conservative and "honest," thus lending confidence to the significance of the results (McDonald, 1999). For the Friedman and the one-way repeated measures ANOVA tests, a statistical significance level of .05 was established as the criterion for either retaining or rejecting the research hypotheses. For the Wilcoxon and the ANOVA paired samples tests, I used the Bonferroni adjustment technique to reduce the risk of a Type I error. Thus, because the Wilcoxon and the ANOVA paired samples tests tested each hypothesis three times, the .05 p value was divided by 3, which yielded .017, which I rounded to .02 (Huck, 2000). Using the Bonferroni technique "leads to a more rigorous alpha level for each of the separate tests being conducted, [and] each of those tests becomes more 'demanding'" (Huck, 2000, p. 223). Thus, Bonferroni-adjusted alpha levels demand more stringent criteria—data even more discrepant from null hypothesis expectations—before rejecting the null is permitted.

The following sections address a summary of this study's results, the meaning of the results (as interpreted by the primary investigator), implications for therapists, limitations of the study, and recommendations for further research.

Results

Of the 71 individuals who had agreed to participate in this study, 58 participants returned research packets. Regarding theoretical orientation, 7 were Adlerian, 6 were person-centered, 4 were psychodynamic, 4 were transpersonal, 3 were multimodal, 3 were existential/humanistic, 2 were integral, 1 was Jungian, and 1 was cognitive. Eight marked "other," of which 4 were eclectic, 2 were Gestalt, 1 was integrative, and 1 was developmental. Finally, I was unable to determine the theoretical orientation of 19 of the participants because they marked two or more different theories. Regarding their professions, 40 of the participants were counselors, 14 were professors of counseling or counselor education, 13 were psychologists, and 8 were professors of psychology; these numbers total more than 58 because some participants marked more than one profession (i.e., a psychologist who is also a professor of psychology).

Findings Regarding the Differences in How Participants Evaluated the Three Inventories

I think it is only fair to stress that participants were evaluating the first (original) version of the Integral Intake, whereas the LI and MI had each been through several revisions (we can assume that instruments are usually improved when they are revised). The original Integral Intake was improved based upon the data from this study; the result is the current Integral Intake, which is included in the Appendix and on the CD.

Quantitative Inquiry

To clarify this discussion, Table 8.2 summarizes the overall rankings and ratings of the three inventories on the 11 dimensions.

Regarding the three primary research questions, the data appear straightforward: participants consistently evaluated the II and MI as more helpful, comprehensive, and efficient than the LI, both overall and relative to the eight specific dimensions. Comparing the II with the LI on the 22 items, participants consistently evaluated the II statistically significantly more highly. Comparing the MI with the LI on the 22 items, participants also consistently evaluated the MI more highly, though not always statistically significantly. The following 11 paragraphs summarize the rankings and ratings of the three inventories, dimension by dimension.

Taken together, the rankings and ratings yielded the same evaluative profiles regarding how well the inventories addressed the dimension of *overall helpfulness*. Although participants ranked and rated the II more highly than the MI, those differences were not statistically significant. However, participants did rank and rate the II statistically significantly higher than the LI. Participants evaluated the MI more highly than

Table 8.2 Summary of Overall Rankings/Ratings of the Three Currently
Published Initial Intake Inventories

Dimension	II	MI	LI
		(3= best, 1= worst)	
Overall helpfulness	3/3	2/2	1/1
Client's thoughts	2/2	3/3	1/1
Client's emotions	2/2	3/3	1/1
Client's behaviors	2/2	3/3	1/1
Physical aspects of the client	2/2	3/3	1/1
Physical aspects of the client's environment	3/3	2/2	1/1
Client's culture	3/3	2/2	1/1
Client's spirituality	3/3	2/2	1/1
What is most meaningful to the client	3/3	2/2	1/1
Overall comprehensiveness	3/3	2/2	1/1
Overall efficiency	3/3	2/2	1/1

the LI, but those differences were statistically significant only on the rankings.

Taken together, the rankings and ratings yielded the same evaluative profiles regarding how well the inventories addressed the dimension of the *client's thoughts*. Although participants ranked and rated the MI more highly than the II, those differences were not statistically significant. However, participants did rank and rate both the II and the MI significantly higher than the LI.

Taken together, the rankings and ratings yielded the same evaluative profiles regarding how well the inventories addressed the dimension of the *client's emotions*. Although participants ranked and rated the MI more highly than the II, those differences were not statistically significant. However, participants did rank and rate both the II and the MI statistically significantly higher than the LI.

Taken together, the rankings and ratings yielded the same evaluative profiles regarding how well the inventories addressed the dimension of the *client's behaviors*. Although participants ranked and rated the MI more highly than the II, those differences were not statistically significant. However, participants did rank and rate both the II and the MI statistically significantly higher than the LI.

Taken together, the rankings and ratings yielded the same evaluative profiles regarding how well the inventories addressed the dimension of *physical aspects of the client*. Although participants ranked and rated the MI more highly than the II, those differences were not statistically significant. However, participants did rank and rate both the II and the MI statistically significantly higher than the LI.

Taken together, the rankings and ratings yielded the same evaluative profiles regarding how well the inventories addressed the dimension of *physical aspects of the client's environment*. Although participants ranked and rated the II more highly than the MI, those differences were not statistically significant. However, participants did rank and rate both the II and the MI statistically significantly higher than the LI.

Taken together, the rankings and ratings yielded the same evaluative profiles regarding how well the inventories addressed the dimension of the *client's culture*. Participants ranked and rated the II more highly than the MI, and those differences were statistically significant on both the ranking and rating sections. Participants also ranked and rated both the II and the MI higher than the LI, but the differences were statistically significant only between the II and LI, not between the MI and LI.

Taken together, the rankings and ratings yielded the same evaluative profiles regarding how well the inventories addressed the dimension of the *client's spirituality*. Participants ranked and rated the II more highly than the MI, and those differences were statistically significant on the ranking section. Participants also ranked and rated both the II and the MI higher than the LI, but the differences were statistically significant only between the II and LI (on the ranking section), not between the MI and LI.

Taken together, the rankings and ratings yielded the same evaluative profiles regarding how well the inventories addressed the dimension of *what is most meaningful to the client*. Participants ranked and rated the II more highly than the MI, and those differences were statistically significant on the ranking section. Participants also ranked and rated both the II and the MI higher than the LI, but the differences were statistically significant only between the II and LI (on the ranking section), not between the MI and LI.

Taken together, the rankings and ratings yielded the same evaluative profiles regarding how well the inventories addressed the dimension of *overall comprehensiveness.* Although participants ranked and rated the II more highly than the MI, those differences were not statistically significant. However, participants did rank and rate both the II and the MI statistically significantly higher than the LI.

Taken together, the rankings and ratings yielded the same evaluative profiles regarding how well the inventories addressed the dimension of *overall efficiency.* Although participants ranked and rated the II more highly than the MI, those differences were not statistically significant. However, participants did rank and rate both the II and the MI higher than the LI, although those differences were statistically significant only between the II and LI.

To summarize, the LI was consistently evaluated as the worst of the three inventories on all dimensions. The MI was evaluated as the best inventory on four dimensions: the client's thoughts, emotions, behaviors, and physical aspects. The II was evaluated as the best inventory on seven dimensions: physical aspects of the client's environment, client's culture, client's spirituality, what is most meaningful to the client, and, notably, on overall comprehensiveness, overall efficiency, and overall helpfulness.

Although the above paragraphs make many distinctions, the more interesting and certainly more subtle distinctions involve the ways participants evaluated the II relative to the MI. On the three dimensions addressing overall helpfulness, comprehensiveness, and efficiency, participants consistently ranked and rated the II more highly than the MI, though the differences were not statistically significant. These differences might have been statistically significant if 13 of the 58 quantitative data sets had not been deemed unanalyzable; after all, of those 13, 7 responded that the II was their inventory of choice, versus 4 for the MI and only 1 for the LI.[1] These findings seem even more noteworthy given that participants who consider themselves "integral" were underrepresented in this study: of those specifying more than one theory—at least one of which was a theory associated with an inventory assessed in this study—and those specifying affiliation with just one inventory-related theory, only 2 and 2 participants, respectively, identified themselves as "integral," compared to 14 and 7, respectively, who marked themselves "Adlerian," and 9 and 3, respectively, who marked themselves "multimodal." I believe that the practical significance of these findings is strengthened by the fact that the II was evaluated as the best overall inventory even though integral participants were underrepresented in this study and integral theory is the least-known theory, compared to Adlerian and multimodal theories. Also noteworthy is that had I not been as conservative in my use of statistical analyses (if I had run the statistical analyses in directional/one-tailed fashion, because that is how I stated my hypotheses), levels of statistical significance would have been more likely to emerge.

Participants both ranked and rated the II statistically significantly higher than the MI on items evaluating client's culture, spirituality, and issues of meaning. They rated no dimensions statistically significantly higher on the MI than the II. This is a highly significant practical finding. Overall, participants—regardless of their theoretical orientation—evaluated the II most highly. Thus, the II was, in its initial version, already the best overall inventory. However, participants did rank the MI more highly than the II on the dimensions of the client's thoughts, emotions, behaviors and physical aspects, although those differences were not statistically significant. Thus, from a practical standpoint, when I revised the II, I paid particular attention to those four dimensions, so that, presently, the II should be, by an even larger margin, the most helpful initial intake inventory available for those therapists who are inclined to use such inventories.

Based on the quantitative results, all 22 research hypotheses were retained. The practical import of this finding is that I, although affiliated with integral theory, was not globally biased in favor of the Integral Intake; I perceived, and participants perceived identically, different strengths and weaknesses among the three inventories. On this basis it might be more safely contended that my analysis of the qualitative data, which tended to favor the II but not exclusively so, was also relatively unbiased.

Qualitative Inquiry

After reviewing the three inventories and providing demographic information, *but before they proceeded to the quantitative section that was described above,* participants responded to six open-ended *"general impressions*" questions that provided the qualitative data for this study. The six questions were:

1. From a clinical perspective, what were your impressions or reactions to reading through these inventories?
2. How do you think clients would react to being asked to complete these inventories?
3. (a) Which of these three inventories would you most likely use with your clients? (b) Why?
4. (a) Were there aspects of any of the three inventories that elicited a negative reaction from you? (b) What were they? (Please specify the inventory and the items.)
5. (a) Do you know of other assessment inventories/instruments that you think are more clinically useful? (b) What are they?
6. Anything else?

Because Marquis & Holden (in press) describes the qualitative analyses in far greater detail, I will here only skim the surface.

In response to question 1, participants remarked that both the II and MI were more comprehensive, helpful, and user-friendly than the LI, with the II being more concise and spiritual than the other two.

In response to question 2, participants remarked that the II would appear more scientific, interactive, and concise to clients than the other two; that the MI would appear more user-friendly than either the II or LI, but also more offensive and twice as overwhelming.

In response to question 3a, 26 participants remarked that they would most likely use the II; 21 participants remarked that they would most likely use the MI; 5 participants remarked that they would most likely use the LI; 5 participants remarked that they would not use any of them; 1 participant would use any of them; and 3 participants remarked that they would prefer to use a combination of all three instruments. In response to question 3b, participants remarked that they chose the II as their preferred instrument because it is comprehensive without being too long, it is more relational and "interactive," and it yields more contextual data; participants remarked that they chose the MI as their preferred instrument because of its format (it was the only instrument that I mailed out in booklet format; the II and LI were merely pages with a staple in the upper left corner) and because it more clearly led to a treatment plan (this can be accounted for because more participants were familiar with the theory behind the MI than the II); participants remarked that they chose the LI as their preferred instrument because it yields more interesting data and it fit with their guiding theory.

In response to question 4, participants remarked that the LI and MI elicited far more negative reactions from them than did the II: 15 participants thought the instructions were too complicated on the LI; 12 participants thought the LI had too much emphasis on siblings and family atmosphere; 10 participants thought the LI had too much emphasis on the past and early recollections; 12 participants thought the MI was too long (3 participants thought the II was too long); 4 participants thought the MI had a heterosexual bias; 2 participants thought the MI was "pathologizing"; 5 participants thought the II had vague or irrelevant questions (all of which have been revised in the current version).

In response to question 5a, all but a few of the participants responded "No." One participant noted using the MMPI-2, which is a completely different type of assessment instrument—nomothetic and geared toward classifying people with regard to psychopathology and personality characteristics and providing inferential information regarding people's behavior (Hood & Johnson, 1991). One participant wrote that most agencies have created their own interview forms specific to their clientele and services. Two participants noted using a genogram-centered interview in their practices, and two others reported using the Beck Depression Inventory. One participant reported using a Myers-Briggs Type Indicator and a Keirsey-Bates Inventory/Keirsey Temperament Sorter. A few of the participants' responses to question 5 follow: "I prefer to have the client's information to largely emerge in the interpersonal context of the therapeutic relationship (other than the first person objective and systemic/objective) and so rarely use extensive inventories at the outset. When called for, I use the Rorschach as an interactive diagnostic tool." Another participant's response: "Not really, and I've seen a lot! I teach clinical interviewing, and see two main choices: (a) comprehensive written intake—works great with some people—lousy with some populations; (b) a guideline for oral interviews that prompts and reminds, gives menu but not exhaustive." Finally: "No, most initial inventories seem to seek to circumvent the process of counseling so that the counselor immediately can focus in on the client's 'problem'! The counselor will gain much more information and focus from developing a relationship with the client and allowing this kind of information to unfold."

The last open-ended question from part 4 of the EF, "Anything else?" elicited some interesting data. One participant wrote that "the II reflects current changes in counseling—requires time and self-analysis to respond, however." Three participants noted that they were influenced by their familiarity with Adlerian and multimodal theories, as well as with the LI and MI, and their total lack of familiarity with integral theory and the II. Regarding the II, one participant wrote that it is "much more aimed at the person as a whole and toward relationship. Spiritually important and useful addition. May be hard for some clients to complete due to writing requirements. I had seen the other two instruments. An interesting study." Another: "MI was too long and detailed. Information that may not be necessary. II was succinct and to the point." Another: "The II is the most balanced, with best comprehensive coverage. It is (surprisingly!) weak in the interpersonal, with a tendency to revert back to client self-experience. The II is also very good in the 'personal-subjective' components, though not as detailed as the MI. The MI gives the most in-depth detail on the client: subjective self-experience (ongoing 'tapes' and emotions). The LI is the strongest in offering a picture of the interpersonal situation and family subculture of the client's family of origin" (I believe I have strengthened the interpersonal/LL dimension of the current II). Another participant wrote that "the II would have an even higher value if some of the information could be secured with a checklist. Higher value in that the client may be more willing to respond and that often checklists trigger info that the client may have not thought was important. I wonder if you could use the II as an oral interview model. I wonder if you would get different info if the intake was oral rather than written? Thought: maybe the II could be sent by mail and client could complete at their leisure. Question—can I use the II now in my practice?"

Compared to the previous ideas, the following two participants presented a different perspective: "I prefer understanding much of what is asked for on the assessments via the existential relationship" and "Rather than putting so much analysis burden on clients, let's do a better job of training practitioners to be intake instruments."

Implications

The results of this study have several implications. First, an initial assessment instrument was created—the Integral Intake—that, in its first version, was ranked and rated by expert participants as the overall best available published intake inventory. Given that I also received constructive feedback relative to improving and clarifying various aspects of the II from this research, I have good reason to believe that the current II appears, overall, to be the most helpful idiographic assessment tool for therapists. The changes that I implemented in the second version of the II range from rewording vague questions into more clear ones to the addition of a few checklists that not only assess similar material in a different manner but also inquire into subpersonalities and developmental issues. As previously stated, particular attention was paid to those dimensions on which participants evaluated the MI more highly than the II. Of course, the MI was also rated as a very helpful and comprehensive inventory. However, the MI is considerably more lengthy than the II, and participants thought that clients would experience the MI as "overwhelming" with twice the frequency of the II or LI. Because some participants reported that the II was overwhelming, I also gave consideration to how some items could be deleted without compromising the comprehensiveness of the II.

Shadows of Assessment

The results of this research also shed light upon some of the "shadows" of assessment. For example, many participants—despite their enthusiasm or fondness for a given inventory—reported that they would prefer to assess their clients via dialogue or informal interview rather than with paper-and-pencil instruments. Their concerns revolved around the potential danger that clients might be put off by having to reveal such personal information prior to establishing a trusting and sound therapeutic alliance. I agree that this is an important and valid concern. Clinicians should use their own best judgment regarding which clients will appreciate filling out a paper-and-pencil inventory versus which clients would be better served by being assessed informally via dialogue; in the latter case, the therapist might use the inventory as a guide to the intake interview.

Another item of interest involves the high correlations reported in Table 8.1. Because all 11 items for each inventory on the EF correlate highly, the correlations appear to be measuring a fairly homogeneous construct. Indeed, factor analysis confirmed that the 11 items loaded onto one primary factor—something akin to the overall utility or helpfulness of each inventory. I consider this important and unexpected data. The one-factor finding also suggests the possibility that something like an instrument-variant of the halo effect may have been in effect, as if the participants' overall reactions to a given inventory colored their evaluations of each individual item for that inventory. That is to say, participants' evaluations *could* have been a reflection of a type of bias, and therefore they would not differentiate as well among the 11 items. However, participants did differentially evaluate the three inventories. In other words, participants did not, for example, evaluate the II best on each dimension. This suggests that participants *did* evaluate each dimension individually, as opposed to being completely biased for or against a given inventory.

One final point involves one of the participant's comments that the II appears "more objective and less theoretically biased." I would certainly like to believe that is the case, and I believe it may be so because the integral perspective, in contrast to the Adlerian or multimodal perspective, is a metatheory—a conceptual scaffolding capable of situating traditional theories of counseling within a more differentiated framework because it embraces multiple perspectives from higher levels of complexity. For an elaboration of this issue, refer to Chapter 2.

Limitations and Recommendations for Further Study

This research was originally proposed as an exploratory study—my dissertation. As such, it has several limitations. First, the participants were not randomly selected and thus are not necessarily representative of the population of practicing therapists.[2] The reasons I opted for volunteer participants, rather than a random stratified sample, involved the high cost of the research packets and, consequently, the need to have a high return rate to ensure an adequate size (N) for data analyses. However, because the volunteer participants could differ systematically from the population of practicing therapists, further research along the lines of this study should use a random stratified sample of participants.

Another limitation of this study revolves around the fact that only the primary investigator analyzed the qualitative data. I did, however, take measures to minimize bias. For example, in addition to my differentially perceiving strengths and weaknesses in the inventories, I used methodological triangulation in the study—using both qualitative and quantitative methods of inquiry and, within the quantitative domain, both rankings and ratings, to form an understanding. Moreover, as mentioned above, I was not globally biased toward the II; in my hypotheses I anticipated that participants would evaluate the MI as the best instrument with regard to assessing clients' behaviors, thoughts, emotions, and physical aspects. Nevertheless, the qualitative results could have been strengthened if Adlerian and multimodal co-investigators had participated in the qualitative analyses. This is suggested in follow-up studies.

Another limitation to bear in mind is that all of the data collected in this research study—both qualitative and quantitative—involved participants' self-reports. Thus, respondent veracity is a crucial factor in the validity of the results. In other words, how truthfully, carefully, or conscientiously did the participants respond to the EF? Given the high levels of internal reliabilities established via Cronbach's alphas, I feel safe in assuming that participants were conscientious and truthful in their evaluations. However, respondent veracity is always an issue of practical significance regarding self-report data.

Also, given that the MI appeared more professional in format—recall that one participant noted her fondness for its booklet format—future research comparing such inventories would ideally have their formats matched more equivalently, that is to say, to have them all either in booklet format or all with a staple in the upper left corner.

In the near future, I intend to replicate my dissertation research, attending to the limitations mentioned above. Over the past few years, I have given presentations on the Integral Intake at national conferences and seminars, and hundreds of therapists have requested to use it, to which I consented. I would also like to interview a sample of those therapists to see how the Integral Intake has been helpful in assessing their clients and facilitating treatment, as well as inquiring into what they perceive as areas for continued improvement. If you are one of those who has been using the Integral Intake for years and would like to participate in further research regarding the Integral Intake, please contact me at amarquis@its.rochester.edu. I will follow with great interest the work of anyone who empirically studies the Integral Intake or other ideas presented in this book, and I look forward to future developments in integral assessment and therapy that such research will stimulate.

Conclusion

In addition to inquiring into how expert participants evaluated the three inventories, I hoped to receive feedback from the participants regarding how to improve the Integral Intake. Both goals were accomplished. Based on the results and discussion of the evaluations reported above, it appears clear that overall the II was evaluated as the best inventory. I can also conclude that the participants' feedback was incorporated into the second (current) version of the II. I am thrilled to have received so much constructive feedback and am excited to have improved upon an inventory that was already very helpful.

Notes

1. These 13 participants did not accurately follow the directions for the ranking and rating sections of the EF. For example, rather than filling in *each* of the fields with a numerical ranking or rating, some of the participants placed a check mark in only one of the fields for a particular inventory per item.
2. I asked colleagues, attendees at professional psychotherapy conferences, and expert therapists referred to me by those expert therapists if they would be willing to participate in the study.

9
CONCLUSION

The primary purpose of integral assessment is to inquire into those dimensions of clients and their circumstances that play influential roles in their suffering, struggles, and pathologies as well as their strengths, resources, and well-being. By more comprehensively understanding clients and the reasons they seek professional help—both as individuals and within the context of their AQAL matrices (including their quadrants, levels, lines, states, and types)—therapists can cull some of the sundry factors that are potentially causative in some people's difficulties and thus more closely pinpoint those factors or circumstances that are actually most relevant to specific clients and their circumstances, thus facilitating optimally serving the full spectrum of clients' needs, from traumatic crises that must be coped with immediately all the way to psychospiritual development across the life course.

Of course, no single (10–12 page) intake instrument will thoroughly assess *every* dimension of AQAL and the self-system. However, together with this book and its explication of integral theory, the Integral Intake should provide clinicians with an assessment instrument and a metatheoretical conceptual framework with which to more fully understand, contextualize, and help their clients—in both their uniqueness and their similarity to the rest of humanity.

At a minimum, integral assessment must address quadrants and developmental levels; ideally, it also attends to lines, states, types, and the self-system. Although integral assessment and treatment are integrative, unifying, "big-picture" approaches, integral therapists also ask, "What's the main problem?" Often, the central problem is developmental (the client's present life-circumstances require developmental transformation, or one or two specific developmental lines are particularly underdeveloped relative to the rest of the client's lines and may need clinical attention). It may also be quadratic: lack of medical care, poor work conditions, an abusive relationship (LR); a meaning-making system that once provided legitimacy no longer seems fulfilling, not feeling connected with or understood by friends and family, unhelpful interpretations of one's experience (LL); problems with self-esteem/self-efficacy/self-concept, depression or anxiety, lacking motivation or purpose or joy in life (UL); the specific behaviors that bring the client to therapy, medical disorders, malfunctioning neurotransmission (UR). Most problems or pathologies are influenced by aspects of all four quadrants (especially in the present and likely from the past as well).

If developmental levels are implicated and there are significant repressions or dissociated aspects of self, uncovering work is indicated. If the pathologies involve previous stages of development (the client's center of gravity is formal-reflexive but she is bothered by disowned subpersonalities that appear prepersonal), 3-2-1 work is indicated. Even if a client just wants to solve an isolated problem or wants a referral so he can get Prozac, integral therapists have an AQAL-informed perspective that integratively contextualizes clients, pathologies, and treatment.

The Integral Intake is primarily an idiographic assessment instrument. An integral approach to therapeutic assessment and treatment also honors nomothetic assessment as well, as evidenced by my lengthy discussion of stage theories of development in Chapter 4 and ego development, in particular, in Chapter 5. A genuine integral approach will always take into account both inside and outside views (idiographic and nomothetic, respectively) of both individuals and the collective systems in which they live. Thus, although I have focused more on idiographic assessment, that is not meant to imply that there is not plenty of room for standardized assessments in integral assessment (but every instrument and book has its scope, limits, and focus, and the focus of the Integral Intake and this book is idiographic assessment).

By creating the Integral Intake, I hoped to provide therapists with an efficient, comprehensive, and clinically useful intake instrument that is capable of accommodating diverse clients with different and multifaceted issues and needs, thus helping therapists expand their theoretical and practical "toolboxes." By writing this book and discussing Integral theory in some depth, I hope I have afforded therapists an integrative conceptual system that will assist them in choosing the optimal "tool" (treatment approach) for each individual client. Nails need to be hammered, but clients do not; some need cognitive restructuring or assertiveness training, some need meditation or contemplative prayer, some need advocacy, and some need only the medium of a therapeutic relationship. May the Integral Intake and this book help therapists be more mindful of the law of the hammer, and not to pound the same approach on people who are better served by a more integrative, compassionate, and embracing—integral—approach.

Appendix A

INTEGRAL INTAKE
Andre Marquis, Ph.D.
University of Rochester

Client's Name _____ Age____ Date First Seen _____
Home Phone (__)_____ (message: Y/N) Work Phone (___)_____ (message: Y/N)
Address _____ City_____ Zip_____
Date of Birth _____ Gender (M/F) Referral Source _____
Emergency Contact: Name _____ Phone (___)_____
(Please use the back side of this form if you need more space to respond to *any* of the questions)

PRELIMINARY ISSUES AND PREVIOUS THERAPY

What is the primary concern or problem for which you are seeking help?

_____

_____

_____

_____

_____

What makes it better? What makes it worse?

_____

_____

_____

_____

_____

Are there any *immediate* challenges or issues that need our attention? Yes/No If yes, please describe.

_____

_____

_____

_____

_____

Copyright © 2008 by Andre Marquis.

Have you had previous counseling or psychotherapy? Yes/No From when to when?
With whom?

_____

_____

What was your experience of therapy? (What was your previous therapy like?)

_____

_____

What was most helpful about your therapy?

_____

_____

What was least helpful about your therapy?

_____

_____

What did you learn about yourself through your previous therapy?

_____

_____

What do you expect from me and our work together?

_____

_____

EXPERIENCE: Individual-Interior

What are your strengths?

_____

_____

_____

What are your weaknesses?

_____

_____

_____

How would you describe your general mood/feelings?

_____

_____

What emotions do you most often feel most strongly?

_____

_____

Copyright © 2008 by Andre Marquis.

What are the ways in which you care for and comfort your self when you feel distressed?

_____

_____

How do you deal with strong emotions in yourself?

_____

_____

_____

How do you respond to stressful situations and other problems?

_____

_____

_____

_____

How do you make decisions (for example, do you use logic and reason, or do you trust your gut and heart)?

_____

_____

_____

Are you aware of recurring images or thoughts (either while awake or in dreams)? Yes/ No If yes, please describe.

_____

_____

_____

Have you *ever* attempted to seriously harm or kill yourself or anyone else? Yes/No If yes, please describe.

_____

_____

_____

Are you *presently* experiencing suicidal thoughts? Yes/No If yes, please describe.

_____

_____

_____

Copyright © 2008 by Andre Marquis.

Has anyone in your family ever attempted or committed suicide? Yes/No If yes, please describe.

_____

_____

_____

Have there been any serious illnesses, births, deaths, or other losses or changes in your family that have affected you? Yes/No If yes, please describe.

_____

_____

_____

_____

_____

What is your earliest memory?

_____

_____

What is your happiest memory?

_____

_____

What is your most painful memory?

_____

_____

Where in your body do you feel stress (shoulders, back, jaw. etc.)?

_____

_____

Do you have ways in which you express yourself creatively and/or artistically? Yes/No If yes, please describe.

_____

_____

Describe your leisure time (hobbies/enjoyment).

_____

_____

Copyright © 2008 by Andre Marquis.

Have you ever been a victim of, or witnessed, verbal, emotional, physical, and/or sexual abuse? If yes, please describe.

_____

_____

_____

In general, how satisfied are you with your life?
Not at all   1   2   3   4   5   6   7   Very

In general, how do you feel about yourself (self-esteem)?
Very bad   1   2   3   4   5   6   7   Very good

In general, how much control do you feel you have over your life and how you feel?
None at all   1   2   3   4   5   6   7   A lot

Please mark any of the following feelings or expressions you've had recently, or have had sometimes in the past:

_____	angry	_____	difficulty concentrating
_____	sad	_____	little interest or pleasure in doing things
_____	lonely	_____	poor or excessive appetite
_____	afraid	_____	excessive tiredness
_____	anxious/worried	_____	feeling helpless
_____	shameful/guilty	_____	having much more energy than normal
_____	jealous	_____	thoughts racing through your head
_____	happy	_____	desire to harm yourself
_____	grateful/thankful	_____	desire to harm someone else
_____	sexual/erotic	_____	hearing or seeing things not actually there
_____	excited	_____	thoughts that seem strange but that you can't
_____	energetic		seem to stop
_____	hopeful	_____	fear that someone is trying to harm you
_____	relaxed/peaceful		
_____	other emotions you often feel:		

_____

BEHAVIOR: Individual-Exterior

Please list any medications you are presently taking (dosage/amount and what the medication is for).

_____

_____

_____

Copyright © 2008 by Andre Marquis.

Do you have a primary care physician? Yes/No If yes, who is it? _____
Height _____ Weight_____ lbs.

When was your last physical? _____Were there any noteworthy results (diseases, blood pressure, cholesterol, etc.)?

_____

_____

_____

Have you ever suffered a head injury or other serious injury? Yes/No If yes, please describe.

_____

_____

_____

What other significant medical problems have you experienced or are you experiencing now?

_____

_____

_____

Please mark any of the following behaviors or bodily feelings that are true of you:

_____   drink too much

_____   use illegal and/or mind-altering drugs

_____   eat too much

_____   eat too little

_____   neglect friends and family

_____   neglect self and your own needs

_____   difficulty being kind and loving to yourself

_____   act in ways that end up hurting yourself or others

_____   lose your temper

_____   seem to not have control over some behaviors

_____   think about suicide

_____   have difficulty concentrating

_____   spend more money than you can afford to

_____   crying

_____   any other behaviors you would like me to know about?

_____

Copyright © 2008 by Andre Marquis.

_____ headaches

_____ menstrual problems

_____ dizziness

_____ heart tremors

_____ jitters

_____ sexual preoccupations

_____ tingling/numbness

_____ excessive tiredness

_____ hear or see things not actually there

_____ blackouts

_____ do you have any other bodily pains or difficulties? Yes/No If yes, what are they?

In general, how would you rate your physical health?

Very unhealthy   1   2   3   4   5   6   7   Very healthy

Describe your current sleeping patterns (When do you sleep? How many hours per 24 hours? Do you sleep straight through or do you wake up during sleep time?).

_____

_____

Do you feel rested upon waking? Yes/No

Describe your usual eating habits (types of food, and how much).

_____

_____

_____

Do you take vitamins and other nutritional supplements? Yes/No If yes please describe.

_____

_____

Describe your drug and alcohol use (both past and present).

_____

_____

_____

Do you engage in some form of exercise (aerobic and/or strength building)? Yes/No If yes, please describe.

_____

_____

Copyright © 2008 by Andre Marquis.

Do you have any communication impairments (sight, hearing, speech)? Yes/No If yes, please describe.

_____

_____

CULTURE: *Collective-Interior*

Describe your relationships, including friends, family, and coworkers.

_____

_____

_____

_____

_____

What is important and meaningful to you (what matters the most to you)?

_____

_____

_____

_____

_____

In general, how satisfied are you with your friendships and other relationships?
Not at all   1   2   3   4   5   6   7   Very

In general, how comfortable are you in social situations?
Not at all   1   2   3   4   5   6   7   Very

In general, how satisfied are you with your religion/spirituality?
Not at all   1   2   3   4   5   6   7   Very

Which emotions were encouraged or commonly expressed in your *family of origin* (family you grew up with)?

_____

_____

Which emotions were discouraged or not allowed in your *family of origin*?

_____

_____

What emotions are most comfortable for you now?

_____

Copyright © 2008 by Andre Marquis.

What emotions are most uncomfortable for you now?

_____

_____

_____

How do you identify yourself ethnically? How important is your ethnic culture to you?

_____

_____

_____

How did your *family of origin* express love and care?

_____

_____

How does your *current family* express love and care?

_____

_____

How did your *family of origin* express disapproval?

_____

_____

How does your *current family* express disapproval?

_____

_____

Describe your romantic/love relationships, if any.

_____

_____

_____

Describe your sex life. How satisfied are you with your sex life?

_____

_____

What beliefs do you have about sex? How important to you are those beliefs?

_____

_____

Do you have a religious/spiritual affiliation and/or practice? Yes/No If yes, please describe.

_____

_____

_____

Copyright © 2008 by Andre Marquis.

What beliefs do you have about religion/spirituality? How important to you are those beliefs?

_____

_____

What are some of your most important morals? How important to you are those morals?

_____

_____

_____

Describe any political or civic involvement in which you participate.

_____

_____

Describe any environmental activities in which you participate (recycling, conserving, carpooling, etc.).

_____

_____

Are you involved with any cultural activities or institutions? Yes/No If yes, please describe.

_____

_____

Have you ever been a victim of any form of prejudice or discrimination (racial, gender, etc.) or felt that you were disadvantaged in terms of power and privilege in society? Yes/No If yes, please describe.

_____

_____

_____

SOCIAL SYSTEMS: _Collective-Exterior_

Describe your current _physical_ home environment. For example, describe the layout of your home, and other general conditions, such as, privacy, is it well-lighted?, do you have A/C?, heating?, etc.

_____

_____

_____

_____

Copyright © 2008 by Andre Marquis.

Describe your neighborhood. (Is it safe/dangerous, nice/unpleasant, quiet/loud, etc.?)

_____

_____

Describe your current *social* home environment (how would an outside observer describe how you get along with those who live with you?).

_____

_____

_____

Describe your work environment (include coworkers and supervisors who directly affect you).

_____

_____

_____

Do you have a romantic partner? Yes/No Have you been married before? Yes/No If yes, please describe.

_____

_____

Do you have pets? (Yes/No) How important are they to you?

_____

_____

Have you served in the military? (Yes/No) If yes, please describe.

_____

_____

Are you currently involved in a custody dispute? Yes/No If yes, please describe.

_____

_____

Have you had any involvement with the legal system (incarceration, probation, etc.)? Yes/No If yes, please describe.

_____

_____

What aspects of your life are stressful to you? Please describe.

_____

_____

_____

_____

Copyright © 2008 by Andre Marquis.

What sort of support system do you have (friends, family, or religious community who help you in times of need)?

_____

_____

_____

List your *family of origin* (family you grew up with), beginning with the oldest, include parents and yourself.

Name	Age	Gender	Relationship to you (include "step" and "half", etc.)
_____	____	____	_____
_____	____	____	_____
_____	____	____	_____
_____	____	____	_____
_____	____	____	_____

What is your educational background?

_____

_____

What is your occupation? _____ How satisfied are you with the type of work you do?

Not at all   1   2   3   4   5   6   7   Very

What is your yearly income? $_____ per year. How satisfied are you with your standard of living?

Not at all   1   2   3   4   5   6   7   Very

List your *current family* or all the people you currently live with (begin with the oldest person and include yourself).

Name	Age	Gender	Relationship to you (include "step" and "half", etc.)
_____	____	____	_____
_____	____	____	_____
_____	____	____	_____
_____	____	____	_____
_____	____	____	_____
_____	____	____	_____

Describe any family history of mental illness.

_____

_____

_____

_____

Copyright © 2008 by Andre Marquis.

Are you involved with any organizations? Yes/No If yes, please describe.

_____

_____

Do you participate in any volunteer work? Yes/No if yes, please describe.

_____

_____

Please mark any of the following that you experienced difficulty or problems with. Also indicate to the right of the problem in the parentheses ( ) your approximate age when the difficulty or problem occurred:

_____   nursing and/or eating ( )

_____   toilet training ( )

_____   crawling or walking ( )

_____   talking ( )

_____   nail biting or other nervous habits ( )

_____   going to school/ separating from caregivers ( )

_____   cruelty to animals or people ( )

_____   serious illnesses or injuries ( )

_____   academic problems ( )

_____   social problems ( )

_____   moves or other family stresses ( )

_____   abuse (emotional, physical, or sexual) ( )

_____   any problems with sexual maturation ( )

_____   being made fun of or joked about at school, home, or elsewhere ( )

_____   self-destructiveness (risky sex, eating problems, drug use, excessive risk-taking, etc.) ( )

_____   fitting into social groups ( )

_____   standing up for what you believe in when it differs from your peers' views ( )

_____   making important decisions, especially when they differ from social norms ( )

_____   any existential dilemmas ( )

_____   any religious and/or spiritual experiences (these could be completely positive) ( )

Copyright © 2008 by Andre Marquis.

The following is a list of various parts, aspects, or *subpersonalities* that many people notice within themselves in certain situations, but not in others. Please mark any of the following that you have experienced difficulty or problems with. Often, it is only after the fact that we notice that we were behaving, thinking, or feeling in a problematic manner. Also, please indicate to the right of the problem the situation or context in which you noticed this part of yourself.

_____ irresponsible child _____

_____ critical parent _____

_____ dominating "top dog" _____

_____ prone-to-fail "underdog" _____

_____ overly harsh judge or critic _____

_____ false or phony self _____

_____ unworthy, not-good-enough self _____

_____ grandiose, better-than-everyone-else self _____

_____ other, please describe _____

Is there anything else you want me to know about? (use the back of the page if you need to).

_____

_____

_____

_____

_____

_____

_____

_____

_____

_____

_____

_____

_____

_____

_____

_____

_____

_____

Copyright © 2008 by Andre Marquis.

References

Alexander, C., Druker, S., & Langer, E. (1990). Introduction: Major issues in the exploration of adult growth. In C. Alexander & E. Langer (Eds.). *Higher stages of human development* (pp. 3–32). New York: Oxford University Press.

American Counseling Association. (2005). *Code of ethics and standards of practice.* [Electronic version]. Retrieved Oct. 21, 2005, from http://www.counseling.org/ethics.

American Psychiatric Association. (2000). *Diagnostic and statistical manual of mental disorders* (4th ed.) (text rev.). Washington, DC: Author.

Ansbacher, H. L., & Ansbacher, R. R. (Eds.). (1956). The individual psychology of Alfred Adler: A systematic presentation in selections from his writings.

Assagioli, R. (1988). Transpersonal development: Dimensions beyond psychosynthesis. San Francisco: Aquarian.

Avabhasa, D. (1985). *The dawn horse testament.* Clearlake: Dawn Horse Press.

Aurobindo, S. (1970). *The life divine, vols. 1 & 2.* Pondicherry: Sri Aurobindo Ashram.

Austin, J. H. (1998). *Zen and the brain.* Cambridge: MIT Press.

Badiner, A. H., & Grey, A. (Eds.). (2002). Zig zag zen: Buddhism and psychedelics. San Francisco: Chronicle Books.

Baillargeon, R., & De Vos, J. (1991). Object permanence in young infants: Further evidence. *Child Development, 62,* 1227–1246.

Basch, M. F. (1988). Understanding psychotherapy: The science behind the art. New York: Basic Books.

Bateson, G. (1972). *Steps to an ecology of mind.* New York: Ballantine.

Battista, J. (1996). Offensive spirituality and spiritual defenses. In B. Scotton, A. Chinen, & J. Barrista (Eds.), *Textbook of transpersonal psychiatry and psychology.* New York: Basic Books.

Beck, A. T., Rush, A. J., Shaw, B. F., & Emery, G. (1979). *Cognitive therapy of depression.* New York: Guilford.

Beck, D. E., & Cowan, C. C. (1996). *Spiral dynamics: Mastering values, leadership, and change.* Malden: Blackwell Publishers.

Beck, D. E., & Cowan, C. C. (2000). *The values test: Mapping the currents of change.* Denton, TX: National Values Center.

Bettelheim, B. (1983). *Freud and man's soul.* London: Vintage.

Beutler, L. E. (1995a). Issues in selecting an assessment battery. In L. E. Beutler & M. R. Berren (Eds.), *Integrative assessment of adult personality* (pp. 65–93). New York: Guilford Press.

Beutler, L. E. (1995b). The clinical interview. In L. E. Beutler & M. R. Berren (Eds.), *Integrative assessment of adult personality* (pp. 94–120). New York: Guilford Press.

Beutler, L. E., & Rosner, R. (1995). Introduction to psychological assessment. In L. E. Beutler & M. R. Berren (Eds.), *Integrative assessment of adult personality* (pp. 1–24). New York: Guilford Press.

Binswanger, L. (1956). Existential analysis and psychotherapy. In F. Fromm-Reichmann & J. Moreno (Eds.), *Progress in psychotherapy.* New York: Grune & Stratton.

Blanck, G., & Blanck, R. (1979). *Ego psychology 2: Psychoanalytic developmental psychology.* New York: Columbia University Press.

Blasi, A. (1976). Concept of development in personality theory. In *Ego development: Conceptions and theories* (pp. 29–53). San Francisco: Jossey-Bass.

Bohart, A. C., & Tallman, K. (1999). *How clients make therapy work: The process of active self-healing.* Washington, DC: American Psychological Association.

Boss, M. (1963) *Psychoanalysis and daseinanalysis.* New York: Basic Books.

Bowlby, J. (1988). A secure base: Parent-child attachment and healthy human development. New York: Basic Books.

Briggs, K. C., & Myers, I. B. (1977). *Myers-Briggs type indicator.* Palo Alto, CA: Consulting Psychologists Press.

Brown, D. P. (1986). The stages of meditation in cross-cultural perspective. In K. Wilber, J. Engler, & D. P. Brown (Eds.), *Transformations of Consciousness: Conventional and contemplative perspectives on development* (pp. 219–284). Boston: Shambhala.

Browning, D. L. (1987). Ego development, authoritarianism, and social status: An investigation of the incremental validity of Loevinger's Sentence Completion Test (short form). *Journal of Personality and Social Psychology, 53,* 113-118.

Campbell, W. H., & Rohrbaugh, R. M. (2006). The biopsychosocial formulation manual: A guide for mental health professionals. New York: Routledge.

Carlozzi, A. F., Gaa J. P., & Lieberman, D. B. (1983). Empathy and ego development. *Journal of Counseling Psychology, 30(1),* 113–116.

Cavanagh, M. (1982). The counseling experience: A theoretical and practical approach. Prospect Heights: Waveland Press.

Chia, M., & Arava, D. A. (1996). The multi-orgasmic man: How any man can experience multiple orgasms and dramatically enhance his sexual relationship. San Francisco: Harper Collins.

Chirban, J. (1986). Developmental stages in eastern orthodox Christianity. In K. Wilber, J. Engler, & D. P. Brown (Eds.), *Transformations of consciousness: Conventional and contemplative perspectives on development* (pp. 285–314). Boston: Shambhala.

Clarkin, J. F., & Levy, K. N. (2004). The influence of client variables on psychotherapy. In M. J. Lambert (Ed.), *Bergin and Garfield's handbook of psychotherapy and behavior change* (5th ed.). New York: John Wiley & Sons.

Cohn, L. D. (1991). Sex differences in the course of personality development: A meta-analysis. *Psychological Bulletin, 109,* 252–266.

Cook-Greuter, S. (2000). Mature ego development: A gateway to ego transcendence? *Journal of Adult Development, 7,* p. 227–240.

Cook-Greuter, S. (2003). Postautonomous ego development: A study of its nature and measurement. Wayland, MA: Harthilll USA.

Cook-Greuter, S., & Soulen, J. (2007). The developmental perspective in integral counseling. *Counseling and Values, 51,* 180–192.

Corey, G. (2001). Theory and practice of counseling and psychotherapy (6th ed.). Belmont, CA: Brooks Cole.

Cormier, S., & Hackney, H. (2005). *Counseling strategies and interventions* (6th ed.). Boston: Allyn and Bacon.

Damasio, Antonio (1999). *The feeling of what happens.* San Diego: Harcourt.

Dameyer, J. J. (2001). Psychometric evaluation of the Riso-Hudson Enneagram Type Indicator. *Dissertation Abstracts International, 62(02),* 1136B.

Dana, R. H., & Hoffman, T. (1987). Holistic health: Definitions, measurement, and applications. In J. N. Butcher & C. D. Spielberg (Eds.), *Advances in personality assessment* (Vol. 6). Hillsdale: Lawrence Erlbaum.

Dattilio, F. M., & Padesky, C. A. (1990). *Cognitive therapy with couples.* Sarasota, FL: Professional Resource Exchange.

Deida. D. (1995). Intimate communion: Awakening your sexual essence. Austin: Plexus.

Deida. D. (2002a). Find god through sex: A spiritual guide to ecstatic loving and deep passion for men and women. Austin: Plexus.

Deida. D. (2002b). Dear lover: A women's guide to enjoying love's deepest bliss. Austin: Plexus.

Deikman, A. (1983). The observing self: Mysticism and psychotherapy. Boston: Beacon Press.

Douthit, K. Z., & Marquis, A. (2006). Empiricism in psychiatry's post-psychoanalytic era: Contemplating DSM's "atheoretical" nosology. Constructivism in the Human Sciences, 11(1), 32–59.

Eckstein, D., Baruth, L., & Mahrer, D. (1992). An introduction to life-style assessment (3rd ed.). Dubuque: Kendall/Hunt.

Engel, G. L. (1977). The need for a new medical model: A challenge for biomedicine. Science, 196, 129–136.

Engel, G. L. (1980). The clinical application of the biopsychosocial model. American Journal of Psychiatry, 137, 535–544.

Erikson, E. H. (1963). Childhood and society. New York: W. W. Norton.

Erikson, E. H. (1968). Identity: Youth and crisis. New York: W. W. Norton.

Erikson, E. H. (1980). Identity and the life cycle. New York: W. W. Norton.

Erikson, E. H. (1982). The life cycle completed: A review. New York: W. W. Norton.

Erickson, M. H., & Rossi, E. L. (1981). Experiencing hypnosis: Therapeutic approaches to altered states. New York: Irvington.

Fall, K., Holden, J. M., & Marquis, A. (2004). Theoretical models of counseling and psychotherapy. New York and Hove: Brunner-Routledge.

Farnsworth, J., Hess, J., and Lambert, M. J. (2001, April). A review of outcome measurement practices in the Journal of Consulting and Clinical Psychology. Paper presented at the annual meetings of the Rocky Mountain Psychological association, Reno, NV.

Fichte, J. G. (1988). Fichte: Early philosophical writings. Ithaca, NY: Cornell University Press.

Fosha, D. (2000). The transforming power of affect: A model for accelerated change. New York: Basic Books.

Foster, D., & Black, T. G. (2007). An integral approach to counseling ethics. Journal of Counseling and Values, 51(3), 221–234.

Freud, S. (1935). A general introduction to psychoanalysis. New York: Liveright.

Freud, S. (1962). The ego and the id. New York: W. W. Norton.

Freud, S. (1963). An outline of psychoanalysis. New York: W. W. Norton.

Freud, S. (1967). Beyond the pleasure principle. New York: Bantam.

Freud, S. (1971). A general introduction to psychoanalysis. New York: Pocket.

Gall, M. D., Borg, W. R., & Gall, J. P. (1996). Educational research: An introduction (6th ed.). White Plains: Longman.

Gamard, W. S. (1986). Interrater reliability and validity of judgments of enneagram personality types. Dissertation Abstracts International, 47(07), 3152B.

Garfield, S. L. (2003). Eclectic psychotherapy: A common factors approach. In J. C. Norcross & M. R. Goldfried (Eds.), Handbook of psychotherapy integration. New York: Oxford University Press.

Gardner, H. (1983). Frames of Mind: The theory of multiple intelligences. New York: Basic Books.

Gardner, H. (1998). Intelligence reframed: Multiple intelligences for the 21st century. New York: Basic Books.

Gebser, J. (1985). The ever-present origin. Athens: Ohio University Press.

Gedo, J. E. (1981). Advances in clinical psychoanalysis. New York: International University Press.

Gendlin, E. (1962). Experiencing and the creation of meaning: A philosophical approach to the subjective. Evanston, IL: Northwestern University Press.

George, L. K. (1994). Multidimensional assessment instruments: Present status and future prospects. In M. P. Lawton and J. A. Teresi (Eds.), Annual review of gerontology and geriatrics: Focus on assessment techniques (Vol. 14). New York: Spring.

Gilligan, C. (1982). In a different voice: Psychological theory and women's development. Cambridge, MA: Harvard University Press.

Glasser, W. (1990). *The basic concepts of reality therapy*. Canoga Park, CA: Institute of Reality Therapy.

Goldberger, N., Trule, J., Clinchy, B., & Belenky, M. (1996). *Knowledge, difference, and power: Women's ways of knowing*. New York: Basic Books.

Goleman, D. (1995). *Emotional intelligence*. New York: Bantam Books.

Goleman, D. (Ed.). (2003). Destructive emotions: How can we overcome them? New York: Bantam.

Graves, C. (1970). Levels of existence: An open system theory of values. *Journal of Humanistic Psychology, 10*, 131–154.

Greenberg, J. R., & Mitchell, S. A. (1983). *Object relations in psychoanalytic theory*. Cambridge, MA: Harvard University Press.

Greenberg, L. S. (2002). *Emotion-focused therapy*. Washington, DC: American Psychological Association.

Grof, S. (1998). *The cosmic game: Explorations of the frontiers of human consciousness*. Albany: State University of New York Press.

Grof, S. & Grof, C. (Eds.) (1989). *Spiritual emergency: When personal transformation becomes a crisis*. Los Angeles: Jeremy P. Tarcher.

Groth-Marnat, G. (1999). *Handbook of psychological assessment*. New York: John Wiley.

Guidano, V. F. (1987). Complexity of the self: A developmental approach to psychotherapy and therapy. New York: Guilford Press.

Hargens, S. (2001). Intersubjective musings: A response to Christina de Quincey's "The promise of integralism." *Journal of Consciousness Studies, 8(12)*, 35–78.

Hauser, S. T., Powers, S. I., & Noam, G. G. (1991) *Adolescents and their families: Paths of ego development*. New York: Free Press.

Heidegger, M. (1962). *Being and time*. New York: Harper & Row.

Herlihy, B., & Corey, G. (1996). *ACA ethical standards casebook*. Alexandria, VA: American Counseling Association.

Hill, C. E. (1996). *Working with dreams in psychotherapy*. New York: Guilford.

Hodges, K. (1993). Structured interviews for assessing children. *Journal of Child Psychiatry and Psychology, 34*, 49–68.

Hohenshil, T. H. (1996). Editorial: Role of assessment and diagnosis in counseling. *Journal of Counseling and Development, 75(1)*, 64–67.

Hollon, S. D., & Beck, A. T. (2004). Cognitive and cognitive behavioral therapies. In M. J. Lambert (Ed.), *Bergin and Garfield's handbook of psychotherapy and behavior change* (5th ed.). New York: John Wiley & Sons.

Hood, A. B., & Johnson, R. W. (1991). Assessment in counseling: A guide to the use of psychological assessment procedures. Alexandria: American Association for Counseling and Development.

Hoyt, M. F. (Ed.). (1998). *Constructive therapies* (Vol. 2). New York: Guilford.

Huck, S. W. (2000). *Reading statistics and research* (3rd ed.). New York: Longman.

Hy, L. X., & Loevinger, J. (1996). *Measuring ego development*. Mahwah, NJ: Lawrence Erlbaum Associates.

Ingersoll, R. E. (2002). An integral approach for teaching and practicing diagnosis. *The Journal of Transpersonal Psychology, 34*, 115–127.

Ingersoll, R. E., & Cook-Greuter, S. R. (2007). The self-system in integral counseling. *Journal of Counseling and Values, 51(3)*, 193–208.

Ingersoll, R. E., & Rak, C. F. (2006). Psychopharmacology for helping professionals: An integral exploration. Belmont: Thomson Brooks/Cole.

Ivey, A. E. (1986). *Developmental therapy*. California: Jossey-Bass.

James, W. (1890/1950). *The principles of psychology*. New York: Dover.

James, W. (1978). *Pragmatism and the meaning of truth.* Cambridge, MA: Harvard University Press.

John, B. F. (1978). Love of the two-armed form: The free and regenerative function of sexuality in ordinary life, and the transcendence of sexuality in true religious or spiritual practice. Clearlake, CA: Dawn Horse Press.

Jordan, J. V., Kaplan, A. G., Baker Miller, J., Stever, I. P., & Surrey, J. L. (1991) *Women's growth in connection.* New York: Guilford Press.

Jung, C. G. (1961). *Memories, dreams, reflections.* New York: Random House.

Jung, C. G. (1968). Analytical psychology: Its theory and practice. New York: Random House.

Kabat-Zinn, J. (1994). Wherever you go, there you are: Mindfulness meditation in everyday life. New York: Hyperion.

Karg, R. S., & Wiens, A. N, (1998). Improving diagnostic and clinical interviewing. In G. P. Koocher, J. C. Norcross, & S. S. Hill (Eds.), *Psychologist's desk reference* (pp. 11–14). New York: Oxford University Press.

Kaufmann, W. (1992). *Discovering the mind: Vol. 3. Freud, Adler, and Jung.* Edison, NJ: Transaction Publishers.

Keating, T. (1986). Open mind, open heart: The contemplative dimension of the gospel. Amity: Amity House.

Keen, S. (1991). *Fire in the belly: On being a man.* New York: Bantam.

Kegan, R. (1982). *The evolving self: Problem and process in human development.* Cambridge, MA: Harvard University Press.

Kegan, R. (1994). In over our heads: The mental demands of modern life. Cambridge, MA: Harvard University Press.

Kernberg, O. (1976). Object relations theory and clinical psychoanalysis. New York: Jason Aronson.

Kernberg, O. (1980). Internal world and external reality: Object relations theory applied. New York: Jason Aronson.

Kernberg, O. (2005). Transference-focused psychotherapy. Paper presented at the Evolution of Psychotherapy Conference. Anaheim, CA.

Kohlberg, L. (1969). Stage and sequence: The cognitive-developmental approach to socialization. In D. Goslin (Ed.), *Handbook of socialization theory and research* (pp. 347–480). Chicago: Rand McNally.

Kohlberg, L. (1990). Which postformal levels are stages? In M. L. Commons, C. Armon, L. Kohlberg, F. A. Richards, T. A. Grotzer, & J. D. Sinnott, *Adult development: Models and methods in the study of adolescent and adult thought* (pp. 263–268). New York: Praeger.

Kohut, H. (1971). *The analysis of the self.* New York: International Universities Press.

Kohut, H. (1977). *The restoration of the self.* New York: International Universities Press.

Kohut, H. (1984). *How does analysis cure?* Chicago: University of Chicago Press.

Kohut, H., & Wolf, E. S. (1978). The disorders of the self and their treatment: An outline. *International Journal of Psychoanalysis, 59,* 413–425.

Kottler, J. A., & Brew, L. (2003). *One life at a time: Helping skills and interventions.* Brunner-Routledge.

Lambert, M. J., & Cattani-Thompson, K. (1998). Key principles in the assessment of psychotherapy outcome. In G. P. Koocher, J. C. Norcross, & S. S. Hill (Eds.), *Psychologist's desk reference* (pp. 22–25). New York: Oxford University Press.

Lazarus, A. A. (1995). Multimodal therapy. In R. J. Corsini & D. Wedding (Eds.), *Current psychotherapies* (5th ed.) (pp. 322–255). Itasca: F. E. Peacock Publishers.

Lazarus, A. A. (1997). Brief but comprehensive psychotherapy: The multimodal way. New York: Springer.

Lazarus, A. A., & Lazarus, C. N. (1991). *Multimodal life history interview.* Champaign, IL: Research Press.

Lazarus, A. A., & Lazarus, C. N. (1998). Clinical purposes of the multimodal life history inventory. In G. P. Koocher, J. C. Norcross, & S. S. Hill (Eds.). *Psychologist's desk reference* (pp. 15–22). New York: Oxford University Press.

LeDoux, J. (1996). The emotional brain: The mysterious underpinnings of emotional life. New York: Simon & Schuster.

Leonard, G., & Murphy, M. (1995). *The life we are given.* New York: G. P. Putnam's Sons.

Levenson, H. (1995). *Time-limited dynamic psychotherapy: A guide to clinical practice.* New York: Basic Books.

Linehan, M. (1993). Skills training manual for treating borderline personality disorder. New York: Guilford.

Loevinger, J. (1966). The meaning and measurement of ego development. *American Psychologist, 21,* 195–206.

Loevinger, J. (1976). *Ego development.* San Francisco: Jossey-Bass.

Loevinger, J. (1979). Construct validity of the Sentence Completion Test of ego development. *Applied Psychological Measurement, 3,* 281–311.

Loevinger, J. (1985). A revision of the Sentence Completion Test for ego development. *Journal of Personality and Social Psychology, 48,* 420–427.

Loevinger, J. (1987). *Paradigms of personality.* New York: Freeman.

Loevinger, J. (Ed.). (1998). Technical foundations for measuring ego development: The Washington University Sentence Completion Test. Mahwah, NJ: Lawrence Erlbaum.

Loevinger, J., & Wessler, R. (1970). *Measuring ego development.* San Francisco: Jossey- Bass.

Mahler, M. S., Pine, F., & Bergman, A. (1975). *The psychological birth of the human infant: Symbiosis and individuation.* New York: Basic Books.

Maharshi, R. (1985). Be as you are: The teachings of Ramana Maharshi. Godman, David (Ed.). London: Penguin Books.

Mahoney, M. J. (1991). Human change processes: The scientific foundations of psychotherapy. New York: Basic Books.

Mahoney, M. J. (2003). Constructive psychotherapy: A practical guide. New York: Guilford.

Mahoney, M. J., & Marquis, A. (2002). Integral constructivism and dynamic systems in psychotherapy processes. *Psychoanalytic Inquiry, 22(5),* 794–813.

Maitri, S. (2001). The spiritual dimension of the enneagram: Nine faces of the soul. New York: Penguin Putnam.

Manners, J., & Durkin, K. (2001). A critical review of the validity of ego development theory and its measurement. *Journal of Personality Assessment, 77(3),* 542–567.

Marquis, A. (2002). Mental health professional's comparative evaluations of the Integral Intake, Life-Style Introductory Interview, and the Multimodal Life History Inventory. Unpublished doctoral dissertation. University of North Texas.

Marquis, A. (2006). *An integral taxonomy of therapeutic interventions.* Manuscript submitted for review.

Marquis, A. (2007). What is integral theory? *Journal of Counseling and Values, 51(3),* 164–179.

Marquis, A., & Douthit, K. Z. (2006). The hegemony of "empirically supported treatment": Validating or violating? *Constructivism in the Human Sciences, 11(2),* 108–141.

Marquis, A., Holden, J. M., & Warren, E. S. (2001). An integral psychology response to Helminiak's (2001) "Treating spiritual issues in secular psychotherapy." *Counseling and Values, 45(3).*

Marquis, A., & Ingersoll, R. E. (in progress). *Handbook of Integral Psychotherapy.*

Marquis, A., & Holden, J. M. (in press). Mental health professionals' evaluations of the Integral Intake, a metatheory-based, idiographic intake instrument. *Journal of Mental Health Counseling.*

Marquis, A., & Warren, E. S. (2004). Integral counseling: Prepersonal, personal, and transpersonal in self, culture, and nature. *Constructivism in the Human Sciences, 9(1),* 111–132.

Marquis, A., & Wilber, K. (in press). Unification beyond eclecticism: Integral psychotherapy. *Journal of Psychotherapy Integration.*

Maslow, A. H. (1970). *Motivation and personality* (2nd ed.). New York: Harper & Row.

Maslow, A. H. (1971). *The farther reaches of human nature.* New York: Viking Press.

Masterson, J. (1981). The narcissistic and borderline disorders. New York: Brunner/Mazel.

Matthews, G., Zeidner, M., & Roberts, R. D. (2002). *Emotional intelligence: Science and myth.* Cambridge, MA: MIT Press.

Maturana, H. R., & Varela, F. J. (1987). *The tree of knowledge: The biological roots of human understanding.* Boston: Shambhala.

May, R. (1977). *The meaning of anxiety* (Rev. ed.). New York: Norton.

May, R., & Yalom, I. (1995). Existential psychotherapy. In R. J. Corsini & D. Wedding (Eds.), *Current psychotherapies* (5th ed.) (pp. 262–292). Itasca: F. E. Peacock.

McDonald, R. P. (1999). *Test theory: A unified treatment.* London: Lawrence Erlbaum Associates.

McCrae, R. R., & Costa, P. T. (1996). Toward a new generation of personality theories: Theoretical contexts for the five-factor model. In J. S. Wiggins (Ed.), *The five-factor model of personality: Theoretical perspectives.* New York: Guilford.

McWilliams, N. (1994). Psychoanalytic diagnosis: Understanding personality structure in the clinical process. New York: Guilford.

Miller, P. (2002). *Theories of developmental psychology.* New York: Worth Publishers.

Miller, R. B. (2004). *Facing human suffering: Psychology and psychotherapy as moral engagement.* Washington, DC: American Psychological Association.

Mosak, H. H. (1995). Adlerian psychotherapy. In R. J. Corsini & D. Wedding (Eds.), *Current psychotherapies* (5th ed.) (pp. 51–94). Itasca: F. E. Peacock.

Murphy, M. (1993). Integral practices: Body, heart, and mind. In Walsh, R. and Vaughan, F. (Eds.), *Paths beyond ego: The transpersonal vision.* Los Angeles: Jeremy P. Tarcher.

Neff, K. (2003a). Self-compassion: An alternative conceptualization of a healthy attitude toward oneself. *Self and Identity, 2,* 85–101.

Neff, K. D. (2003b). The development and validation of a scale to measure self-compassion. *Self and Identity, 2,* 223–250.

Nietzsche, F. (1966). Beyond good and evil: Prelude to a philosophy of the future. New York: Vintage Books.

Novy, D. M., & Francis, D. J. (1992). Psychometric properties of the Washington University Sentence Completion Test. *Educational and Psychological Measurement, 52,* 1029–1039.

Palmer, H. (1988). Enneagram: Understanding yourself and the others in your life. New York: HarperCollins.

Palmer, S. (1997). Modality assessment. In S. Palmer & G. McMahon (Eds.), *Client Assessment* (pp. 134–167). London: Sage.

Pearson, W. (2007). Integral counseling and a three-factor model of defenses. *Journal of Counseling and Values, 51(3),* 209–220.

Perry, W. G. (1970). Forms of intellectual and ethical development in the college years. New York: Holt, Rinehart & Winston.

Persons, J. B. (1991). Psychotherapy outcome studies do not accurately represent current models of psychotherapy: A proposed remedy. *American Psychologist 46,* 99–106.

Piaget, J. (1926). *Language and thought of the child.* New York: Harcourt Brace Jovanovich.

Piaget, J. (1928). *Judgment and reasoning in the child.* New York: Harcourt Brace Jovanovich.

Piaget, J. (1948). *Moral judgment of the child.* Glencoe: Free Press.

Piaget, J. (1977). *The essential Piaget.* H. E. Gruber & J. J. Voneche (Eds.). New York: Basic.

Popper, K. R. (1963). *Conjectures and refutations: The growth of knowledge.* London: Routledge and Kegan Paul.

Pressly, P. K., & Heesacker, M. (2001). The physical environment and counseling: A review of theory and research. *Journal of Counseling and Development 79(2),* 148–160.

Prochaska, J. O., & DiClemente, C. C. (1982). Transtheoretical therapy: Toward a more integrative model of change. *Psychotherapy: Theory, Research, and Practice, 19(3),* 276–288.

Prochaska, J. O., & DiClemente, C. C. (2003). The transtheoretical approach. In J. C. Norcross & M. R. Goldfried (Eds.), *Handbook of psychotherapy integration.* New York: Oxford University Press.

Prochaska, J. O., & Norcross, J. C. (2003). *Systems of psychotherapy: A transtheoretical analysis.* Pacific Grove, CA: Brooks Cole.

Riso, D. R., & Hudson, R. (1999). The wisdom of the Enneagram: The complete guide to psychological and spiritual growth for the nine personality types. New York: Bantam.

Robinson, T. (1997). Insurmountable opportunities. *Journal of Counseling and Development, 76,* 6–7.

Rogers, C. R. (1957). The necessary and sufficient conditions of therapeutic personality change. *Journal of Consulting Psychology, 21,* 95–103.

Rogers, C. R. (1961). On becoming a person: A therapist's view of psychotherapy. Boston: Houghton Mifflin.

Rogers, C. R. (1986). A client-centered/person-centered approach to therapy. In I. Kutash & A. Wolf (Eds.), *Psychotherapist's casebook* (pp. 197–208). San Francisco: Jossey-Bass.

Ruddell, P. (1997). General assessment issues. In S. Palmer & G. McMahon (Eds.), *Client Assessment* (pp. 6–28). London: Sage.

Sartre, J. P. (1976). *The emotions: Outline of a theory.* Secaucus, NJ: Citadel Press.

Sartre, J. P. (1998). *Existentialism and human emotions.* Secaucus, NJ: Citadel Press.

Schwartz, J., & Begley, S. (2002). The mind and the brain: Neuroplasticity and the power of mental force. New York: HarperCollins.

Schwartz, T. (1995). What really matters: Searching for wisdom in America. New York: Bantam.

Scotton, B. W., Chinen, A. B., & Battista, J. R. (Eds.). (1996). *Textbook of transpersonal psychiatry and psychology.* New York: Basic.

Segal, Z. V., Williams, J. M. G., & Teasdale, J. D. (2002). Mindfulness-based cognitive therapy for depression: A new approach to preventing relapse. New York: Guilford.

Selman, R. (1980). The growth of interpersonal understanding. New York: Academic.

Shapiro, F. (2001). Eye movement desensitization and reprocessing: Basic principles, protocols and procedures. New York: Guilford.

Sharp, P. M. (1994). A factor analytic study of three enneagram personality inventories and the vocational preference inventory. *Dissertation Abstracts International, 55(05),* 1228A.

Shertzer, B., & Linden, J. D. (1979). Fundamentals of individual appraisal: Assessment techniques for counselors. Boston: Houghton Mifflin.

Short, B. (2005). AQAL: Beyond the biopsychosocial model. *AQAL Journal of Integral Theory and Practice 1(3),* 2–14.

Siegel, D. J. (2001). Toward an interpersonal neurobiology of the developing mind: Attachment relationships, "mindsight," and neural integration. *Infant Mental Health Journal, 22,* 67–94.

Solomon, R. (2007). True to our feelings: What our emotions are really telling us. New York: Oxford University Press.

Steindl-Rast, D. (1983). *A listening heart: The art of contemplative living.* New York: Crossroad.

Steindl-Rast, D. (1984). Gratefulness, the heart of prayer: An approach to life in fullness. New York: Paulist Press.

Stolorow, R. D., Atwood, G. E., & Orange, D. M. (2002). *Worlds of experience: Interweaving philosophical and clinical dimensions in psychoanalysis.* Hillsdale, NJ: Analytic Press.

Stolorow, R. D., Brandchaft, B., & Atwood, G. E. (1987). *Psychoanalytic treatment: An intersubjective approach.* Hillsdale, NJ: Analytic Press.

Sullivan, C., Grant, M. Q., & Grant J. D. (1957). The development of interpersonal maturity: Applications to delinquency. *Psychiatry, 20,* 373–385.

Sullivan, H. S. (1953). *The interpersonal theory of psychiatry.* New York: Norton.

Vacc, N. A., & Juhnke, G. A. (1997). The use of structured clinical interviews for assessment in counseling. *Journal of Counseling and Development, 75(6),* 470– 480.

Van Audenhove, C., & Vertommen, H. (2000). A negotiation approach to intake and treatment choice. *Journal of Psychotherapy Integration, 10(3),* 287–299.

Visser, F. (2003). *Ken Wilber: Thought as passion.* Albany: State University of New York Press.

Wachtel, P. L. (1993). *Therapeutic communication: Knowing what to say when.* New York: Guilford Press.

Walsh, R. (1982). Psychedelics and psychological well-being. *Journal of Humanistic Psychology, 22(3),* 22–32.

Walsh, R. (1993). Meditation research: The state of the art (pp. 60–67). In R. Walsh & F. Vaughan (Eds.), *Paths beyond ego: The transpersonal vision* (pp. 212–213). Los Angeles: Jeremy P. Tarcher.

Walsh, R., & Vaughan, F. (Eds.). (1993). *Paths beyond ego: The transpersonal vision.* Los Angeles: Jeremy P. Tarcher.

Walsh, R., & Vaughan, F. (1994). The worldview of Ken Wilber. *Journal of Humanistic Psychology, 34(2),* 6–21.

Washburn, M. (1988). *The ego and the dynamic ground: A transpersonal theory of human development.* Albany: State University of New York Press.

Washburn, M. (1994). *Transpersonal psychology in psychoanalytic perspective.* Albany: State University of New York Press.

Watts, A. (1966). *The book: On the taboo against knowing who you are.* New York: Vintage.

Weil, A. (1986). *The Natural Mind: An Investigation of Drugs and the Higher Consciousness.* Boston, Houghton Mifflin.

Weil, A. (1998). *8 weeks to optimum health.* New York: Ballantine Books.

Weil, A. (2001). *Eating well for optimum health: The essential guide to bringing health and pleasure back to eating.* New York: Collins.

Welwood, J. (Ed.). (1985). *Awakening the heart: East/West approaches to psychotherapy and the healing relationship.* Boston: Shambhala.

Welwood, J. (2000). *Toward a psychology of awakening: Buddhism, psychotherapy, and the path of personal and spiritual transformation.* Boston: Shambhala.

Westen, D., & Morrison, K. (2001). A multidimensional meta-analysis of treatments for depression, panic, and generalized anxiety disorder: An empirical examination of the status of empirically supported therapies. *Journal of Consulting and Clinical Psychology,* 69, pp. 875–899 (downloaded from Ovid Web gateway, pp. 1–36).

Westen, D., Novotny, C. M., & Thompson-Brenner, H. (2004). The empirical status of empirically supported psychotherapies: Assumptions, findings, and reporting in controlled clinical trials. *Psychological Bulletin, 130,* pp. 631–663 (downloaded from Ovid Web gateway, pp. 1–65).

White, J. (1984). *What is enlightenment: Exploring the goal of the spiritual path.* Los Angeles: Jeremy P. Tarcher.

Wilber, K. (1980). *The atman project: A transpersonal view of human development.* Wheaton, IL: Quest Books.

Wilber, K. (1983). Where it was, there I shall become: Human potentials and the boundaries of the soul. In R. Walsh & D. H. Shapiro (Eds.). *Beyond health and normality: Explorations of exceptional psychological well being.* New York: Van Nostrand, pp. 67–123.

Wilber, K. (1984a). The developmental spectrum and psychopathology: part I, stages and types of pathologies. *Journal of Transpersonal Psychology, 16(1),* 75–118.

Wilber, K. (1984b). The developmental spectrum and psychopathology: part II, treatment modalities. *Journal of Transpersonal Psychology, 16(2)*, 137–166.

Wilber, K. (1999a). *The collected works*: Vol. 1. *The spectrum of consciousness, no boundary, selected essays*. Boston: Shambhala.

Wilber, K. (1999b). *The collected works*: Vol. 2. *The atman project, up from Eden*. Boston: Shambhala.

Wilber, K. (1999c). *The collected works:* Vol. 3. *A sociable god, eye to eye*. Boston: Shambhala.

Wilber, K. (1999d). *The collected works*: Vol. 4. *Integral psychology, transformations of consciousness, selected essays*. Boston: Shambhala.

Wilber, K. (2000a). *The collected works:* Vol. 5. *Grace and grit*. Boston: Shambhala.

Wilber, K. (2000b). *The collected works:* Vol. 6. *Sex, ecology, spirituality*. Boston: Shambhala.

Wilber, K. (2000c). *The collected works*: Vol. 7. *A brief history of everything, the eye of spirit*. Boston: Shambhala.

Wilber, K. (2000d). *The collected works*: Vol. 8. *The marriage of sense and soul, one taste*. Boston: Shambhala.

Wilber, K. (2000e). Integral psychology: Consciousness, spirit, psychology, therapy. Boston: Shambhala.

Wilber, K. (2001). On the nature of a post-metaphysical spirituality: Response to Habermas and Weis. Retrieved October, 20, 2001 from wilber.shambhala.com.

Wilber, K. (2003). Waves, streams, states, and self: An outline of an integral psychology. *Journal of Humanistic Psychology 31(2–3)*, 22–49.

Wilber, K. (2005a). *Introduction to integral theory and practice*. http://integralnaked.org.

Wilber, K. (2005b). *Integral life practice starter kit*. Boulder, CO: Integral Institute.

Wilber, K. (2006). Integral spirituality: A startling new role for religion in the modern and postmodern world. Boston: Integral Books.

Wilber, K., Engler, J., & Brown, D. (1986). Transformations of consciousness: Conventional and contemplative perspectives on development. Boston: Shambhala.

Yalom, I. D. (2002). The gift of therapy: An open letter to a new generation of therapists and their patients. New York: Harper Collins.

Index

1-2-3 process, 159
3-2-1 process, 159

A

Aborted self-actualization, 86
Actualization hierarchies, 97
Adlerian personality priorities, 34, 142
Aesthetic development, assessing, 115
Altered states of consciousness, 36, 131–136
Altitudes of development, 31, 42, 74–75, 90
Antecedent self, 156–157
Anxiety, 173, 260
  existential, 86
AQAL (all quadrants, all levels), 24–38, 59,
    140, 160, 259
  case example assessment, 185–186,
    214–216
  matrix, 171
  model, xiii
Archaic-unconscious, 161
Assessment, 259
  as process, 4–5
  attunement, 5–6
  behavioral queries, 49–52
  biographical inventories, 14–15
  cultural queries, 52–55
  diagnosis and, 12–14
  effect of diversity and multicultural issues
    on, 19–20
  evaluation of instruments, 239–253
  experiential, 46–49
  idiographic and nomothetic, 3, 9–12,
    129–130
  instruments, 2–3
  integral, 20–22
  Integral Intake, 6, 18–19 (See also Integral
    Intake)
  Life-Style Introductory Interview (LSII),
    10, 16–18
  lines of development, 107–117
  multidimensional instruments for, 15–19

Multimodal Life History Inventory
    (MLHI), 10, 17–18
  outcome, 12
  paper-and-pencil vs. clinical interviews,
    7–8
  Personal Experience Report (PER), 10
  shadows of, 7, 254–255
  social/systemic queries, 56–57
Autopoietic systems, 72–73
Awareness, 31, 46, 62, 68, 72, 76, 79–80,
    86, 88, 99, 106–107, 109–110,
    114, 116, 126–127, 134–135, 141,
    155–156, 163–166, 237

B

Basic structures, 153–154
Beck Depression Inventory (BDI), 10
Behavior, 26. See also UR (upper right)
    quadrant
  assessment of, 49–52
  case example of, 189–190, 218–219
Biographical inventories, 14–15
Biopsychosocial formulation, 50
Body, mind, and spirit, 59–60
Borderline (F-2) disorders, 84
  case example, 214–236
  use of structure-building therapy for, 88

C

California Psychological Inventory (CPI), 10
Caring, 35, 55
Case formulation, 4
Causal cognition, 107
Center of gravity, 101, 238
  developmental, 63
  stage development and, 93
Centering techniques, 237
Change. See also development; horizontal
        growth; vertical development
  Bateson's notions of, 170–171
  transtheoretical theories of, 99–100

Clinical interviews, 7–9
Cognitive development, 28–32, 42, 78–81
  line of, 105–107
  universality of Piaget's stages of, 92
Cognitive interventions, 60, 238
Cognitive therapy, 87
  mindfulness-based, 137
  use of for F-4 disorders, 88
Collaboration, 82
Consciousness development, 29–32, 91
  ego development and, 124
Constructive development, 15
Constructivism, 70, 139
Contemplative practice, 82
Contemplative states of consciousness, 136
Cook-Greuter, Susanne, 71, 83, 95
Counseling styles, 64, 127–128
Culture, 19–20, 26. *See also* LL (lower left)
    quadrant
  assessment of, 52–55
  case example of, 190–192, 219–220
  worldviews as a function of, 110–111
Cultures of embeddedness, 71, 73–74

D

Death terror, 164
Deep sleep, 36, 131
Deep structures/features, 91–92, 102
Defenses, 81–83
  against transcendence, 164
Deity mysticism, 133
Depression, 27, 86, 137, 173, 260
  existential, 86
Desacralization, 164
Development
  assessing levels of, 83
  dynamics of, 119
  human, 61 (*See also* human development)
  linear ladder *vs.* nested concentric
    spheres, 43, 95
  lines of, 33–34, 100, 104–105 (*See also*
    lines of development)
  logic *vs.* dynamics of developmental
    models, 94, 97, 103, 119
  psychopathology and, 102
  spectrum approach to, 29–32
  stage theories of, 28, 76–78 (*See also* stage
    theories of development)
  structural theory of, 124
  theories of, 62
  treatment and, 63–64, 81, 87, 100
Developmental dynamics
  integral principles of, 71–73
  principles of, 68–70
Developmental psychology, clinical practice
    and, 64–67
Diagnosis, differentiating from assessment,
    12–14
*Diagnostic and Statistical Manual of Mental
    Disorders (DSM-IV-TR)*, 12
  axis II disorders of, 148–153
  diagnostic examples, 187, 217
Dialectic of progress, 75
Differentiation, 68, 73–74, 80, 83, 95, 127,
    156–157
Disidentification, 31, 157, 159
Distal self, 72, 155–156
Diversity, issues surrounding, 19–20
Domination hierarchies, 97
Dream work, 137
Dreaming, 36, 131

E

Ego, 33
  development, 81, 83, 110, 120–129
    (*See also* self-identity)
  meaning-making and, 64
Egocentric values, 112, 120
Embedded-unconscious, 162
Embeddedness, 155–156
  cultures of, 71, 73–74
Emergent-repressed-unconscious, 163–164
Emergent-unconscious, 162–163
Emotional development, assessing, 116–117
Emperically Supported Treatments (ESTs),
    14
Enduring traits, 134
Enneagram, 34–35, 143–153
Ericksonian Hypnosis, 137
Ethnocentric, 20, 71, 133
Existential (F-6) pathologies, 86
Experience, 26. *See also* UL (upper left)
    quadrant
  assessment of, 46–49
  case example of, 188–189, 217–218
Eye Movement Desensitization
    Reprocessing, 137

F

Feminine type, 34–35
Five-factor model, 34, 142
Forgetting, 160
Formal assessment, 3
Formal-operational thinking, 92
Formal-reflexive structure, 30

Freud, Sigmund, 71–72, 122
Fulcrum of development, 73

G

Gardner, Howard, 103–104
Gender types, 34–35, 142
Genetics, 72, 144
Gilligan, Carol, 34–36
Gross cognition, 107
Ground-unconscious, 161
Gurdjieff, George Ivanovich, 143

H

Hierarchical stage models, 42
    dangers of, 97–98
Hierarchies, natural vs. pathological, 97
Holarchy, 42, 97
Holding environments, 73–74
Holism, 39
Holons, 33, 97
Horizontal growth, 80
Human development, 61. See also
        development
    principles of, 68–70
    spectrum of, 81–83

I

Ichazo, Oscar, 143
Identity (F-5) neuroses, 85
Idiographic assessment, 3, 9–12
Inauthenticity, 86
Informal assessment, 3
Ingersoll, Elliott, ix–xii
Intake assessment. See also assessment
    case formulation approach to, 4
    negotiation approach to, 4
Integral assessment, 20–22
Integral Intake, 6, 18–19
    assessment form, 263–276
    case examples, 174–184, 202–212
    evaluation of, 239–253
    flexibility in the use of, 8–9
    personality types and, 150–153
    possibilities and perspectives, 109–110
    quadratic assessment queries, 45–57
    state of consciousness queries on, 138
Integral life practices (ILPs), 170–173
Integral methodological pluralism (IMP),
        38–40
Integral operating system (IOS), 38–40
Integral psychographs, 117–120

Integral taxonomy of therapeutic
        interventions (ITTI), 57–60
Integral theory, 70–73, 76
Integral treatment planning, 170–173
Integration, 31, 67–68, 73–74, 100, 127
    interpersonal, 122, 125
Integrative, semistructured interviews, 7
Intersubjective field theory, 117
Introspection, 82
Ipsative assessment instruments, 9
Isolation, 164
    existential, 86
Ivey, Allan, 63–64, 68–70, 77–81

K

Kegan, Robert, 71, 73–74, 155–156
Kohut, Heinz, 1, 232, 233
Kosmic philosophy, 40, 43, 91

L

Levels of change, 99–100
Levels of development, 28–32, 69, 76,
        78–81. See also stage theories of
        development; structures; waves of
        development
    meaning-making and, 62
    relationship with psychopathology, 83
Life-Style Introductory Interview (LSII),
        10, 16–17
    evaluation of, 18, 239–253
Lines of development, 33–34, 78–81, 100,
        104–105
    assessing, 107–117
    cognitive, 105–107
LL (lower left) quadrant, 25, 27, 55, 59–60,
        111, 132, 237, 260. See also culture
    case example, 186, 190–192, 216,
        219–220
    cultural queries, 52–55
Loevinger, Jane, 110, 121–129
LR (lower right) quadrant, 25, 27, 39, 47,
        55, 59–60, 132, 237, 260. See also
        social systems
    case example, 186, 192, 197, 216,
        220–221
    social/systemic queries, 56–57

M

Mahoney, Michael, 9–10, 22, 68, 170, v
Masculine type, 34–35
Meaning-making, 62

Meditation, 81, 136
Mental disorders, classification of, 12–13
Meta-mental altitude of development, 32, 133
Millon Clinical Multiaxial Inventory (MCMI), 10
Mindfulness, 139, 170, 198–200, 237
    cognitive therapy and, 137
Minnesota Multiphasic Personality Inventory (MMPI-2), 10
Moral development, 114–115
Morals, 111–112
Motivation, assessing, 111
Mountain metaphor, 74–75
Multiculturalism, issues surrounding, 19–20
Multidimensional assessment instruments, 15–19
Multimodal Life History Inventory (MLHI), 10, 17–18
    evaluation of, 239–253
Multiple intelligences, 103–104
Myers-Briggs Type Indicator (MBTI), 34–35, 142

N

Naranjo, Claudio, 143
Narcissistic (F-2) disorders, 84–85
    use of structure-building therapy for, 88
Natural states of consciousness, 36, 131
Needs, assessing, 111
Negotiation approach to intake, 4
Neurotic (F-3) disorders, 85
    use of uncovering therapy for, 88
Nomothetic assessment, 3, 9–12

O

Observing self, 156
Organismic theories, 123
Outcome assessment, 12
Over-mental altitude of development, 32

P

Paper-and pencil assessment instruments, 7–9
Para-mental altitude of development, 31–32
Pathological hierarchies, 97
Peak experiences, 36–37, 132–134
Personal data records, 14–15
Personal Experience Report (PER), 10
Personal mythology, 16–17
Personal stages of development, 28, 30–31

    disorders of, 85–86
    emotional development in, 117
Personality disorders, typologies in, 35
Personality organization, 121
Personality typologies, 34–36, 140–153
    meaning-making and, 62
Perspectives, 24, 26–27, 31, 46, 86, 101, 109–110, 109–111, 113, 117, 126, 255. *See also* altitudes of development; quadrants
    client, 5
Phantasmic/emotional structure, 30, 236
Phenomenology, 135
Piaget, Jean, 30, 42, 69, 78–81, 92
Plateau experiences, 134
Pre/trans fallacy, 133, 167
Prepersonal stages of development, 28–30
    disorders of, 84–85
    emotional development in, 117
Prime directive, 81
Problem, pattern, process work, 170–171
Processes of change, 99
Projection, 85, 121, 159
Pronouns (1st-, 2nd-, and 3rd-person), 154, 157–159
Proximate self, 72, 110, 154–155
Psychodiagnosis. *See* diagnosis
Psychographs, 117–120
    case examples, 187, 216
Psychopathology
    defenses and treatment for, 82
    relationship with levels of development, 83, 102
    relationship with treatment, 87–89
Psychosexual development, assessing, 115–116
Psychotherapy, ego development and, 127–128
Psychotic (F-1) disorders, 84
    use of structure-building therapy for, 88
Pure ego, 156

Q

Quadrant absolutism, 27, 39, 55
Quadrants, 25–27
Quadratic assessment, 45–60
Quadratic balance, 59
Quadrivium, 46
Quantitative *vs.* qualitative assessment, 10

R

Rational emotive behavior therapy, 88

Rationalization, 164
Referral, 6
Representational mind structure, 30
Repression, 160
Riso, Don, 144
Riso-Hudson Enneagram Type Indicator
 (RHETI), 144. *See also*
 Enneagram
Rogers, Carl, 37, 137
Rule-role/script (F-4) disorders, 85
 use of cognitive therapy for, 88
Rule/role mind structure, 30

S

Script (F-4) disorders, 85, 87
 use of cognitive therapy for, 88
Script analysis, 82
Self, 38, 122
 antecedent, 156–157
 center of gravity, 63, 93, 101, 238
 conscientious, 30
 disorders of, 84–85
 distal, 72, 155–156
 proximate, 72–73, 110, 154–156
Self-actualization, aborted, 86
Self-assessment, 14–15
Self-compassion, 46, 198
Self-identity, 110
Self-psychology, 232
Self-referent instruments, 9
Self-related lines of development, 106–107
Self-report questionnaires, 14–15
Self-sense, 153
Self-system, 38, 153–166, 259
 development of, 123
 pathology, 157–159
Sensoriphysical structure, 30
Sentence completion tests (SCTs). *See also*
 Washington University Sentence
 Completion Test (WUSCT)
 integral (SCTi), 83
 semiprojective, 125
Sexuality, 115–116
Shadows of assessment, 7, 254–255
Social systems, 26. *See also* LR (lower right)
 quadrant
 assessment of, 56–57
 case example of, 192, 220–221
Sociocentric values, 112, 120
Socratic dialogue, 66, 82
Spectrum approach, 28–32

Spiral dynamics, 71, 112
Spiritual experiences, interpreting, 132–133
Spirituality, assessing, 113–114
Stabilization, 102
Stage theories of development, 28, 69, 76–78.
 See also levels of development;
 structures; waves of development
 directionality and irreversibility of stages,
 93–94
 ego development, 123
 universal *vs.* context-bound, 90–93
 value of later stages, 94–96
State-stages, 134–136
State-training, 134
States of consciousness, 36–38, 77–78,
 131–134
Streams, 97. *See also* lines of development
Structural development theory, 123
Structuralism, 135
Structure-building approaches, 82
 use of for F1 and F2 disorders, 88
Structure-stages, 134–136. *See also* structures
Structures, 29, 69, 76. *See also* levels of
 development; stage theories
 of development; waves of
 development
 basic and transitional, 153–154
 definition of, 42
 progress and, 124
 universal, 90–93
Style-shift counseling, 64
Subject/object balance, 157
Submergent-unconscious, 161–162
Subpersonalities, 164–166
Substitution, 164
Subtle cognition, 107
Subtle experiences, interpretation of, 133
Suicidal ideation, 139–140
Super-mental altitude of development, 32
Suprapersonal stages of development, 29, 163
 disorders of, 86–87
 emotional development in, 117
 peak experiences and, 36–37
Surface structures/features, 91–92
Symptom Checklist-90-Revised (SCL-90-
 R), 10
Systems. *See* social systems

T

Tender-minded personalities, 132, 142
Therapeutic processes

developmental dynamics and, 68–76
integral principles of, 71–73
Therapeutic work, Mahoney's levels of,
        170–171
Therapies
    behavioral, 88
    cognitive, 87
    constructive, 139
    dream work, 137
    Ericksonian Hypnosis, 137
    existential, 2, 82
    existential-humanistic, 89
    existential-interpersonal, 139
    Eye Movement Desensitization
        Reprocessing, 137
    integral constructive approach to, 70–71
    introspective, 88, 121, 194
    person-centered, 3
    psychodynamic, 88, 102, 224, 238
    self-psychological, 232
    transpersonal, 89, 102, 167, 238
    transtheoretical therapy (TTT), 98–100
    uncovering, 82, 88
Tough-minded personalities, 132, 142
Transactional analysis, 88
Transcendence, defenses against, 164
Transcendent self, 156
Transformation, 29, 39, 71, 80–81
    spirituality and, 113–114
Transitional structures, 153–154
Translation, 80–81
    spirituality and, 113–114
Transtheoretical therapy (TTT), 98–100
Treatment modalities, 82
    relationship between psychopathology
        and, 87–89
Treatment planning, 170–173
    case examples, 192–194, 221–225
    classes of, 173
Truth value, 28
Types, 34–36, 140–153. See also personality
        typologies
Typological systems, evolution of, 141–142

U

UL (upper left) quadrant, 25, 27, 39, 47–48,
        50, 53, 55–56, 59–60, 111, 132,
        237, 260. See also experience
    case example, 186, 188–189, 197, 215,
        217–218
    experiential queries, 46–49
Uncanniness, 86

Unconsciousness, types of, 160–164
Uncovering approaches, 82
    use of for F3 disorders, 88
Uneven development, 103
Unity-in-diversity, 24
UR (upper right) quadrant, 25, 27, 47–48,
        55, 59–60, 132, 237, 260. See also
        behavior
    behavioral queries, 49–52
    case example, 186, 189–190, 197, 215,
        218–219

V

Values Test, 112
Values, assessing, 111–112
Vertical development, 80
Vision-logic structure, 31, 86, 163
VMEMEs, 112–113, 129

W

Waking, 36, 131
Washington University Sentence Completion
        Test (WUSCT), 83, 125–126
Waves of development, 29, 69, 76, 96.
            See also levels of development;
            stage theories of development;
            structures
    irreversibility of, 93–94
Wechsler Adult Intelligence Scale
        (WAIS-R), 10
Wechsler Intelligence Scale for Children
        (WISC-III), 10
Wilber, Ken, 28–34, 39, 63, 71–73, 86, 91,
        95, 100–101, 153–166, 173, xiii
Witness, 107, 237
    antecedent self, 156–157
    exercise, 158
Witness-consciousness, 32, 156
Worldcentric, 117, 120, 133
Worldviews, 154
    assessing, 110–111
    cultural, 23 (See also LL (lower left)
        quadrant)
    development of, 62, 68, 70
    shared, 26
WUSCT, scoring of, 128–129

Y

Yalom, Irvin, 139
Yoga, 116, 136, 173, 194

About the Author

Andre Marquis is an assistant professor of counseling and human development at the University of Rochester who practices therapy, teaching, supervision, and research from an integral-constructive perspective. He holds licenses as a professional counselor in Texas and a mental health counselor in New York and has taught 20 different courses in both psychology and counseling and human development programs (Northeastern State University and University of Rochester, respectively). Andre has served several editorial roles, including associate editor, for the journal *Constructivism in the Human Sciences* and has authored 11 articles in peer-reviewed journals. In addition to being a founding member of the Integral Institute, he currently serves on the Advisory Board of *AQAL: Journal of Integral Theory and Practice*.

Given that Andre's primary work involves developing an integrative approach to counseling and psychotherapy, it is meaningful to him that he has been able to publish in journals that span a spectrum from *Journal of Psychotherapy Integration, Psychoanalytic Inquiry,* and *Studies in Gestalt Therapy* to *Counseling and Values, Journal of Mental Health Counseling, Constructivism in the Human Sciences,* and *Journal of Humanistic Psychology*. He has also coauthored articles with both Ken Wilber and Michael Mahoney, and a book, *Theoretical Models of Counseling and Psychotherapy,* also published by Routledge. He is currently coediting *The Handbook of Integral Psychotherapy*.

CD Contents

Integral Intake
Introductory Letter to New Clients
Integral Intake (Psychiatric Version)
Integral Intake (French Version)
Introductory Letter to New Clients (French Version)
Integral Intake (Spanish Version)
Introductory Letter to New Clients (Spanish Version)